1985

The World of *Piers Plowman*

THE MIDDLE AGES
Edward Peters, general editor

The World
of
Piers Plowman

Edited and translated by
Jeanne Krochalis
&
Edward Peters

University of Pennsylvania Press/1975

Copyright © 1975 by the University of Pennsylvania Press, Inc.
Cover illustration from Trinity College, Cambridge, Ms R. 3. 14.
Courtesy of the Master and Fellows of Trinity College,
    Cambridge.
Library of Congress Catalog Card Number 75-11167
All rights reserved
ISBN (cloth): 0-8122-7699-x
ISBN (paper): 0-8122-1085-9
Printed in the United States of America

To
Morton W. Bloomfield
and
E. Talbot Donaldson
Magistris nostris

Contents

CONTENTS

Introduction

Between 1370 and 1399 an English poet and clerk in minor orders named William Langland composed three versions of a long poem in alliterative Middle English which he himself seems to have called by several titles, but which is generally known as *Piers Plowman*. The three versions, designated conventionally A, B, and C, contain about 2400 lines, 7200 lines, and 7300 lines respectively. They survive in fifty-one manuscripts, in approximately even division—a very large number for any alliterative poem in Old or Middle English. The poem appears to have found considerable immediate favor, particularly among clergy and pious laypeople, and it retained its interest into the sixteenth century, being printed by Crowley in 1550 and by Rogers in 1561. Although the work was not edited again until 1813, thus allowing its language to become more and more obscure to modern readers, William Langland retained a modest reputation as a poet and devotional writer during the seventeenth and eighteenth centuries. In 1886 all three texts were edited in an elaborate and learned edition by W. W. Skeat, and Skeat's edition, reprinted in 1961, has remained the standard text of the best-known version of the poem. In 1960 George Kane published what will probably be the definitive edition of the A-Text. Kane and E. T. Donaldson are at work on the B-Text, and G. H. Russell is preparing an edition of the C-Text. Thus, about six hundred years after Langland wrote, his great work will become available to English readers in the best form it has had since it left the poet's hand (see Bibliographical Note below).

The poem was divided by the poet into two main sections. The A-Text contains only the first of these, the *Visio* (*The Vision of William concerning Piers the Plowman*). The B and C-Texts contain both the *Visio* and the *Vita* (*The Life of Dowel, Dobet and Dobest*). The whole poem is divided into *Passus*, a Latin term that approximates the English *fitt*, or section, and there are twenty of these in the B-Text: *Passus* I–VII contain the *Visio*, and *Passus* VIII–XX the *Vita*. Langland took considerable pains with structure, and the two main parts, as well as the twenty subordinate parts, are carefully made.

Langland's audience was not the court audience of Chaucer and Gower, nor was it the learned magnatial audience of such contemporary works as *Sir Gawain and the Green Knight*. As Morton Bloomfield describes it,

> *Piers Plowman* is a monument to the struggles of a perplexed but hopeful sensitive fourteenth-century Englishman for a solution to the problems of his time and of all time in the attainment of a Christian perfection which must, to his apocalyptic mind, be a social solution which would involve the setting up of the Kingdom of God on earth, very much as his master Jesus had Himself promised in the New Testament.[1]

Many other fourteenth-century Englishmen, poets or not, shared similar feelings. Whatever their diverse origins, complaint and

1. Morton W. Bloomfield, "*Piers Plowman* as a Fourteenth-Century Apocalypse," *Centennial Review* 5 (1961): 281–95, rpt. in Bloomfield, *Essays and Explorations: Studies in Ideas, Language, and Literature* (Cambridge, Mass., 1970), 159–72. See also Bloomfield, *Piers Plowman as a Fourteenth-Century Apocalypse* (New Brunswick, 1962). A good general introduction to the poem is Elizabeth Salter, *Piers Plowman: An Introduction* (Cambridge, Mass., 1963).

satire became in the fourteenth and fifteenth centuries a virtually continuous cry against those abuses and institutions which seemed to prevent the establishment of a just order in the world. Never before had the tools and vehicles of salvation appeared so close, and never before were so many people of all ranks of life so acutely conscious of their society's failure to use them properly. *Piers Plowman*, the work of a single and highly distinctive poet, nevertheless may be said to speak about the strongest, most deeply-rooted hopes of a considerable part of English society in the late fourteenth and fifteenth centuries. Of this society, F. R. H. Du Boulay has recently remarked:

> The splendor and virtue of the late Middle Ages reside in this, that a vast mass of mankind in western Europe was raising itself to a higher level of education, a better individual standard of living, a more lively hope for the future, than were enjoyed by the majority of men and women in the twelfth and thirteenth centuries.[2]

Out of a part of this world of heightened hopes and disappointments, Langland made a great poem. He made it out of a dubious education, a humble and generally unsuccessful career, an improbable rhetorical tradition, and a generally dismal, but full and versatile experience of London life. He also possessed immense literary and devotional genius.

Concerning Langland himself, the clearest evidence is found at the end of a manuscript of the C-Text, written around 1400, now in Trinity College, Dublin. At the end of the page there occurs the notation:

> It is known that Stacy de Rokayle the father of William de Langlond was generous and lived in Shipton under Wichwood, holding from the lord Le Spenser in the county of Oxford. The aforesaid William made the book that is called Piers Ploughman.

Professor George Kane has examined this and all other relevant documentation concerning Langland and, with E. T. Donaldson,

2. *An Age of Ambition: England in the Late Middle Ages* (New York, 1970), 144.

has provided a powerful argument, not only that the same poet wrote all three versions of the poem, but that that poet was probably William Langland.[3]

Langland was probably born between 1330 and 1340, received a primary education and perhaps initial training for the priesthood at a monastery, but appears to have broken off his studies, possibly because of poverty and the withdrawal of patronage or the death of his patrons, and wandered in and out of southern England for much of his adulthood. He lived much of his life in London, apparently in great poverty, earning a living by singing offices for the dead, copying manuscripts, and begging. Langland seems to have been known as an eccentric, as a beggar distinctively costumed, and as an outspoken, if bizarre, social critic. The last thirty years of his life, from 1370 to 1399, were spent working and reworking his poem, and virtually nothing is known of the circumstances of his death.

Clerical proletarian, beggar, social critic, and general eccentric Langland may well have been, but he was also extraordinarily devout and a bitter, meticulous observer of social mores. Allegorical personifications that turn wooden and ridiculous in much other literature become lively and distinctive characters in *Piers Plowman*. In spite of his lack of general education, Langland reveals considerable sensitivity to literary styles and to complex theological problems.

Although satire and complaint had been directed at ecclesiastical institutions since the twelfth century, the period after 1250 witnessed both a heightening of intensity and a spreading of various forms of orthodox and heterodox dissent. Criticism of the Crusade, furious ecclesiastical infighting in universities and dioceses, and the series of remarkable documents solicited by Pope Gregory X for the Second Council of Lyons in 1274 brought forth considerable criticism even before the end of the thirteenth century. The fourteenth century opened with the quarrel between Philip IV of France and Boniface VIII (and Philip's subsequent triumph), his later destruction of the Templars,

---

3. George Kane, *Piers Plowman: The Evidence for Authorship* (London, 1965); E. Talbot Donaldson, *Piers Plowman: The C-Text and Its Poet* (New Haven, 1949; rev. ed., London, 1966).

and the long papal residence in Avignon, which ended just as Langland was completing the B-Text of *Piers Plowman*. That century also witnessed the material disasters of widespread war, famine, and the recurring incidences of the Black Death after 1348. The war between Edward III of England and Philip VI of France began in 1337, and by the end of the fourteenth century, after intermittent truces and renewals of hostilities, was on the verge of breaking out once more, this time as a war of armies, political factions, and the extensive mobilization of state resources, rather than a pretty war of kings. With much of this, of course, Langland had little to do. But the deterioration of public order during the last years of Edward III (1327–1377) called forth much comment in England and was reflected in the troubled reign of Richard II (1377–1399). On an entirely different level from Langland, the sermons of Thomas Brinton, Bishop of Rochester from 1373 to 1389, and the consideration of public crises in the House of Commons during the turbulent period during and after Richard's minority reflect broad discontent, criticism of public life and private morals, and widespread passions for reform in spiritual and temporal affairs. A great poet with a spiritual passion for moral reform had much to work with in England from the Treaty of Brétigny in 1360 to the death of Richard II in 1399. Langland was indeed such a poet, and *Piers Plowman* indeed reflects a world in which spiritual discontent and civil dissension often formed ephemeral, but persistent alliances. This book attempts to suggest some of the documentary evidence for the relationships of that poem to that world.

In "The Present State of Piers Plowman Studies," a magisterial survey published in 1939, Morton Bloomfield suggested that the most profitable directions that future study of the poem might take would be in three areas: textual criticism, "the study of the meaning of Langland's words and lines," and "a general study of the backgrounds in folklore, art, theology, homilies, religious tractates, and various literatures, as well as in social and economic history. The basic purpose is not to find sources necessarily, but to make possible a new understanding of the intellectual and social atmosphere of fourteenth-century England. Much remains to be done in that field."[4] Since Bloomfield's article appeared, a considerable amount of all three types of work has been produced.[5] As noted above, a new edition of the A-Text appeared in 1960, and soon there will be new versions of the B and C-Texts as well. Many studies have considered Langland's semantics, language, and prosody, and the label created by J. A. Burrow, "Ricardian poetry," has suggested a significant re-evaluation of Langland's style in the light of other related four-teenth-century works.[6] Finally, a large and diffuse literature has touched on parts, at least, of what Bloomfield called "the social and intellectual atmosphere of fourteenth-century England."

This book is addressed to Bloomfield's third area. It presents a number of extracts from larger works and some shorter works in their entirety that reflect either the techniques or the concerns that shaped Langland's somber vision of the condition of English humanity in the last quarter of the fourteenth century. We hope that these documents, many of them often cited in connection with *Piers Plowman* and often hard to come by, may shed some light on the perceptions of the poet and his audience. The documents printed below are certainly not "sources," if, indeed, any "sources" for *Piers Plowman* can be said to exist, nor can it safely be said that Langland knew all, or indeed any of them. The concerns they reflect, however, indeed touch upon those of Langland in *Piers Plowman*, and some of them may be said to be a part of the common intellectual, emotional, and spiritual property of a large body of literate and semi-literate Europeans generally between 1250 and 1550.

The best information concerning the common attitudes and ideas of fourteenth-century Englishmen does not often come di-rectly from that tradition which in the twelfth and thirteenth centuries had constituted the high road of intellectual history. Going directly to St. Augustine or St. Thomas Aquinas often does not help to clarify the thought of those who had acquired

---

4. *Speculum* 14 (1939): 215–232 at 232.
5. The best guide through the bibliography is Kathleen Proppe, "*Piers Plowman: An Annotated Bibliography for 1900–1968*," *Comitatus* 3 (1972): 33–88. For further suggestions, see the Bibliographical Note above.
6. J. A. Burrow, *Ricardian Poetry: Chaucer, Gower, Langland and the Gawain Poet* (New Haven, 1971).

their learning in the schools of the fourteenth century and refreshed it, when they felt the need or could be persuaded, out of *thesauri, florilegia, summae,* and random collections of *sententiae* that comprise the bulk of fourteenth-century manuscript production. We have, therefore, selected not the best known works of the most eminent medieval thinkers, but samples of the popularized, abridged, sometimes confused and fragmentary versions of high learning that circulated widely and often constituted the sole access to collections of formal learning of writers whose works colored the thought of the later Middle Ages in England. We do not argue for the supreme literary merit of many of the selections printed below, but we do argue for their widespread familiarity and their faithfulness in reflecting many of the social and spiritual concerns of late fourteenth-century Englishmen. Finally, by juxtaposing texts that are commonly separated by the disciplinary labels of "historical" and "literary," we wish to suggest that the casual familiarity with, or ignorance of, each discipline by practitioners of the other does justice to the riches of neither. Historians and literary critics must both ask "What is grace," whether they find it in a coronation order or personified in an allegorical poem. And social ideas are no less social because they are found in a poem, nor more social when found in a speech in Parliament. The documents printed below offer simply the suggestion of interdisciplinary co-operation, a suggestion that the editors, as students and teachers, have found very useful.

Although the division of these documents into distinctive sections is the work of the editors of this volume, we have tried whenever possible to use texts found in manuscripts that are roughly contemporary with *Piers Plowman* or indeed contain the poem itself bound in with other materials. Because *Piers Plowman,* particularly in the B and C versions, is a long poem, it often takes up a whole manuscript by itself. In many instances, however, the poem is not alone, and the texts with which it is bound may occasionally shed some light upon the audience for the poem and the minds of its readers. At least half a dozen of these manuscripts contain, besides *Piers Plowman,* either lists of, or treatises on, virtues and vices, religious poems of varying length and quality, moral or political treatises, chronicles, and one even contains Sir John Mandevilles's *Travels*. Cambridge University Library Ms. Ll. 4. 14, for example, contains *Piers Plowman* in the B-Text with a glossary of difficult dialect words and *The Wise Book of Philosophy and Astronomy* (Below, nos. 1 and 22), a handy compendium of astronomical, astrological, and characterological information. Trinity College, Cambridge, B. 15. 17 contains *Piers Plowman* in the B-Text and "Wrecchednesses" (Below, No. 28). We have selected *The Wise Book* to introduce common late medieval notions of cosmology and its place in the understanding of human behavior and "Wrecchednesses" to illustrate the much-discussed attitude toward death in the fourteenth and fifteenth centuries. These are probably the same reasons that led to their being copied in with *Piers Plowman* in the first place. Codicology, the study of the archaeology of the book, suggests that not only the contents of individual manuscripts, but the layout of the text on the page (as well as scribal and readers' marks), stress the didactic moral interest the poem generated in the fourteenth and fifteenth centuries. Langland's frequent biblical citations are often marked off in red, lest the reader miss them; and the scripts, although not often the work of elegant professional scribes and elaborate *scriptoria*, are usually clear, workmanlike productions written for an enlarged, literate lay audience that could not afford to spend much money on their books, but wanted books and obviously read them. Almost none of the manuscripts, for example, are illustrated, except for occasional marginal drawings, usually by non-professional artists. Perhaps the only drawing of professional caliber in a *Piers Plowman* manuscript is the illustration from Trinity College, Cambridge, Ms. R. 3. 14 reproduced on the cover of this book.

One way of regarding this book, although it may stretch the reader's imagination somewhat to do so, might be as a commonplace book containing texts illustrative of social and moral reform, of the kind that might have grown up in late fourteenth-century England and been owned by someone who also owned a manuscript of *Piers Plowman*.

The seven sections into which these readings are divided follow an intelligible fourteenth-century order. Section One deals with ideas concerning the heavens, the universal Church, England, and the city of London, the macrocosm and microcosm, except for human beings, familiar to most medieval thinkers. Section Two attempts to catalogue representative views of material and spiritual abuses in England and on the Continent, including the Peasants' Rebellion of 1381. Section Three offers examples of two of the most influential forces in late fourteenth-century England, the voices of the Preacher and the Heretic, in this case Thomas Brinton, Bishop of Rochester from 1373 to 1389, and John Wyclif, the most important religious figure of the age. Section Four illustrates some of the immense variety of the world of moral *exempla*, tales from hagiography, sermon literature, and tracts on moral theology. Section Five suggests some of the kinds of practical instruction and proposals for conduct available to the devout layman or laywoman, from handbooks of general knowledge, to the schoolbook containing the moral *Disticha Catonis*, to the regulations of guilds and fraternities, organizations that had spiritual as well as social and economic dimensions. Section Six suggests the world of multiple meaning in many devotional and literary works, from brief extracts of single images to the allegorical devotional poems of Robert Grosseteste and Guillaume de Deguilleville. The final section reminds the reader of one of the greatest concerns of fourteenth- and fifteenth-century people, aging and the approach of death, graphically described by Langland in *Passus* XX, in Will's encounter with Elde (Old Age), as well as the consideration of judgements on the soul and the rewards and punishments of the afterlife.

The very character of fourteenth-century literature invites a wide sampling, rather than longer selections from a few works, particularly in illustrating the social and economic aspects of Langland's world, and there are few anthologies that offer such a representation. *Piers Plowman* is a difficult poem linguistically and textually, and the works sampled below are of the sort that generally get mentioned in the notes to various editions and translations of the work but are rarely available for beginning, and sometimes even for advanced readers of the poem.

All Latin and French texts have been translated here, and Middle English texts have been given in the original, usually with glossarial notes. None of the Middle English printed here, however, is much more difficult than that of Chaucer; probably none of it is as difficult as Langland's own language. Spellings have been kept as they are in the manuscripts used. Most scribes are inconsistent, and many of the selections are not long enough to give any sense of what a scribe's most common spelling of a word would be—if, indeed, he had one. Punctuation has sometimes been altered for the convenience of the reader. The medieval unit of thought is much more the clause, and then the paragraph, than anything approximating the modern sentence. And there are places where no modern punctuation seems quite faithful to the author's logical flow of thought, but we have tried to achieve a workable compromise. The translations attempt to catch something of the tone of the original languages, the editors having to settle often for an English that portrays dismally flat French or Latin.

❧ Acknowledgements and Abbreviations

The following pamphlets from the series Translations and Reprints from the Original Sources of European History (Philadelphia, 1894f) have been reprinted in their entirety: Dana C. Munro, *Monastic Tales of the XIII Century* (sometimes entitled *Medieval Sermon Stories* vol. 2, no. 4 [1895]) and E. P. Cheney, *England in the Time of Wycliffe*, vol. 2, no. 5 (1895). The following pamphlets have provided excerpts: James Harvey Robinson, *The Pre-Reformation Period*, vol. 3, no. 6 (1896), pp. 9–10, 19–21, 25–30, 32; J. H. Robinson and Merrick Whitcomb, *Period of the Early Reformation in Germany*, vol. 2, no. 6 (1895), pp. 4–10; E. P. Cheney, *English Towns and Gilds*, vol. 2, no. 1 (1895), pp. 21–25, 29–35.

The editors express their gratitude to the Early English Text Society (E.E.T.S.) for permission to reprint nos. 19, 25, and 26. *Chronicles and Memorials of Great Britain and Ireland during the Middle Ages, Rerum britannicarum medii aevi scriptores*, is the full title in English and Latin for the Rolls Series, 253 vols. (London, 1858–1911). *Société des anciens textes français* is abbreviated S.A.T.F.

The editors also wish to thank a number of people without whose generous and learned help this book would not have been written. M. Wescott Driver, M. Kathryn Taylor, and Laurie Finke provided transcriptions of some of the manuscript material. Maureen Quilligan and Christina Hanson of Yale University helped check editions of Deguilleville. Ruth J. Dean and Thomas G. Waldman offered us help in problems of translation, comprehensibility, and, as they always do, intelligibility. We also wish to thank the staffs of the Van Pelt Library of the University of Pennsylvania, the British Museum, Cambridge University Library, Trinity College Cambridge, the Bodleian Library of Oxford, and Yale University. The glossarial notes were compiled by Laurie Finke and Stephen Lappert.

❧ Bibliographical Note

The vast corpus of *Piers Plowman* scholarship may conveniently be traced in two locations. W. W. Skeat, ed., *The Vision of William Concerning Piers the Plowman* . . . , by William Langland, 2 vols. (London, 1886; rpt. ed., Oxford, 1961) describes much of the early criticism and mis-criticism of the poem. Indispensable for twentieth-century scholarship, however, is Kathleen Proppe, "*Piers Plowman:* An Annotated Bibliography for 1900–1968," *Comitatus* 3 (Los Angeles, 1972): 33–88. Proppe's extensive listings make further detailed bibliographical guidance unnecessary, and they also include a few listings from 1969. Since 1968, however, several more works should be noted. See also J. A. W. Bennett, *Langland, Piers Plowman: The Prologue and Passus I–VII of the B-Text as found in Bodleian Ms Laud Misc. 581* (Oxford, 1972), a new edition of the prologue and first seven passus of the poem based upon Skeat's main manuscript. *Langland, Piers the Ploughman*, trans. J. F. Goodridge (Baltimore, 1959), is a modern Englishing primarily of Skeat's B-Text. George Kane, *Piers Plowman: The A Version. Will's Visions of Piers Plowman and Do-Well* (London, 1960), is the standard

A-Text. Parts of the C-Text have been edited in Elizabeth Salter and Derek Pearsall, *Piers Plowman* (London, 1967).

In addition to the convenient collections of articles edited by Blanch and Vasta (Proppe, nos. 57 and 221), S. S. Hussey, ed., *Piers Plowman: Critical Approaches* (London, 1969), is a fine collection of important recent articles. Among recent book-length studies, particularly interesting is Elizabeth D. Kirk, *The Dream Thought of Piers Plowman* (New Haven, 1972). Ruth M. Ames, *The Fulfillment of the Scriptures: Abraham, Moses, and Piers* (Evanston, Ill., 1970) and Mary Carruthers, *The Search for St. Truth: A Study of Meaning in Piers Plowman* (Evanston, Ill., 1973), offer distinctive views of different aspects of the work. William M. Ryan, *William Langland* (New York, 1968), is a general introduction in the *Twayne's English Author's Series*. A number of essays by Morton Bloomfield have been collected in his *Essays and Explorations: Studies in Ideas, Language, and Literature* (Cambridge, Mass., 1970), and several by Alfred L. Kellogg in his *Chaucer, Langland, Arthur: Essays in Middle English Literature* (New Brunswick, 1972).

Denys Hay, *Europe in the Fourteenth and Fifteenth Centuries* (New York, 1966) is the best general period history in English. Although May McKisack, *The Fourteenth Century, 1307–1399* (Oxford, 1959) is still the standard history of England during Langland's period, F. R. H. Du Boulay, *An Age of Ambition: English Society in the Late Middle Ages* (New York, 1970), is a lively and fascinating summary of recent scholarship guided by a fine critical intelligence and a lively style. Edith Rickert, *Chaucer's World* (New York, 1948), offers an extensive collection of useful documents. The works of Jacques Heers, particularly *L'Occident aux XIVe et XVe siècles: aspects économiques et sociaux* (Paris, 1970), offer excellent discussions of relevant topics, as do the papers collected in John Hale, Roger Highfield, and Beryl Smalley, eds., *Europe in the Late Middle Ages* (Evanston, Ill., 1965). An important, but slightly later focus upon popular religion, culture, and physical and spiritual environments is that found in the first few chapters of Keith Thomas, *Religion and the Decline of Magic* (New York, 1971). Convenient bibliographical information may be found in the relevant essays in Elizabeth Chapin Furber, ed., *Changing Views on British History* (Cambridge, Mass., 1966) and in the volumes of the Conference on British Studies series Bibliographical Handbooks.

John A. Burrow, *Ricardian Poetry: Chaucer, Grower, Langland and the Gawain Poet* (New Haven, 1971), is the most recent, stimulating, and controversial general view of the literary aesthetic of late fourteenth-century England.

On literacy generally and the audience of such works as *Piers Plowman*, see M. B. Parkes, "The Literacy of the Laity," in D. Daiches and A. K. Thorlby, *Literature and Western Civilization*, vol. 2 (London, 1973), pp. 555–77 and H. J. Chaytor, *From Script to Print* (Cambridge, 1945); J. A. Burrow, "The Audience of *Piers Plowman*," *Anglia* 75 (1957): 373–84.

PART I:

Macrocosm
and Microcosm

In the eyes of most fourteenth-century thinkers, and indeed most thinkers before the late seventeenth century, the smallest and largest parts of creation possessed intimate and harmonious relationships that extended throughout its entire fabric. These relationships formed the structure of what C. S. Lewis has felicitously called "a complex mental Model of the Universe," a concept that imparted a particular meaning—a proportional and hierarchical significance—to diverse aspects of the material universe, human behavior, states of mind, and concepts of time and order. Although Langland himself was no practicing cosmologist, certainly not the equal of such twelfth-century figures as Alain de Lille and Bernard Silvestris, the figures—earthly and celestial, material and mental, in time or transcending time—who appear throughout the poem stretch the narrative setting to embrace hopes, fears, and opposing forces whose significance can only be understood in terms of a cosmos whose structure Lewis and others have described in such detail.

The five selections that follow suggest the mastering idea of the unity and interrelatedness of all creation and the influence of that idea of cosmological unity upon the two largest and most theoretically developed human societies, the Church and the Empire. The last two selections narrow the scope of the macrocosm down to England and to London. Not all people thought constantly about the relations between macrocosm and microcosm, but each element in the following series takes on particular significance because of its place in a hierarchy of organizational categories. Although these selections certainly do not describe the particular universe of William Langland, they certainly describe universal relationships that were recognized by many in the fourteenth and fifteenth centuries. A good introduction to cosmology is C. S. Lewis, *The Discarded Image* (Cambridge, 1964).

1

The Universe:
The Wise Book of
Philosophy and Astronomy

Introductory Note: "The Wise Book of Philosophy and Astronomy" follows *Piers Plowman* in Cambridge University Library Ms. Ll.4. 14. The author is unknown. The work purports to be the teaching of the wisest philosopher ever known, an Englishman who lived in Greece and "compiled this book out of spells graciously into Englissh." This cleverly devised literary persona would make him the heir of Aristotle, the only author he cites by name. The work itself has certain similarities to Book VIII of Bartholomaeus Anglicus, *De Proprietatibus Rerum* (*On the Properties of Things*) which was Englished by John of Trevisa in the fourteenth century and later printed at Westminster by Wynkyn de Worde around 1495. Bartholomaeus, however, is more philosophical, more distinctly religious, and more learned than our author. His eighth book begins:

> After that we have by the help of God ended þe treatyse of
> mannes body, of God, and of proprytees of angelles and of men,
> and of accidentes and condicions of men, Now we shal speke of
> the proprytees of þe worlde that we se and fele, by the help
> of God, whyche is sende to us fro above: þat we maye drawe

> matere to þe prasing of God of the proprytees of werkynge of
> þe maker and condytour of thinges that ben made and under-
> stonde, as the apostle saythe; and therefore we shal shortly put
> to this werke some proprytees of this worlde and thinges that
> ben therin, that we maye by lyknesse of bodyly proprytees þe
> more easely understonde mystyk and spyrituall meanynge in
> holy writte. And we shal begynne atte the proprytees of the
> worlde.

He digresses to enlighten his reader on the properties of matter, and
how it can exist without quality or quantity. He cites Martianus
Capella, Rabanus Maurus, John of Damascus, and Plato—all within
a few pages. Our author, on the other hand, despite his grandiloquent
opening, is much more modest and practical. He tells us what the
heavenly bodies are and what effect we can expect them to have on
our characters and lives.

He cannot have anticipated too learned an audience. At the
beginning of his discussion of the planets, he notes that the three-
hour ascendency of each planet during the day is as long as "a good
reeder and a devoute shulde rede twies þe 7 psalmus with þe letayne"
—fairly slow going by modern standards.

The relationship between planets and human character had a
long history before our author, but one of the virtues of this kind of
text is that it put into very plain English much of the learned doctrines
of philosophy. When we are told that "Saturne is a planete derke and
malicious, colde and drie; undir þe constellacioun of whyche þe man
þat is bore, is bore dredffull, and a nygard," it becomes easier to
envision the response of a Middle English-speaking audience to those
many literary works that take such knowledge for granted.

On several occasions in the poem, particularly in the description
of the Field full of folk in the *Prologue* and in *Passus* XI during and
following Nature's great exhortation to Will "thorw the wondres of
this worlde wytte for to take," Langland suggests that common body
of general knowledge, which includes cosmology, natural history, and
allegorical geography, that some of the documents in this section
illustrate. Even straightforward topographical descriptions, such as
William Fitzstephen's description of London, can be converted into
honorific landscapes, and the extensive claims to the rule of a universal
ecclesiastical society made in Boniface VIII's *Unam Sanctam* is echoed

in the conclusion of *Passus* VIII. Langland's landscape, beginning on the Malvern hills and including the busy streets of fourteenth-century London, is realistic as well as allegorical, and although the poet is not always concerned with the widest aspects of ecclesiastical authority, he, no less than Boniface, thinks in terms of a universal spiritual community. The *Wise Book of Philosophy and Astronomy* might have been the sort of learning that Will the Dreamer referred to in *Passus* XV, when he tells Anima that he wants to know about "Alle the sciences under sonne and alle the sotyle craftes."

�֍ The Wise Book of Philosophy and Astronomy

Here bigynneth the wyse boke of philosophie and astronomye conteyned and made of the wyseste philisophre and astronomer þat evere was sythe þe world ffrist bygan; þat is ffor to say of þe lond of Greece, ffor in þat lond was an Englissh man, ffull wyse and well undirstandynge of philosophie and astronomye, studied and compylid þis boke out of spells graciously in to Englissh.

Friste þis boke tellith how many hevenes þer beth, and afterwarde he pronuncyth and declared of þe cours and þe governaunce of þe planetys; afterwarde of þe signes and sterres of þe ffirmament; afterwarde of þe elementys and complexions and þe maners of man, without wyche science and knowynge, no man may come to perfitt wurchinge[1] of astronomye and philosophie, ne surgere[2], ne of no oþer science. Ffor þer is non lyche[3] in the lond þat may trewly wurche his crafte, but if he have þe science and kunnynge of þis boke.

And it is to undirstande þat þer beth 11 hevenes, and 9 ordris of angelus, and after þe day of dome[4] þer shalt be 10 ordris, as it was at þe bigynninge whan God made hem. Ther beth also 7 planetis movynge and werchinge[5] in 7 hevenes, and ther beth 7 daiez, þe wyche þat takyn her propir names of þe 7 planetis, þat is to saye: Sol, luna, Mars, Mercurius, Jupiter, Venus, Saturnus.

Also þer beth 12 signes in þe hieste hevene, whyche beth mevable, þat is to saye: Aries, Taurus, Gemini, Cancer, Leo, Virgo, Libra, Scorpio, Sagittarius, Capricornius, Aquarius, Pisces. And these 12 signes be not propir bestis, as it schewiþ here, but be wey of

1. *wurchinge*: performance, action   2. *surgere*: surgery
3. *lyche*: physician   4. *dome*: doom, judgement   5. *werchinge*: operating

philosophie, þey ben lykened to swiche bestes; and þey beth no more to saye in Englissh but 12 parties of þe formament, of þe wyche iche parte hath a serteyne noumbre sterris asigned to hym. And þese 12 sygnes beth cleped[6] þe propre housis of þe 7 planetis in wiche þei reste and abide a serteyne tyme, as þe constellacion fully declareth. And a planete is to saie a sterre wyche is discordaunt[7] ffrom oþer sterris, ffor he is gretter, and more of power þan oþer þat beth lesse.

Also þer beth 12 monthes, acordynge to þe 12 signes in þe wiche þe signes regnen and werchin; þat is ffor to saye: Marche, Aprill, May, Jun, July, August, Septembre, Octobre, Novembre, Decembre, Januare, Feverere. And þese 12 signes travaylin and worchyn togedir in þe monthe, but on of hem principali regneþ and hath his dominacion in his propre monthe, and is lord þerof.

The frist signe is Aries, and he regneþ in þe monthe of Marche, ffor in þat signe God made þe world. And þis signe Aries is cleped þe signe of þe ram, for as moche as Abraham made his offringe to God of a ram for his sone Ysaac, whoo so ys born in þis signe schall be dredffull,[8] and he shall have grette grace.

The 2 signe is Taurus, and he regneth in Aprill, and ys þe signe of a bulle, for as moche as Jacob þe sone of Isaac wrastelid and stroff with þe angell in Bedlem as a bulle, whoo so is born in þat signe shall have grace in alle bestis.

The 3 signe is Gemini, and he regneþ in May and is clepid þe signe of man and of woman, ffor as moche as Adam and Eve were made and fformed of on kynde, whoo so ys bore in þis signe, pore and ffeble he shall be and he shall lyve in poverte and waylinge and in dissesse.

The 4 signe is Cancer and he regneþ in Juin (ms. Juil) and is ciepid þe signe of þe crabbe, or ellis of þe kanker[9] þat is a worme, for as muche as Job was lepre and ffull of cankris[10] by þe honde (ms. sonde) of God, who so ys borne in thys sygne shall be ffeblee, but he shalle have grace in paradise.

The 5 signe is Leo, and he regneþ in July, and ys cleped þe signe of a lyon, ffor as moche as Danyell þe prophete was put in to þe depe pitte among lyouns, whoo so ys born in þis signe shall be a bolde theef and an hardy.

6. *cleped:* called   7. *discordaunt:* different   8. *dredffull:* inspiring awe
9. *kanker:* insect larva, worm   10. *cankris:* sores

The 6 sygne is Virgo, and he regneþ in Auguste, and it is cleped þe signe of a mayde, ffor as moche as oure Lady Seint Marie in þe burthe and biffor þe burthe, and after þe burthe of Our Savyoure was clene mayde, who so ys borne in þat signe shall be a wyse man and with som gyle or cause he shall be blamed.

The 7 signe is Libra, and he regneth Septembre, and it is cleped þe signe of a balance, ffor as moche as Judas Ichariot made his conseyl with þe Juwes and graunted hem þat þey shulde take Goddis Sone of hevene, who so ys borne in þat signe shall be a wicked man and traytor, and of evyll deth shall deie.

The 8 signe is Scorpio, and he regneth in Octobre and is clepid þe signe of a schorpion, ffor as moche as þe childrin of Ysrael passide þorugh out þe Reed See, who so is borne in þis signe shall have many angris[11] and tribulacions.

The 9 signe is Sagittarius, and he regneth in in Novembre, and it is clepid þe signe of an archer, ffor as moche as Kynge David þe prophit ffaught with Golyas, who so is borne in this signe shall be hardy and leccherouse.

The 10 signe ys Capricornius, and he regneth in Decembre, and it is cleped þe signe of a goatt, ffor as moche as þe Jewis leften þe blessinge of Crist, who so ys borne in this signe shal be riche and lovynge.

The 11 signe is Aquarius, and he regneth in Januere, and is clepid þe signe of a man heldynge out water of a poote,[12] for as moche as Seint John Baptiste baptized Jhesu oure Savyoure in fflom Jordan, who so ys borne in þis signe shall be necclygent[13] and lese his þingis.

The 12 signe is Pisces, and he regneth in Feverere, and it is clepid þe signe of ffisshe, ffor as moche as Jonas þe prophete was caste into þe see, and 3 daies and 3 nythes lay in þe wombe of a whale, who so ys borne in þis signe shall be graciouse and happy. [There is a series of marginal glosses with this section, which read:

Aries Regneth in þe heed
Taurus Regneth in þe necke
Gemini Regneth in þe schildris[14] and in þe armes
Cancer Regneth in þe brest
Leo Regneth in þe bowell and stomac

11. *angris:* distress, tribulation   12. *poote:* pot   13. *necclygent:* negligent
14. *schildris:* shoulders

Virge Regneth in þe ribbis and in þe sidis
Libra Regneth in þe reynez[15]
Scorpio Regneth in þe membris[16]
Sagittarius Regneth in þe thyes
Capricornius Regneth in þe kneys
Aquarius Regneth in þe sparler[17]
Pisces Regneth in þe ffeete]

Here beth þe 7 planetis, as is rehersid before, and it is to undirstande þat whatte man is borne in any oure of þe day in þe wiche regneth any of þe 7 planetis, he shalle be apte and disposid to good or to evell after þe enffluence and þe constellacion of þe planete in þe whiche he is borne in, but never þe latter it is to knowe þat non of hem constreyneth a man to good or to evyll, ffor why be a manys owen good wille, and þe grace of God comynge beffor; and by his owen good levynge may do good, thow he were disposide to do evyll after þe nature and inffluence of his planete.

On þe same maner evere contrarie by a manys owen ffre wyll and by þe coveytinge of a manys herte and his eyn, he may do evell all thowh he were disposid by his planete to do good. Uppon þis argument a phelisophre disputid with another, and axid wheþer a manys predestinacion myght seneste (stonde) by þe preff of þis argumente, and he proved it myght stonde sothe by these wordis Powle rehersid in Holy Scripture, þat þer beth evell daiez, and bi þis it semeth þat þer beth many of hem. And in þe kalender also it is declared þat þer beth many dismalis, þat is to say evell daies and ungracioz, and þat is sothe. It may well be preved be þe philisophrez of þe elde lawe. For whan men wente to bataile, if þei were spedde and hadde þe victorie, þan lovyd þey and þankyd God, and wurshepid þat day; and if þey were scomfited,[18] þan made þei þat day dismoll in here kalenders. And þan answerid þe oþer philisophre and said þus, þat God made all þing good in here kynde[19] withoute ffauȝte and lacke, as þe planetis and þe sterres, and þe elementis, þe monthez and þe daiez, man and beste and all oþer þingz beneþe hem. And bi þis while he arguede, þat þer was no day, ne non oþer þing evyll.

Than þat oþer philisophre answeride aȝeyn, and saide þat whan þat God had made in þe biginnynge 11 hevenes and 10 ordris of

15. *reynez:* reins, kidney, loins   16. *membris:* members   17. *sparler:* legs
18. *scomfited:* defeated   19. *kynde:* nature

angelus ffor to governe hem, and þe planetis, signes and þe elementis, and þe 7 daiez, and man after his owyne schappe[20] and likennesse; and afterwarde in þe mene while, þat he satte up on þe watris, and dividid and made ffisshis and ffoulis to manys ffode. The 10 ordre and þe hiest of þe 10 hevenes, of þe wyche ordre Luciffer was scheff[21] next God, þorugh his pride ffelle doune with many legiouns of his ffelawis þat helden with him in to þe depeste parte of helle; and iche of hem after þat þey had sunned,[22] ffellan, some heyere and somme lowere. Where þorugh þe sterris þe planetis and þe elementis beth enffecte and corrupte, and by þis cause summe beth good and summe evell, after þat inffluence. And þe multitude of spiritus þat ffillen at þat tyme doune oute of þe 10 hevene; and be þis argument þe fforsaide philisophre proved and conclutide þat manys predestinacione ys sothe if it be well determynyd by wey of philosophie. Ffor yche man levynge is made of 3 þingis in generall, þat is to say of 7 planetis, of 12 signes, and 4 elementis, and by þe whiche he hath his ffortune and his inffortune, his boncheff[23] and his myscheff, his maners and his complexions.

For to knowe alle þe serclez of þe ffyrmamente, and þe sterris, it is ffor to witte þat hevene is rounde in þe maner of a rerid[24] spere, in þe myddis of wyche hangyth þe erthe, of a centre of all þe world. Hevene is devytid in 12 spiris, þat makith 11 hevenes, as it is tofforesaid. Of þe whiche þe ffrist and þe heieste is clepyd in Latyn þus: *Celum emperium-ffyoum et motum.*[25] In þe wiche is þe trone of Oure Savyoure; and it is þe place of Oure Lorde of holy seyntis.

The 10 hevene is clepid in Latyn þus: *Celum medium inter cristallum et corporum.*[26]

The 9 hevene is clepid in Latyn: *Cristallum vel applanes,*[27] þat is unmovable.

The 8 spere is clepid in Latyn: *Celum signorum et siderum,*[28] in þe whiche be sette þe 12 signes, with all þe sterris. And þat spere is mevable, and it is clepid also in Latyn *primum mobile,*[29] of þe whiche philisophres ffyndyn in here bokis to werk þer with many craftis.

20. *schappe:* shape, image   21. *scheff:* chief   22. *sunned:* sinned
23. *boncheff:* prosperity   24. *rerid:* upright
25. Lat. heaven of the empyrean
26. Lat. heaven midway between the crystalline (10th) sphere and the earth
27. Lat. crystalline and unmoving   28. Lat. heaven of signs and stars
29. Lat. First mover (ninth sphere of the Ptolemaic system)

The 7 spere is clepid in Latyn *celum saturnum*, in þe whiche Saturnus dwellith and goth abouȝte at onys in ȝe wynter. And Saturne is a planete maliciouse and wickid, cold and drie, and þerffor he is sette heigest of all his ffellawis. Ffor if he stode lowest as þe mone dothe, he shulde distroie man and best, and all þat were yfformed growynge uppon þe erthe. To þe wyche beth ordeyned of kynde þese 4 þingis, þat is to saye: malancolie, elde, hervest and colde wyndis and drie as Northerne Wyndis beth in erthe.

The 6 spere is clepid in Latyn *Celum Jovis*, in whiche regneth Jupiter, and he sercleth it onys in 12 yere, and it is a planete well-willide and good hete, and moiste mesurable. He is to whom is ordeyned blood, beere, drinke and eyre.

The 5 sercle or spere is clepid *Celum martis*, in wyche Mars regneth, and serclyde it onys in 12 yere. And þis planete is hote and drie, to whom is ordeined colere, drrynnk, and ffyre.

The 4 spere or sercle is clepid *Celum solis*,[30] and to þis spere of philisophres in dyverse placis beth diverse names. Summe clepiþ it in Latyn *zodicus;* summe clepiþ *circulus animalium*,[31] and summe *circulus generacionis et corrupcionis*[32] and sume *Circulus obliqus.*[33] In þe myddis of þis zodiacus goth þe sonne evermore in suche a lyne, wyche is clepid in Latyn *Eclyptica;*[34] ffor whan þe mone is in þe lyne, yt is cleped Eclyptica in þe heed or in þe tayle of dracons. And þe sonne be even ffor aȝens it of þat oþer side, þan ffallyth þe eclipse of þe mone þorughout all þe world. Whereffore it shewith þe clipse of þe mone is not ellis but an interposiscion of þe erthe is bitwixe þe sonne and þe mone.

The 3 spere is *Celum veneris*, in þe wyche alwey goth Venus and goth abouȝte at onys in 345 daiez, and he is a planete colde and moiste, in mesure to whom beth ordeyned ffleme, wynde, water and childhode.

The 2 spere is clepid *Celum mercurii*, in þe wyche þis planete Mercury dwelliþ and serclith it onys abouȝte in 330 daies. And Mercurie is a planete colde with cold and hote with hote, and so to yche complexicion he may be likened.

The laste of all and nexte þe erthe of þese 7 planetis ys þe spere of þe mone, and þis spere is clepid in Latyn *Celum lune*. And þis

30. Lat. heaven of the sun   31. Lat. circle of animals
32. Lat. circle of generation and corruption   33. Lat. slanting circle
34. Lat. ecliptic

planete goth abouȝte þe signe 12 tymes in þe yere, and þis is þe cause and þe makynge of þe 12 monthes in þe yere; to whiche planete is ordeyned by kynde fflume,[35] schildehode,[36] and water.

Now it is to knowe and to witte þat þer beth 4 elementis, þat is to saye ffyre, eyre, water and erthe. And ffrist þe spere of þe ffire is hieste, and in kynde it is hote and drie, and makith reed bloode. Coler and þynne be engendrid sicknesse of ffever tercian,[37] and þe agu[38] in somer tyme, abouȝte mydde over none.[39] The 2 is þe spere of þe eyre, whiche is hote and moiste in kynde, and yeldiþ reed bloode sanguyne and thicke, and engendride of kynde evelles in man, whiche be clepid in Latyn *Sinocum*. Sins came of þe ffilthe and corrupcioune of þe bloode.

The 3 is þe spere of þe watere, which is colde and moiste and makiþ of kynde[40] pale bloode, fflematik[41] and watrie above.

The 4 is the spere of þe erthe, whyche is in kynde colde and drie, and ȝeldith blake bloode, malancolie and a partie waterie; and þis is þe laste elemente and lowiste. Þis is hanginge and movynge in þe myddill of þe rounde spere of þe ffirmament as a centre þat is sette in þe myddis of a sercle. And þis element, erth, is round as an appull, as all oþer beth. In þe myddis of þe wyche erthe is þe pitte of helle, rith as þe blake kyrnell lythe in þe myddis of an appull; and as holy wriȝtte declareth after þe day of dome, all þingis shall be round, and þis fforsaid erthe element þan shall be a 1000 tymys brighter þan any Cristall or precious ston, so ffer fforth þat þey þat beth in bittir peynes of helle shull see ever more thoruh þe briȝtenesse of þis element erthe alle þe blisseffull joies of hevene. And þat sight shall be more peyne un to pain þan all þe peynes of hell.

Now it is to undirstande þat every man levynge here in erthe hath 4 complexcionis whiche bithe in him, þat is to saye: colre,[42] sanguyne,[43] ffleme and malancolie, without whiche he may not lyve. Never þe latter, if evere man have alle þese 4, ȝit hath he but on complexcion þat hath his dominacion and maystry over him, by þe wyche yche man is rewlid and governed in kynd. As summe men have moste of colre, and þey ben in complexion colrik men. And ffor

---

35. *fflume:* stream   36. *schildehode:* childhood
37. *tercian:* fever characterized by paroxysms every third day
38. *agu:* ague, fever   39. *none:* ninth (the canonical hour)
40. *of kynde:* by nature   41. *fflematik:* phlegmatic (one of the four humors)
42. *colre:* choler   43. *sanguyne:* sanguine

þey have so moche of colre, here blode is reed and thinne. Sanguine men have most of bloode, and þey ben in complexicion sanguine, and here blode is rith[44] thycke and reed. Summe men also moste of fflemne, and þei ben in complexion fflemnatik, and here blood is pale and waterey, and a partie þynne. Summe men have moste of malancolie, and þei beth in complexion malancolious, and here blode is blac, and thycke in kynde. And þese 4 complexcionis in all þingis ben acordinge in kynde to þe 4 elementis. That is to say, þe ffrist complexicion be cause of hete he luste muste, and because of drinesse he may litill. The 2 complexcion is sanguine, and it is in kynde hote and moyste acordinge to þe elemente of eyre. Who so is of þis complexcion, bi cause of hete him luste moche, and be cause of moystenesse he may moche in kynde. The 3 complexcion is fflemne, and it is in kynde colde and moiste acordynge to þe elemente of watir. Who so is of þis complexcion, be cause of coldenesse him lust litill, and be cause of moysstenesse he may moche. The 4 complexcion is malancolie, and it is in kynde colde and drie acordynge to þe element of erthe. Who so is of þis complexcion, by cause of coldenesse him luste litill, and be cause of drynesse he may but litill in kynde.

Now I shall declare and determyne of þe sercles and of þe regnacion[45] of þe 7 planetis. And ffrist it is to knowe þat þe day naturall bygynnyth in þe morwenynnge of þe day next suwynge,[46] and he hath 24 houris, and iche planete regneth 3 houris a point[47] of þe day and of þe ny3ht, and þat makyth 24 houris. And it is to witte þat þe planete regneþ be estimacion as long tyme as a good reeder and a devoute shulde rede twies þe 7 psalmus with þe letayne. And þerffor Y saye, as by rewle, þat is ffallith not be estimacion, and ffor as moche as yche man may not have þe astrolabe, þerffor it is ychosyn a mesure and point þat men may litgly[48] knowe þe houris and þe planetis. Ffrist bigynneth þe sonne to regne in his owen day, þat is to say þe sonday, in þe morwenynge of þe day, and regneþ as longe tyme as it is to fforsaid. Afterward regneth Venus as longe; than Mercurie as longe; þan þe mone as longe; þan Saturnus as longe. With þat ben 7 houris with here 7 points[49] þat makiþ an houre. Also þe sonne regneþ on his owen day eftsonys[50] þe 8 houre, þan Venus,

---

44. *rith:* right   45. *regnacion:* predominancy, reign   46. *suwynge:* following
47. *point:* fourth part of the day   48. *litgly:* lightly, easily, readily
49. *point:* divisible part of an hour. In this Ms. the 7th part of an hour
50. *eftsonys:* again

þan Mercurius, þan Luna, þan Saturnus, þan Jupiter, þan Mars. And so now þey have regnede 14 houris with here poyntis, þe wyche maken 16 houris. Also þe sonne regneth eftsones in his day þe 15 houre, þan Venus, þan Mercurie, luna, Saturnus, Jupiter, Mars. And so 7 houris ben ffulfillid with her 7 poynts, whiche maken an hour. And so whan alle þese be gaderid togederis, þan is þer 24 houris in þe natural day. Also afterwarde regneþ þe mone on þe Monday, on þe ffrist houre as it dede on þe Sonday. And after þe mone, Saturnus, þan Jupiter, Mars, Sol, Venus, Mercurius, and ffulfillid þe 24 houris with here pointis, and beth þe 7 planets regnande 7 daiez, eche in here naturall day, houris and poyntis, wyche maken 24 houris. And it is to undirstande þat þer beth two maner of daiez: þe day naturall, and þe day artificiall. The artificiall day lasteþ ffro þe sonne rise till þe sonne sette. The naturall day lastiþ 24 houris, þat is to say all þe nyȝth and all þe day. It is to witte also þat if þe plantene regne not retrogarde, as it is tofforsaid, þan myght þey never be made even as by here course. *Post sim, sum sequitur; ultima luna datur.*[51]

Now it is to declare of þe 7 planetis, and of þe houris of hem, wyche beth good, and whiche beth evell, and wyche þe good to begynne, or make any werk, craft, or any oþer science or kunnynge þat longiþ to philosophie, wheder it be good or evell. Where ffor it is to knowe þat þe Sonday is convenable, prophetable, and holsum alle maner of þinges to begynne þat longeth to goodnesse, to love, or to grette werke. And it is prophetable to begynne a werk, or to go on pilgrimage or any longe wey; þat is ffor to say þe ffrist hour on þe Sonday. The 2 houre on þe same day is þe hour of þe planete Venus, which is in nede joyned with Mercurie, and þat is evell and perlous. The 3 houre is Mercure, and also evell. The 4 houre is Luna, and þat is good. The 5 houre is Saturne, and is good, þe whiche is joyned with Jubiter (sic). The 6 houre is Jubiter, and is good. The 7 houre is Mars and is evell. And þe 8 houre is Sol aȝeyn, and is good as þe ffrist. þe 9 houre is Venus. The 10 Mercurie, the 11 Luna, the 12 Saturne. The ffrist houre of þe nyght ffolwynge is þe houre of Jupiter, and þe 2 Mars, þe 3 Sol, þe 4 Venus, þe 5 Mercurius, þe 6 Luna, þe 7 Saturnus, þe 8 Jupiter, þe 9 Mars, þe 10 Sol, þe 11 Venus, þe 12 Mercurius. The ffrist houre on þe M[o]n day is Luna,

---

51. Lat. After "I maybe," "I am" follows; the last moon is given.—the reference is obscure.

and is good; þe 2 Saturnus, and is evell; þe 3 is Jupiter, and is good; þe 4 Mars, and is evell. The 5 is Soll, and is good. The 6 is Venus, and is good. The 7 is Mercurus, and is yvell. The 8 hour is Luna and is good. The 9 is Saturnus, and is yvell. The 10 is Jupiter, and is good. The 11 is Mars, and is yvell. The 12 is Sol, and is good. The ffriest houre of þe ny3th suwinge is Venus, þe 2 Mercurie, þe 3 Luna, þe 4 Saturnus, þe 5 Jupiter, þe 6 Mars, þe 7 Sol, þe 8 Venus, þe 9 Mercurius, þe 10 Luna, þe 11 Saturnus, þe 12 Jupiter. The ffrist hour on þe Twesday is Mars, and þat is evell; þe 2 Soll, and is good; þe 3 Venus, and is good. The 4 is Mercurius and is evyll, þe 5 luna, and is good, þe 6 Saturne, and is evyll. þe 7 is Jupiter and is good; þe 8 Mars, and is evell. The 9 sol, and is good, þe 10 Venus, and is good, þe 11 Mercurie, and is yvell, þe 12 Luna, and is good. þe ffrist houre on þe nyght suwinge is Saturnus, and so fforth be ordre all þe daies in þe weke. And so þou maiste knowe þe planetis, how þey regnen in here houris, whiche ben good and whiche ben evell, as þe gonne be ordre abou3te.

Now it is to declare of þe 7 daiez in þe weke, þe whiche taken here names of þe 7 planetis, as it is afforsaid. And þis is þe cause ffor iche planete regne on þe ffrist houre on his owyn day: as þe sonne þat is clepid Sol on þe Sonday, and Luna on þe Monday, and so of all oþer. And it is to witte, þat what man is borne in ony houre of þe day, in whiche on of þe 7 planetis hath lordschipe he shall be lyghter[52] to turn to good or to evell after þe inffluence of þe same planete þat he is borne in. Now 3e shulle knowe well þat þe sonne is þe eye of þe world, þe ffayreste of þe ffirmament, the lyghter of þe mone, and of alle oþer planetis, of whom þe day takiþ his leynge.[53] Ffor þe day is no þinge but þe spredinge of þe sonne uppon erthe. Ffor þe philosopre seith þat men may not come fforthe ne be norshid withoute vertu of þe sonne. Undir swiche constellacion, a man þat is bore levynge ffayre spechid, meke, swifte, a sotell lerner, and hie of witte, and well duringe, a ffaire softe speker, moche good gaderinge, and with glad chere dispendinge, without boste, abell moche to be lovede, wyse, save he loveth moche wommen, and alle oþer þingis doynge with grette discrecioun. The tokenes of þe sonne in a mannys body ben þese: a clere fface, and a redy; a mene mouþe, lippis reed and sumdell boluynge;[54] and all þe bodi well schapen.

52. *lyghter:* more likely   53. *leynge:* length   54. *boluynge:* curving

The mone is like to sonne, lyghtnyd with þe sonne bemes, a gladner of weyffaring men, of vixid men a relevere; undir þe wiche constellacion a man þat is borne is unsteffast, moche wakynge, moch thenkynge in him self, spekinge without sotilte and litghly wexinge seke with colde; of lithe causis makinge grette, and lightliche levynge wronge; not gladliche partinge his good; moche gaderinge of silvere, and nauȝth expendinge; nott sittinge ne restinge with his owen good wille, and biholdinge unstable in every side. The tokenes of þe mone be þese: a pale fface, þat is to saie to whitnes bowyinge;[55] a litill mough;[56] a blonte nose; sone wexinge hore[57] and studinge[58] in erthli þingz without mesure.

Mars is a bitter and a malicious planet. It is undir þe constellacioun of whom batellus[59] kyngis be borne; cursinge a man shall be þat is borne undir him, and mysseledinge and sley, ffor þey wull gladely disceyve; and þei be coveitous of preisinge, and bostinge of here owyn werkis and preisinge, and depravynge of oþere menys werkis, or deffilinge. And holde þis ffor verri trewþe, þat what man þat is borne undire þe planete of Mars, wheder he be kyng or pore man, he shall be hasti, and batellous; his hondis shall be aȝeins hym. The tokenes of Mars in a manys body ben þese: a black fface and a lene; and moche mouþe, and ofte openyd to styves[60] and backbitynges; a longe nose and knobbid in þe myddill. And holde þis ffor verri truþe, þat what man þat haþe a long nose and lyfte up in þe myddill lyke an heren or a kyte, he is naturaliche ffals.

Mercurie is a good planete, and with oþer good planetis he accordith undir þe constellacion of whiche planete all coveitous men of liberall science ben borne, and also lewde men of oþer craftis ben right wyse. Mercurie makith men þat be borne undir him prout, ffaire spekers, good of witte, and good of mynde, and lyghliche mevynge to dyverse regionns, and goynge pylgrimage; desiringe alwey to lerne newe thyngis, and not þingz herde affore. Merccurie makyth men trowynge to here owyn conceyll; it makith men grette geters, and gladliche spendinge. The tokenes of Mercurie in a manys body ben þese: ffayre fface and a clere, and lightliche waxinge reed; grette lyppis and swellynge; even teeþ; blake eyne; a streghte nose, not knobbid; and a grette lovyer of wommen.

---

55. *bowyinge:* tending   56. *mough:* mouth   57. *hore:* grey
58. *studinge:* studying   59. *batellus:* warlike   60. *styves:* strifes

Jupitere ys a good planete, and a clere to all manere temper-
aunce of myrthe, and of elthe;[61] undir þe wyche constellacioyn þe
man þat is borne shall gladliche of religiouse, and a holy man; of
what condidion þat he be Jupiter makyth men large, glade cherid,[62]
and hardy; grettely to be loved, and also gracyous; and knytte with
knotte of Venus, naturaliche desiringe, but clevynge[63] to wylfull
chastite; speritualiche naþeles[64] uneþe[65] comynnge to age. The signe
of Jupiter in a manis body ben þese: citrine[66] eyne; uneven teth and
thynne ysette; a streghte nose, not knobbid; in goynge with tem-
peraunce and mekenesse.

Venus ys a bryght sterre, and in þe lower þingis gracious; tem-
perache colde and moiste; undir þe whiche constellacion þe man þat
is borne, he is ffayre, but he is rith lecherouse, fful of pley, joynge,
desiringe divers kyndes of instrumentis, þat is to saye organs, harpis
and trumpis. Þat man shall be a delicious man, and noble; lovynge
geftis; and he shall desire veyne preysingis. He shall be rith angry,
and sone ffor3evynge. He shall leve more his owen conceyll þan
oþer menys. And if he be a riche man, and he shall 3eve moche good
to pore men; and if he be a pore man, þat he may not do he shall
ffullffylle with mercy and good wylle and compassion. Also he shall
be rith riche and large, and þat more to pore men þan to riche. And
he shall be of good witte, and þat he lerneth, he shall lyghtly sone
ffor3ete. The sygenes of Venus ben þese: a mene[67] fforheed and
smale browis; laughynge eyen; a white nose and scharpe; a large
mouþe, and reed lippis; a semblaunte[68] chaungeable; and þey lobeth[69]
whyyt[70] cloþis.

Saturne is a planete derke and malicious, colde and drie; undir
þe constellacion of wyche þe man þat is bore, is bore dredffull, and
a nygard. O þing he hath in hert, anoþer in þe mouþe. Þat man shall
be envyous and soruffull, a traytor, and solitarie; ffewe wordis
malicious in spekinge. When it semeth þat he spekith good, he
drawith be sotilte into evyll, þe whiche is werste of all þinge. And
lyghtly he wulle be offendid, and evell to be pleside, and unneþe he

61. *elthe:* age   62. *cherid:* cherry in demeanour
63. *clevynge:* cleaving, clinging   64. *naþeles:* nevertheless
65. *unneþe:* scarcely   66. *citrine:* yellow-green
67. *mene:* moderate, medium   68. *semblaunte:* demeanor
69. *lobeth:* love   70. *whyyt:* white

wille be plesid. Unneþe he will conseyne[71] any science, but whan he hath conseyned, he wull not lyghtly lese it. The tokenes of Saturne ben þese: a lowringe chere; ofte tymes grette browis, and hangynge ȝelowe eyne; a thynne berde; a grette nose; stable eyne; slow in goynge. His chere is alwey to þe erthe; he þenkyth moste on erthely þingis; blake cloþinge he loveth moste.

71. *conseyne:* learn

2

The Papal Letter
Unam Sanctam, 1302

Introductory Note: Pope Boniface VIII (1294–1303) issued the bull *Unam Sanctam* in November, 1302, as a step in his dispute with Philip IV, King of France, The particular conflict that elicited this specific, highly juridical expression of a theory of Christian unity and the supremacy of the pope has been widely studied from many points of view. It is included here to suggest the particular ways in which the unity and hierarchical order of the Church were considered in the early fourteenth century. For a general introduction to the document and its context, see Charles T. Wood, *Philip the Fair and Boniface VIII* (New York, 1967), which offers a good bibliography. This translation is that of James Harvey Robinson, *The Pre-reformation Period*, Translations and Reprints from the Original Sources of European History, vol. 3, no. 6 (Philadelphia, 1897), pp. 19–21. The Latin text may be found in E. Friedberg, ed., *Corpus Iuris Canonici* (Leipzig, 1881), 2: cols. 1245–46.

❖ *The Decretal Unam Sanctam of Pope Boniface VIII*

That there is one Holy Catholic and Apostolic church we are impelled by our faith to believe and to hold—this we do firmly believe and openly confess—and outside of this there is neither salvation or remission of sins, as the bridegroom proclaims in Canticles, "My dove, my undefiled is but one; she is the only one of her mother; she is the choice one of her that bare her." The church represents one mystic body and of this body Christ is the head; of Christ, indeed, God is the head. In it, is one Lord, and one faith and one baptism. In the time of the flood, there was one ark of Noah, pre-figuring the one church, finished in one cubit, having one Noah as steersman and commander. Outside of this, all things upon the face of the earth were, as we read, destroyed. This church we venerate and this alone, the Lord saying through his prophets, "Deliver my soul, O God, from the sword; my darling from the power of the dog." He prays thus for the soul, that is for Himself, as head, and also for the body which He calls one, namely, the church on account of the unity of the bridegroom, of the faith, of the sacraments, and of the charity of the church. It is that seamless coat of the Lord, which was not rent, but fell by lot. Therefore, in this one and only church, there is one body and one head—not two heads as if it were a monster—namely, Christ and Christ's Vicar, Peter and Peter's successor, as the Lord said to Peter himself, "Feed my sheep:" *my* sheep, he said, using a general term and not designating these or those sheep, so that we must believe that all the sheep were committed to him. If, then, the Greeks, or others, shall say that they were not entrusted to Peter and his successors, they must perforce admit that they are not of Christ's sheep, as the Lord says in John, "there is one fold, and one shepherd."

In this church and in its power are two swords, to wit, a spiritual and a temporal, and this we are taught by the words of the Gospel, for when the Apostles said, "Behold, here are two swords" (in the church, namely, since the apostles were speaking), the Lord did not reply that it was too many, but enough. And surely he who claims that the temporal sword is not in the power of Peter, has but ill understood the word of our Lord when he said, "Put up thy sword in its scabbard." Both, therefore, the spiritual and the material swords, are in the power of the church, the latter indeed to be used for the church, the former by the church, the one by the priest, the other by the hand of kings and soldiers, but by the will and sufferance of the priest. It is fitting, moreover, that one sword should be under the other, and the temporal authority subject to the spiritual power. For when the apostle said, "there is no power but of God and the powers that are of God are ordained," they would not be ordained unless one sword were under the other, and one, as inferior, was brought back by the other to the highest place. For according to the Holy Dionysius, the law of divinity is to lead the lowest through the intermediate to the highest. Therefore, according to the law of the universe, things are not reduced to order directly, and upon the same footing, but the lowest through the intermediate, and the inferior through the superior. It behooves us, therefore, the more freely to confess that the spiritual power excels in dignity and nobility any form whatsoever of earthly power, as spiritual interests exceed the temporal in importance. All this we see fairly from the giving of tithes, from the benediction and sanctification, from the recognition of this power and the control of these same things. For the truth bearing witness, it is for the spiritual power to establish the earthly power and judge it, if it be not good. Thus, in the case of the church and the power of the church, the prophecy of Jeremiah is fulfilled: "See, I have this day set three over the nations and over the kindgoms"—and what follows. Therefore, if the earthly power shall err, it shall be judged by the spiritual power, if the lesser spiritual power err, it shall be judged by the higher. But if the supreme power err, it can be judged by God alone and not by man, the apostles bearing witness saying, the spiritual man judges all things but he himself is judged by no one. Hence this power, although given to man and exercised by man, is not human, but rather a divine power, given the divine lips to Peter, and founded on a rock for Him and his successors in Him [Christ] whom he confessed; the Lord saying to Peter himself, "Whatsoever thou shalt bind" etc. Whoever, therefore, shall resist this power, ordained by God, resists the ordination of God, unless there should be two beginnings, as the Manichaean imagines. But this we judge to be false and heretical, since, by the testimony of Moses, not in the *beginnings*, but in the *beginning*, God created the heaven and the earth. We, moreover, proclaim, declare and pronounce that it is altogether necessary to salvation for every human being to be subject to the Roman Pontiff.

Given at the Lateran the twelfth day before the Kalends of December, in our eighth year, as a perpetual memorial of this matter.

3

"Engelond his a wel god lond . . ."
Robert of Gloucester, 1300

Introductory Note: This description of England opens Robert of Gloucester's Metrical Chronicle of the history of England. This version, from the A-text, is taken from British Museum ms. Cotton Caligula A. xi. fol. 3; in this manuscript, the chronicle precedes *Piers Plowman*. The chronicle goes from Brutus, son of Aeneas, to Henry III. For a complete text of Robert of Gloucester, see *The Metrical Chronicle of Robert of Gloucester*, ed. William Aldis Wright, Rolls Series, vol. 86 (London, 1887). While not a brilliant piece of versification, the thirteenth-century chronicle is obviously the work of one who took pride in cataloguing his country's advantages and detailing its history. Although Langland's landscape is universal and allegorical in *Piers Plowman*, it is clear, (e.g., in the *Prologue* and *Passus* VI) that England is the literal landscape in the poem.

 "Engelond his a wel god lond . . ."

> Engelond his a wel god lond;[1] ich wene at londe best.[2]
> yset in þe on[3] ende of þe worlde, as al in þe west.

1. *a wel god lond:* a very good land
2. *ich wene at londe best:* I think it the best of lands   3. *on:* one

þe see geþ[4] him al aboute; he stond as in an yle.[5]
Of for hii dorre þe lasse doute, bote hit be þorȝ gyle
Of file of þe suive lond, as me haþ iseye ȝwile.   5
Fram souþe to norþ he is long eiȝte houndred mile
And two hundred mile brod, fram est to west to wende[6]
A midde þe lond as hit be,[7] and noȝt as biþe on ende.
Plente me[8] may in Engelond, of alle gode ise
bote volc hit vorgulte,[9] oþer ȝeres þe worse be,   10
Vor[10] Engelo(n)de is vol[11] inoȝ of frut, and els of tren,[12]
Of wodes and of parkes, þet joye hit is to sen;
Of fowles and of bestes, of wylde and tame also;
Of salt fichȝ[13] and eke verss, of vaire[14] rivers þerto;
Of wellen[15] swete and olde inouȝ; of lesen[16]
     and of mede;   15
Of selver or[17] and of gold, of tyn and eke of lede;
Of stel, of yre,[18] and of bras; of god corn[19] gret won;
Of wit[20] and of wolle god—betere ne may be non.
Wateres he haþ el inoȝ; ac at vore all oþere þre[21]
Out of þe lond in to þe se, armes as þei it be.   20
I ware be þe ssiþes mowe come[22] fram þe se, and wende
And bringe a londe god inoȝ, about in eche ende.
Severne and Temese,[23] Homber is þet þridde[24]
And þaime is al ȝwo sen þat þur lond amidde[25]
Homber bringȝ bi Norþe, muche god and wide;   25
Severne bi west souþ; Temese bi þe est side.
So þat of god inoȝ þat in oþer londes his
Per bi weneþ to Engelond, þat non defaute nis.

4. *see geþ:* sea goes   5. *yle:* isle, island   6. *to wende:* to go, journey
7. *as hit be:* as it is   8. *me:* men
9. *bote volc hit vorgulte:* unless people (folk) indulge in gluttony
10. *Vor:* For   11. *vol:* full   12. *tren:* trees   13. *fichȝ:* fish
14. *vaire:* fresh, fair   15. *wellen:* wells   16. *lesen:* leas
17. *selver or:* silver ore   18. *yre:* iron   19. *corn:* grain   20. *wit:* wheat
21. *ac at vore all oþere þre:* but before all others, three
22. *ssiþes mowe come:* voyagers must come
23. *Severne and Temese:* Severn and Thames (rivers)
24. *Homber is þet þridde:* Humber (river) is the third
25. *þur lond amidde:* through the middle of the land

4

William Fitzstephen's Description of London, 1180

Introductory Note: This text was written by William Fitzstephen in the last quarter of the twelfh century and was first printed in John Stow's *Survey of London* in 1598. Although there are many later descriptions of the city, the Fitzstephen text suggests some of the early vigor of the city and the early attraction it had for the life of power, wealth, and thought throughout the kingdom. This translation is that by H. E. Butler, in Sir F. M. Stenton, *Norman London: An Essay*, Historical Association Leaflets, no. 93 (London, 1934), pp. 26–32. The Latin text may be found in J. C. Robertson, *Materials for the History of Thomas Becket*, Rolls Series, vol. 67 (London, 1878). Two different approaches to London in Langland's age are those of Sylvia Thrupp, *The Merchant Class of Medieval London* (rpt. Ann Arbor, 1962) and D. W. Robertson, Jr., *Chaucer's London* (New York, 1968). Both contain useful bibliographical references. By Langland's day London had become the center of English political life and its economy, and many of the characters in *Piers Plowman* (e.g., the sins in *Passus* V and the world around Lady Meed in *Passus* III–IV) sound very much like figures out of late fourteenth-century London life.

✤ A Description of the Most Noble City of London

Among the noble cities of the world that are celebrated by Fame, the CITY OF LONDON, seat of the Monarchy of England, is one that spreads its fame wider, sends its wealth and wares further, and lifts its head higher than all others. It is blest in the wholesomeness of its air, in its reverence for the Christian faith, in the strength of its bulwarks, the nature of its situation, the honour of its citizens, and the chastity of its matrons. It is likewise most merry in its sports and fruitful of noble men. Of these things it is my pleasure to treat, each in its own place.

There

"the mild sky doth soften hearts of men,"

not that they may be "weak slaves of lust," but that they may not be savage and like unto beasts, nay, rather, that they may be of a kindly and liberal temper.

In the Church of St. Paul is the Episcopal See. Once it was Metropolitan, and it is thought that it will be so again, if the citizens return to the island, unless perchance the Archiepiscopal title of the Blessed Martyr Thomas and the presence of his body preserve that honour for all time at Canterbury, where it now resides. But since St. Thomas had adorned both these cities, London by his rising and Canterbury by his setting, each city has, in respect of the Saint himself, something further that it may urge, not without justice, one against the other. Also as concerns Christian worship, there are both in London and the Suburbs thirteen greater Conventual churches, and a hundred and twenty-six lesser Parochial.

On the East stands the Palatine Citadel, exceeding great and strong, whose walls and bailey rise from very deep foundations, their mortar being mixed with the blood of beasts. On the West are two strongly fortified Castles, while thence there runs continuously a great wall and high, with seven double gates, and with towers along the North at intervals. On the South,

London was once walled and towered in like fashion, but the Thames, that mighty river, teeming with fish, which runs on that side with the sea's ebb and flow, has in course of time washed away those bulwarks, undermined and cast them down. Also up-stream to the West the Royal Palace rises high above the river, a building beyond compare, with an outwork and bastions, two miles from the City and joined thereto by a populous suburb.

On all sides, beyond the houses, lie the gardens of the citizens that dwell in the suburbs, planted with trees, spacious and fair, adjoining one another.

On the North are pasture lands and a pleasant space of flat meadows, intersected by running waters, which turn revolving mill-wheels with merry din. Hard by there stretches a great forest with wooded glades and lairs of wild beasts, deer both red and follow, wild boars and bulls. The corn-fields are not of barren gravel, but rich Asian plains such as "make glad the crops" and fill the barns of their farmers "with sheaves of Ceres' stalk."

There are also round about London in the Suburbs most excellent wells, whose waters are sweet, wholesome and clear, and whose

"runnels ripple amid pebbles bright."

Among these Holywell, Clerkenwell and Saint Clement's Well are most famous and are visited by thicker throngs and greater multitudes of students from the schools and of the young men of the City, who go out on summer evenings to take the air. In truth a good City when it has a good Lord![1]

This City wins honour by its men and glory by its arms and has a multitude of inhabitants, so that at the time of the calamitous wars of King Stephen's reign the men going forth from it to be mustered were reckoned twenty thousand armed horsemen and sixty thousand foot-soldiers. The citizens of London are everywhere regarded as illustrious and renowned beyond those of all other cities for the elegance of their fine manners, raiment and table. The inhabitants of other towns are called

---

1. A hit at Henry II. Cf. the pointed reference to his son "Henry the Third" below, note 7.

citizens, but of this they are called barons. And with them a solemn oath ends all strife.

The matrons of London are very Sabines.

In London the three principal churches, to wit the Episcopal See of the church of Saint Paul, the church of the Holy Trinity, and the church of Saint Martin, have famous schools by privilege and in virtue of their ancient dignity. But through the personal favour of some one or more of those learned men who are known and eminent in the study of philosophy there are other schools licensed by special grace and permission. On holy days the masters of the schools assemble their scholars at the churches whose feast-day it is. The scholars dispute, some in demonstrative rhetoric, others in dialectic. Some "hurtle enthymemes,"[2] others with greater skill employ perfect syllogisms. Some are exercised in disputation for the purpose of display, which is but a wrestling bout of wit, but others that they may establish the truth for the sake of perfection. Sophists who produce fictitious arguments are accounted happy in the profusion and deluge of their words; others seek to trick their opponents by the use of fallacies. Some orators from time to time in rhetorical harangues seek to carry persuasion, taking pains to observe the precepts of their art and to omit naught that appertains thereto. Boys of different schools strive one against another in verse or contend concerning the principles of the art of grammar or the rules governing the use of past or future. There are others who employ the old wit of the cross-roads in epigrams, rhymes and metre; with "Fescennine License," they lacerate their comrades outspokenly, though mentioning no names; they hurl "abuse ad gibes," they touch the foibles of their comrades, perchance even of their elders with Socratic wit, not to say

"bite more keenly even than Theon's tooth,"

in their "bold dithyrambs." Their hearers

"ready to laugh their fill,"
"With wrinkling nose repeat the loud guffaw."

---

2. *enthymeme:* an argument consisting of a single premise and conclusion as opposed to a "syllogism" made up of major and minor premises and conclusion.

Those that ply their several trades, the vendors of each several thing, the hirers out of their several sorts of labour are found every morning each in their separate quarters and each engaged upon his own peculiar task. Moreover there is in London upon the river's bank, amid the wine that is sold from ships and wine-cellars, a public cook-shop.[3] There daily, according to the season, you may find viands, dishes roast, fried and boiled, fish great and small, the coarser flesh for the poor, the more delicate for the rich, such as venison and birds both big and little. If friends, weary with travel, should of a sudden come to any of the citizens, and it is not their pleasure to wait fasting till fresh food is bought and cooked and

"till servants bring / Water for hands and bread,"

they hasten to the river bank, and there all things desirable are ready to their hand. However great the infinitude of knights or foreigners that enter the city or are about to leave it, at whatever hour of night or day, that the former may not fast too long nor the latter depart without their dinner, they turn aside thither, if it so please them, and refresh themselves each after his own manner. Those who desire to fare delicately, need not search to find sturgeon or "Guinea-fowl" or "Ionian francolin," since all the dainties that are found there are set forth before their eyes. Now this is a public cook-shop, appropriate to a city and pertaining to the art of civic life. Hence that saying which we read in the Gorgias of Plato, to wit that the art of cookery is a counterfeit of medicine and a flattery of the fourth part of the art of civic life.

In the suburb[4] immediately outside one of the gates there is a smooth field, both in fact and in name. On every sixth day of the week, unless it be a major feast-day on which solemn rites are prescribed, there is a much frequented show of fine horses for sale. Thither come all the Earls,[5] Barons and Knights

---

3. This "cookshop"—for the word *coquina* can hardly mean a "cookshop quarter" —was presumably near the Vintry: the ships would probably come to Dowgate.
4. (West) Smithfield.
5. "Earls." The Latin is *Consules*, sometimes used in an Earl's formal style in the twelfth century. (F.M.S.)

who are in the City, and with them many of the citizens, whether to look on or buy. It is a joy to see the ambling palfreys, their skin full of juice, their coats a-glisten, as they pace softly, in alternation raising and putting down the feet on one side together; next to see the horses that best befit Esquires, moving more roughly, yet nimbly, as they raise and set down the opposite feet, fore and hind, first on one side and then on the other; then the younger colts of high breeding, unbroken and

"high-stepping with elastic tread,"

and after them the costly destriers of graceful form and goodly stature, "with quivering ears, high necks and plump buttocks." As these show their paces, the buyers watch first their gentler gait, then that swifter motion, wherein their fore feet are thrown out and back together, and the hind feet also, as it were, counter-wise. When a race between such trampling steeds is about to begin, or perchance between others which are likewise, after their kind, strong to carry, swift to run, a shout is raised, and horses of the baser sought are bidden to turn aside. Three boys riding these fleet-foot steeds, or at times two as may be agreed, prepare themselves for the contest. Skilled to command their horses, they

"curb their untamed mouths with jagged bits,"

and their chief anxiety is that their rival shall not gain the lead. The horses likewise after their fashion lift up their spirits for the race; "their limbs tremble; impatient of delay, they cannot stand still." When the signal is given, they stretch forth their limbs, they gallop away, they rush on with obstinate speed. The riders, passionate for renown, hoping for victory, vie with one another in spurring their swift horses and lashing them forward with their switches no less than they excite them by their cries. You would believe that "all things are in motion," as Heraclitus maintained, and that the belief of Zeno was wholly false, when he claimed that motion was impossible and that no man could ever reach the finish of a race.

In another place apart stand the wares of the country-folk, instruments of agriculture, longflanked swine, cows with swollen udders, and

> "wooly flocks and bodies huge of kine."

Mares stand there, meet for ploughs, sledges and two-horsed carts; the bellies of some are big with young; round others move their offspring, new-born, sprightly foals, inseparable followers.

To this city, from every nation that is under heaven, merchants rejoice to bring their trade in ships.

> Gold from Arabia, from Sabaea spice
> And incense; from the Scythians arms of steel
> Well-tempered; oil from the rich groves of palm
> That spring from the fat lands of Babylon;
> Fine germs from Nile, from China crimson silks;
> French wines; and sable, vair and miniver
> From the far lands where Russ and Norseman dwell.

London, as the chroniclers have shewn, is far older than Rome. For, owing its birth to the same Trojan ancestors, it was founded by Brutus before Rome was founded by Romulus and Remus. Wherefore they both still use the ancient laws and like institutions. London like Rome is divided into wards. In place of Consuls it has Sheriffs every year; its senatorial order and lesser magistrates; sewers and conduits in its streets, and for the pleading of diverse causes, demonstrative, deliberative and judicial, it has its proper places, its separate courts. It has also its assemblies on appointed days. I do not think there is any city deserving greater approval for its customs in respect of church-going, honour paid to the ordinances of God, keeping of feast-days, giving of alms, entertainment of strangers, ratifying of betrothals, contracts of marriage, celebration of nuptials, furnishing of banquets, cheering of guests, and likewise for their care in regard to the rites of funeral and the burial of the dead. The only plagues of London are the immoderate drinking of fools and the frequency of fires.

To that which I have said this also must be added, that almost all Bishops, Abbots and Magnates of England are, as it were, citizens and freemen of the City of London, having lordly habitations there, whither they repair and wherein they make lavish outlay, when summoned to the City by our Lord the King or by his Metropolitan to councils and great assemblies, or drawn thither by their own affairs.

Furthermore let us consider also the sports of the City, since it is not meet that a city should only be useful and sober, unless it also be pleasant and merry. Wherefore on the seals of the High Pontiffs down to the time when Leo was pope, on the one side of the signet Peter the Fisherman was engraved and over him a key stretched forth from heaven as it were by the hand of God, and around it the verse,

"For me thou left'st the ship; take thou the key.

And on the other side was engraved a city with this device, "Golden Rome." Also it was said in praise of Caesar Augustus and Rome,

"All night it rains; with dawn the shows return.
Caesar, thou shar'st thine empery with Jove."

London in place of shows in the theatre and stage-plays has holier plays, wherein are shown forth the miracles wrought by Holy Confessors or the sufferings which glorified the constancy of Martyrs.

Moreover, each year upon the day called Carnival—to begin with the sports of boys (for we were all boys once)—boys from the schools bring fighting-cocks to their master, and the whole forenoon is given up to boyish sport; for they have a holiday in the schools that they may watch their cocks do battle. After dinner all the youth of the City goes out into the fields to a much-frequented game of ball. The scholars of each school have their own ball, and almost all the workers of each trade have theirs also in their hands. Elder men and fathers and rich citizens come on horse-back to watch the contests of their juniors, and after their fashion are young again with the young; and it seems that the motion of their natural heat is kindled by the contemplation of such violent motion and by their partaking in the joys of untrammelled youth.

Every Sunday in Lent after dinner a "fresh swarm of young gentles" goes forth on war-horses, "steeds skilled in the contest," of which each is

> "apt and schooled to wheel in circles round."

From the gates burst forth in throngs the lay sons of citizens, armed with lance and shield, the younger with shafts forked at the end, but with steel point removed. "They wake war's semblance" and in mimic contest exercise their skill at arms. Many courtiers come too, when the King is in residence; and from the households of Earls and Barons come young men not yet invested with the belt of knighthood, that they may there contend together. Each one of them is on fire with hope of victory. The fierce horses neigh, "their limbs tremble; they champ the bit; impatient of delay they cannot stand still." When at length

> "the hoof of trampling steeds careers along,"

the youthful riders divide their hosts; some pursue those that fly before, and cannot overtake them; others unhorse their comrades and speed by.

At the feast of Easter they make sport with naval tourneys, as it were. For a shield being strongly bound to a stout pole in mid-stream, a small vessel, swiftly driven on by many an oar and by the river's flow, carries a youth standing at the prow, who is to strike the shield with his lance. If he break the lance by striking the shield and keep his feet unshaken, he has achieved his purpose and fulfilled his desire. If, however, he strike it strongly without splintering his lance, he is thrown into the rushing river, and the boat of its own speed passes him by. But there are on each side of the shield two vessels moored, and in them are many youths to snatch up the striker who has been sucked down by the stream, as soon as he emerges into sight or

> "once more bubbles on the topmost wave."

On the bridge and the galleries above the river are spectators of the sport "ready to laugh their fill."

On feast-days throughout the summer the youths exercise themselves in leaping, archery and wrestling, putting the stone, and throwing the thonged javelin beyond a mark, and fighting with sword and buckler. "Cytherea leads the dance of maidens and the earth is smitten with free foot at moonrise."

In winter on almost every feast-day before dinner either foaming boars and hogs, armed with "tusks lightning-swift," themselves soon to be bacon, fight for their lives, or fat bulls with butting horns, or huge bears, do combat to the death against hounds let loose upon them.

When the great marsh that washes the Northern walls of the City is frozen, dense throngs of youths go forth to disport themselves upon the ice. Some gathering speed by a run, glide sidelong, with feet set well apart, over a vast space of ice. Others make themselves seats of ice like millstones and are dragged along by a number who run before them holding hands. Sometimes they slip owing to the greatness of their speed and fall, every one of them, upon their faces. Others there are, more skilled to sport upon the ice, who fit to their feet the shin-bones of beasts, lashing them beneath their ankles, and with iron-shod poles in their hands they strike ever and anon against the ice and are borne along swift as a bird in flight or a bolt shot from a mangonel. But sometimes two by agreement run one against the other from a great distance and, raising their poles, strike one another. One or both fall, not without bodily hurt, since on falling they are borne a long way in opposite directions by the force of their own motion; and wherever the ice touches the head, it scrapes and skins it entirely. Often he that falls breaks shin or arm, if he fall upon it. But youth is an age greedy of renown, yearning for victory, and exercises itself in mimic battles that it may bear itself more boldly in true combats.

Many of the citizens delight in taking their sport with birds of the air, merlins and falcons and the like, and with dogs that wage warfare in the woods. The citizens have the special privilege of hunting in Middlesex, Hertfordshire and all Chiltern, and in Kent as far as the river Cray. The Londoners, who are called Trinobantes, repulsed Gaius Julius Caesar, who

> "rejoiced
> To make no way save with the spilth of blood."

Whence Lucan writes,

> "To the Britons whom he sought / He showed his coward back."

The City of London has brought forth not a few men who subdued many nations and the Roman Empire to their sway, and many others whom valour has

> "raised to the Gods as lords of earth,"

as had been promised to Brutus by the oracle of Apollo.

> Brutus, past Gaul beneath the set of sun,
> There lies an isle in Ocean ringed with waters.
> This seek; for there shall be thine age-long home.
> Here for thy sons shall rise a second Troy,
> Here from thy blood shall monarchs spring, to whom
> All earth subdued shall its obeisance make.

And in Christian times she brought forth the treat Emperor Constantine,[6] who gave the city of Rome and all the insignia of Empire to God and the Blessed Peter and Silvester the Roman Pope, to whom he rendered the office of a groom, and rejoiced no longer to be called Emperor, but rather the Defender of the Holy Roman Church. And that the peace of the Lord Pope might not be shaken with the tumult of the noise of this world by reason of his presence, he himself departed altogether from the city which he had conferred on the Lord Pope, and built for himself the city of Byzantium.

And in modern times also she has produced monarchs renowned and magnificent, the Empress Matilda, King Henry the Third,[7] and Blessed Thomas, the Archbishop, Christ's glorious Martyr,

> "than whom
> She bore no whiter soul nor one more dear"

to all good men in the Latin world.

6. For the forged Donation of Constantine see Gibbon, *Decline and Fall*, chapter 49.
7. King Henry the Third is the "Young King," second son of Henry II. He was crowned at Westminster (1170) and again, with his queen, at Winchester (1172).

PART II:

Abuses in the Church and the World

There is no more varied or ubiquitous medieval literary genre than that of satire and complaint. From the most powerful institutions to prominent and wholly anonymous individuals, the period between the eleventh and sixteenth centuries witnessed a vast outpouring of savage, profound, often highly literate indictments of the failure of the Church and the world to fulfill the purposes for which they were created. Wholly outside of that stream of complaint and dissent that led toward heresy, the critics of Church and society whose works are reprinted below remained firmly, although sometimes truculently, within the Church whose failures they articulated in precise and frequently colorful detail and within the world whose evils they itemized with savagery and humor, understanding and incomprehension, visionary prophecies of the future and nostalgic backward glances at a better, simpler, more virtuous, evangelical past.

The period between 1100 and 1250 witnessed many general
complaints against the institutionalization of ecclesiastical authority. From 1250 on, however, the critics of Church and society
found a wide variety of targets for their outrage. The social utopi-
anism of ecclesiastical thinkers, the crises of the Church between
the second Council of Lyons in 1274 to the Council of Constance
of 1415–1418, and the series of dramatic transformations in material culture between the famines of the late thirteenth century
(through the Black Death) and the social restoration processes
of the late fourteenth and early fifteenth centuries all generated
harsh and profound criticism of the human condition from those
who were primarily witnesses to its deterioration ·and from those
who were its most frequent victims. The selections below, with
the exception of the twelfth-century "Revelation of Golias the
Bisshoppe," come from the fourteenth and fifteenth centuries.
The well-known sixteenth-century materials in 6E and 6F are
included to show both the continuity of some abuses and the
art carried to its most professional peak. There is considerable
literature on the subject of medieval satire, but a good general
introduction is John A. Yunck, *The Lineage of Lady Meed:
The Development of Medieval Venality-Satire* (Notre Dame,
Ind., 1963).

Langland's catalogue of abuses surely parallels the various
kinds of complaint and satire reprinted here. In the *Prologue,*
a "Goliardeys, a glotoun of wordes," talks back to the angel
who has just admonished the king, and the poem is elsewhere
full of characters who speak their minds on all possible occasions
and with the greatest possible bluntness. *Passus X* inveighs against
the increasing superficiality of the ecclesiastical establishment and
the growing wealth of ecclesiastical institutions, abuses that were
viewed by others besides Langland, from the critics of curial
life and papal financial authority to the complaints reflected in
the Statutes of *Provisors and Praemunire* reprinted below in
chapter 7. The whole *Visio* (B-Text, *Prologue-Passus* VII), traces
the difficulties of material life, the search for "treasure," and
the problems of social order on earth. In chapter 8, the heavy-
handed attempts on the part of the royal government to control
the mobility and the cost of labor reflects much of the hard

life depicted in the *Prologue*. *Passus* VI illustrates some of the general concern over laborers that the documents in chapters 8 and 9 share. The *Visio* generally takes up some of the same themes that are discussed in chapters 10 and 11. The small cast of characters satirized in chapter 11, the Sloane Satires, echoes the passage in *Passus* VI in which "Iakke the iogelure, and Ionet of the stews, / And Danyel the dys-playere, and Denote the baude, / And frere the faytoure, and folk of this order, / And Robyn the rybaudoure" are all denied food by the honest laborers and excluded from human commerce. At the end of *Passus* VI, the ominous appearance of Hunger looms over the world of workers and wasters alike. The savagery of Langland's indictment of bad friars in *Passus* XX comes as no surprise to a world that had witnessed Chaucer's bitter portrayal of the friars as well as the anti-friar satires in chapter 12 below.

The last two documents in this section, nos. 6E and 6F, although they come from the early sixteenth century, shed considerable light on the later development of the practice of pardons and indulgences and dispensations that Langland excoriates in *Passus* VII.

5

"The Revelation
of Golias the Bisshoppe"

Introductory Note: The Latin original of this poem was probably composed in the cosmopolitan circle of scholars associated with the court of Henry II of England. Although it has often been attributed to Walter Map, one of the most intelligent, articulate, and imaginative members of that circle, it is certainly not his. Satire and complaint such as this, although most of it does not reach the level of the "Revelation," poured forth in verse, parody, and sermon from the twelfth century on. Some general introductory material may be found in HelenWaddell, *The Wandering Scholars* (London, 1927; rpt. London, 1968) and F. J. E. Raby, *A History of Secular Latin Poetry in the Middle Ages*, vol. 2 (Oxford, 1957). The following translation, which dates from around 1600, is printed in Thomas Wright, ed., *The Latin Poems attributed to Walter Mapes* (London, 1841), pp. 271–81.

"Golias" himself was a legendary figure to whom many medieval Latin satirical poems were at one time or another ascribed. The name may come from Goliath, the giant Philistine who fought David, but if it does, the connection with poetry or satire is obscure indeed. Somewhat more plausibly, the name may be a derivative of *gula*, gluttony, one of the deadly vices in moral theology, and with drunkenness, a favorite vice of the satirists. There may also be some derivation from a Germanic verb, *golijan*, to greet, or, secondarily, to sing; a word, unfortunately, attested to only in Gothic. The Elizabethan translation printed here is one of the surprising gems of the translator's art.

The complete Latin text and a discussion of the various versions in which the poem circulated can be found in Karl Strecker, ed., *Die Apokalypse des Golias* (Rome, 1928).

 "The Revelation . . ."

> WHEN that the shyninge sonne from Taurus downe
>   had sent
>   His fieri burninge dartes, and beames so whot by
>   kynde,[1]
> Into the woodes anon and shadowes darke I went,
>   There for to take the ayr, and pleasaunt westerne
>   wynde.
>
> And as I laye me downe undir an oken tree,   5
>   About the midtyme just, even of the somers daie,
> Pithagoras his shape me thought that I did see,
>   But that it was his corpes, God wott, I cannot saie.
>
> Pithagoras his shape in deede I did behold,
>   Withe divers kindes of art i-painted well about;   10
> But yet this sight, God wotte, by me canot be told
>   Whether it were in deede, in bodie, or without.
>
> Upon his foreheade faire Astrologie did shine,
>   And Gramer stode alonge upon his teethe arowe,[2]
> And Retheroick did springe within his hollowe eyen, 15
>   And in his tremblinge lippes did art of Logick flowe.
>
> And in his fingers eke did Arithemetick lie,
>   Within his hollowe pulse did Musick finelie plaie,

1. *whot by kynde:* hot by nature   2. *arowe:* on a row

And then in bothe his eien stode pale Geometrie;
   Thus eche one of these artes in his owne place did
      staie. 20

In reason is conteynd morall philosophie,
   And then upon his backe all handie craftes were writ;
At lengthe muche like a booke unfolded his bodie,
   And did disclose his hand, and badd me looke in it.

And then he did shewe fourthe his right handes secrets
      cleare, 25
   Whiche I beheld right well, and after ganne to reade;
Withe letters blacke as incke, thus found I written there,
   "I will the leade the waie, to followe me make speede."

And fourthe he passed then, and after followed I,
   Into another world anon bothe we twoo fell,[3] 30
Where manie wonderous thinges and straunge I did behold,
   And people mo therto then anie man can tell.

And whiles I strode in doubt what all this folke might be,
   Upon their foreheades all I cast myne eyen anon,
And there I found their names, which I might
      clearlie se 35
   As it had bene in leade, or els in hard flint stone.

Then sawe I Priscian first, beatinge his scolers hand,
   And Aristotle eke against the aire did fight,
But Tullius his wordes with conninge[4] smoothelie scand,[5]
   And Ptolemie upon the sterres did set his sight. 40

Boetius was there, and did his nomber tell,
   And Euclid measured the space of place hard by,
Pithagoras likewise his hamer handeled well,
   By sound whereof the notes of musick he did trye.

There sawe I Lucane eke,[6] or warlicke writers
      cheife, 45
   And Virgill then did shape the small bees of the aire,
And Ovid with his tales to many was reliefe,
   Perseus his tauntes and satyres did not spare.

3. *fell:* passed into   4. *conninge:* cunning   5. *scand:* scanned   6. *eke:* also

Whiles I of all this rowte[7] the gesture did espie,
   An angell cam to me, with countenaunce full cleare,   50
And said to me, "Behold, and looke into the skie,
   And thowe shalt se therein what shortlie shall appeare."

Upon the skie anon my sight I quicklie bent,
   And by and by I fell into a suddaine traunce,
And all alonge the aire was marvailouslie hent,[8]   55
   But yet at lengthe I was set in the heaven's entraunce.

But suche a suddaine flashe of lighteninge did appeare,
   That it bereft from me the sight of bothe myne eyen,
Then did the aungell saie, that stode fast by me there,
   "Stand still and thowe shalt se what John before
      hathe sene."   60

And as I stode thus still, all in a doubt and feare,
   One thundered in the aire, and air me thought it was,
Like to a thundringe wheele right terrible to heare,
   Or like a trumpet shrill, of horne or els of brasse.

And aftir that this sound has peirst[9] the aire saw I   65
   A goodlie personage, that held in his right hande
Seven candlestickes by tale,[10] and eke seven sterres[11]
      therbie;
   And then this angele said, "Marke well and undirstand.

"Theis candelstickes thowe seest are Churches vij,"
      said he,
   "And Bisshoppes bene the sterres; but all these same
      this daie   70
The shyninge light of grace, wherbie all men should se
   Under a busshel hidd, and kepe out of the waie."

And when he had thus done he did bringe out a booke,
   Whiche booke had titles seven, and seven sealles
      sealled well,
And withe a stedfast eye badde me therein to looke,   75
   And se therbie what I to all the world should tell.

---

7. *rowte:* company   8. *hent:* affected   9. *peirst:* pierced   10. *tale:* count
11. *sterres:* stars

Of bisshopes' life and trade this booke hathe right good
   skill,
  As by the sealles thereof more plainlie dothe appeare,
For in the inner part is hidd all that is ill,
  But to the outeward shewe all godlie thinges
    appeare.   80

Anon a certaine power there was that opened cleare
  The formost chapter's seale, and then I did espie
Foure beastes, whose shape eche one unlike to other were,
  But nothinge yet at all in gesture[12] contrarie.

The first of theise foure beastes a lion semde to be,   85
  The secund like a caulfe, the third an eagle stout,
The fourthe was like a man; and they had wings to flie,
  And full of eyen they were, and turnd like wheeles about.

And when unclosed was the first sealles knotte anon,
  And I perused well the chapter thorough cleare,   90
And aftir that I bent my whole sight thereupon,
  Whereof the title was as here it may appeare.

The lion is the Pope, that useth[13] to devoure,
  And laiethe his bookes to pledge, and thirsteth aftir gold,
And dothe regard the marke,[14] but sainct Marke
    dishonor,   95
  And while he sailes alofte on coyne takes anker holde.

And to the Bisshoppe in the caulfe that we did se,
  For he dothe runne before in pasture, feild, and fenne,
And gnawes and chewes on that where he list best to be,
  And thus he filles himselfe with goodes of other
    men.   100

Th'Archedeacon is likewise the egell that dothe flie,
  A robber rightlie cald, and sees a-farre his praie,
And aftir it with speed dothe follow by and by,
  And so by theft and spoile he leades his life awaie.

The Deane is he that hathe the face and shape of man,   105
  Withe fraude, deceipt, and guile fraught full as he
    may be,

12. *gesture:* manner   13. *useth:* is accustomed   14. The mark of gold

And yet dothe hide and cloke the same as he best can,
Undir pretence and shewe of plaine simplicitie.

And theis have winges to flye, eche one of these said foure,
Because they flye abrode, and lie about affaires,   110
And they have eyes eche one, because that everye houre
They looke about for gaine, and all that may be theires.

And everie one of them withe rollinge wheele dothe goe,
For that their chaunginge mynde on tickell axeltree [15]
Is rold and tost about with straunge thoughtes to
and froe,   115
As in a wheele the like we may all plainlie see.

And when I had perusde this title I did reade
The chapter that was next, and as I there abode,[16]
I learnde the Bisshoppes' lives, that ought the people leade,
But they do them misslike,[17] and let them
straie abrode.   120

Woe to the horned[18] guydes of this poore mangled flocke,
That dothe bothe hurt and mayme the same with armed
head,
Whiles on their hornes they beare eche one of them a locke
And doe not feede their sheape, but with their sheape
are fedd.

And dothe not thincke so much on his poore sillie[19]
flocke,   125
That be bothe blynde and lame, and torne with brushe
and breare;[20]
And he dothe of the count of milke and flece take kepe,
And on his shoulders his lost shepe he dothe beare.

And yf he anie fault amonge the people finde,
That our faithe is broken, to saye he will not spare,   130
And drawe them to the lawe, and fast there dothe them
bynd,
Till he hathe pulde their fleece, and made their purses
bare.

15. *tickell axeltree:* unstable axle   16. *abode:* remained   17. *misslike:* dislike
18. *horned:* the bishop's mitre   19. *sillie:* innocent   20. *breare:* briar

And thus his wandringe flocke dothe followe their blind
    guyde,
  Leade from the perfect waye, even as their sheaperd
    goes;
And when he hathe the fleece he leaves both flesh
    and hide   135
  To feede the raveninge woulfe, or els the gredie croes.

Full evill dothe the ringe upon his finger touche,
  And eke the sheperdes staffe wurse in his hande is laid,
Synce he beares nothinge els but cannons[21] in his purse;
  And thus when I had reade this chapter there
    I staid.   140

Uppe rose the cloudes about, on fire was set the skye,
  The lighteninge flasht abrode, and aftir cam a peale
Of thundringe rollinge wheeles, and then I did espie
  That when this storme was done unclosed the secund
    seale.

I read the chapter next, and there did undirstand   145
  Th'Archedeacons trade and life, whose course was next
    of all,
If anie thinge by chaunce did scape the Bisshoppes hand,
  Withe toothe and naile to snatche, and teares in peices
    small.

This man is full of eyen when he at synode sittes;
  A lynx for to deceyve, for game a Janus right,   150
And Argus when he dothe on misscheefe set his witte,
  But in all art and skill hathe Poliphemus sight.

And when he heares the pleas of persons at debate
  In forme of canon lawe he workethe subtiltie,
For he the canon lawe can turne, even in like sorte   155
  To Symon's court, which is th'Archdeacon's Mercurie.

And of the churches right he maketh open sale,
  But till he have sold more this may be pardoned well;
But that then not obteynd, when all thinges els do faile,

21. *cannons:* canon, rule

He will not sticke[22] at length the churche it selfe
    to sell.   160

And by the craftie meanes of his good messenger
    Some concubyne he gettes, wherbie he may have happe
To wynne her to his bedd, and so yt may prosper
    That his convoy may bringe more lucke into his lappe.

He dothe commaunde the deane, if anie preest be
    known   165
A datyve[23] case to make, by anie gendringe state,
That then the plaintyve shall him call and bringe full lowe
    To save his bretheren's lyves, and kepe them from hell
    gate.

And suddainlie the sonne and moone did lose their light,
    With darke and mistie wyndes oppressed was
    the skie,   170
The darkenes was as thicke as if yt had bene night,
    And then the third seale was disclosed by and by.

The Aungell badde me then to reade what I should fynde,
    And straight I reade and founde a man of wicked shiftes,[24]
That runnes and romes abrode to hunt for
    Venus kynde,   175
A byrder[25] of reproche, and fissheth all for shiftes.[26]

This ys the Deane, that hathe the face and shape of man,
    But is no man in deede, but poyson rancke and fell,
And rageth upon men withe all the force he can,
    Yet counterfaiteth[27] man with face of man
    right well.   180

The Deane is th'Archdeacons dogge, that waighteth neare
    and farre,
    But with the canon lawe his barkinge grees not well,
For he dothe discord singe, and from the rule doth jarre,
    And is to Symon like that did bothe buye and sell.

22. *sticke:* refrain
23. *datyve:* giving/dative (pun on the verb "dō," to give, and the grammatical category dative).
24. *shiftes:* plots   25. *byrder:* hunter   26. *shiftes:* frauds
27. *counterfaiteth:* counterfeits

The Deane is like a hound that can the foote find out,   185
  And by the sent can seke where he may luker get,
And can by sleight[28] bringe in clerkes' purses all about,
  Whom he had caught before within his maister's nette.

He will the promisse helpe if thowe wilt give him hire,
  But when his burninge heat, that all thinges swallowes
    up,   190
Withe coyne thowe shalt have solvd,[29] and quenched his
    desire,
  Yet shalt thowe have no cause at lengthe to praise
    the cuppe.

He will yowe promisse helpe if ought you to him bringe,
  But if y'anoynt as well as anie surjaunt can
The itchinge of his hande with gifte of anie thinge,   195
  He goethe about your worke muche like a gowtie[30] man.

He kepethe downe the just, and dothe advaunce the badde,
  And holdethe with the right if gaine therbie doe springe;
But yf there be no hope of luker to be hadd
  He is a cheeftan right to eche ungodlie thinge.   200

And then appeard from highe a hand of gold anon,
  Whiche hand upon his booke toke hold with fingers
    three,
And did unclose the seale, and suddainlie was gone;
  And then the chapter fourthe appeared unto me.

Of Officialls I found the trade and customes there,   205
  Their raven[31] and their rapes and swollowinge excesse,
Their fraude and their deceipt to filthie for to heare,
  Which passe the margynes large of volumes to expresse.

These are they whom the world abhorreth for to hold,
  And at the sight of whom the earthe dothe quake for
    feare,   210
Whose myndes are whet on missechefe to be bolde,
  As bread in Rodope amonge the whetstones there.

---

28. *sleight:* cunning   29. *solvd:* salved   30. *gowtie:* afflicted with gout
31. *raven:* robbery

What missecheefe of themselves by natures onelie[32] gifte,
   Or els what harm they may by their office contrive,
What writer's penne can shewe, though he be nere so
      swift,   215
   What tounge, what voice express, of anie man alyve?

Small faultes in other men abrode are quicklie blowen,[33]
   But thoughe these men doe rage, and never out of
      square,
Non murmurs, all is husht, their missecheefe is not
      knowen,
   Non, non there is of them once to complaine
      that dare.   220

These bene the Bisshopp's hunt,[34] and birdes at assaie,[35]
   That wise men doe deceyve, and fooles from tyme to
      tyme;
At fooles they shoote their shaftes, for wise men nettes
      they laie,
   And for the unwarie snares, and for the wilie lyne.

The Bisshoppes chambers thus gaine muche, bothe
      farre and wide,   225
   A thowsand pence at once, which poore men undirstand;
But yet ten thowsand moe doe fall downe by his side,
   The which doe never come unto the Bisshoppes hand.

Ob signifiethe against, and is against eche thinge,
   And contrarie to that that it is put unto;   230
And from this worde their name th'Officialls do bringe,
   And office to offende, for they nought els can doe.

Then boisterous wyndes arose, and earthequakes by
      and by,
   And there was harde a voice of thunder from above,
That sounded Ephata, whiche woorde dothe signifie   235
   An openinge, and anon the fifthe seale did remove.

When I the chapter sawe I reade the preface than,
   And there the life and trade of preistes I marked well,

32. *onelie:* single   33. *blowen:* exposed   34. *hunt:* hunters
35. *assaie:* attack

Which doe dishonor God, that all thinges first beganne,
    Whiles for one penyes gaine the Trinitie they sell.   240

Full filthelie the priest dothe service celebrate
    Withe voyce, and breathes on God his surfet's[36]
        belchinge cheere;
And hathe twoo Latin names, but not bothe of one rate,
    Sacerdos is the one, the other's Presbiter.

He cannot brooke[37] so well Sacerdos name by right,   245
    For by the other name men ought to call him more,
When he gives holie thinges then he Sacerdos hight,
    But Presbiter when he hathe drunck well thrise before.

He is more bolde to synne, because he heares in Lent
    The people's greivous crymes, and all their synnes at
        large,   250
And all the faultes for whiche they ought for to be shent,[38]
    And thus he countes his owne to be of smallest charge.

Good dothe this bloudie man abhorre above all thinge,
    For he desires mens deathe more then their life to save;
A[39] covettes more a whoore that may him children
        bringe,   255
    The eleven thowsand virgins or maides for to have.

When masse is done the priest his vestment dothe forsake,
    And to some harlottes ile[40] descendeth by and by;
So on a hayfor[41] faire his pleasure for to take
    Cam Jubiter from heaven, or els the fables lye.   260

And for a stedfast rule he teacheth women this,
    That no soule can be lost that well his tithe dothe paie,
And so unles they paie their bodies tithe I wisse
    Of them non can be saved at the last dredfull daie.

And thus the wilye foxe from hole to hole
        dothe playe,   265
    And dothe not children get for lust, but muche the more
Because that he wold have soules of his owne to paie,
    And raunsome suche withall as he had lost before.

36. *surfet's:* surfeit   37. *brooke:* bear   38. *shent:* cursed
39. *A:* He   40. *ile:* evil   41. *hayfor:* heifer

And then a ladie faire from heavne herselfe did shewe,
　　Withe goodlie countenaunce, as freshe as
　　　　anie rose,   270
And when she tutcht the booke, with hand as white as
　　snowe,
　　I might perceyve right well the sixthe seale did disclose.

This chapter was all writ withe figures short and fine,
　　And eke with letters small, couched as in a presse,
Havinge a narrowe glose[42] drawen betwen
　　　　everie line,   275
　　And therein was conteynde the clergies great excesse.

For drowsie slothefulness and swellinge pride likewise,
　　And all unclenlie lustes and fervent vaine glorie,
Unfittinge pleasure eke and filthie actes arise
　　Out of the shameful rowte[43] of clergis
　　　　companye.   280

The person dothe commit the soules of all our sheepe
　　Into the vicares handes, withe spiritual power;
But to himselfe the rentes and profittes he dothe kepe,
　　Which boldlie without feare he lettes[44] not to devowre.

He dothe his wandringe soule in manye partes
　　　　devide,   285
　　And dothe tenne churches hold or moe within his handes,
And yet he cannot well in eche of these abide,
　　Muche like an accedent, that in no case[45] still stands.

And higher is the roofe advaunced of his hawle
　　Then is Allhollowes churche, made highe with hands
　　　　of men,   290
In valewe eke much more did cost his wenches pall,
　　Then all th'atter[46] is worth that covereth altres tenne.

He maketh toyles[47] and parkes and buyldinges conninglie,
　　And coynes and other toyes and ringes to weren on
　　　　hande,

42. *glose:* gloss   43. *rowte:* band   44. *lettes:* ceases
45. *accedent . . . case:* inflection, ending (grammatical pun)
46. *th'atter:* the attire   47. *toyles:* tools

And all this he doethe make of Goddes patrimonie, 295
  Whom he fees[48] at his doore, and lettes him naked stand.

The vicare rules the soules committed to his charge,
  Even as he dothe his owne, for to the end he maye
More freelie other leese, he lettes his own at large
  First to be lost, and thus to missecheefe leeds
    the waie. 300

Thus all enormitie[49] dothe from the clergie rise,
  And where they ought on God to set their mynde and
    care,
They myddle with affayres and forbidden marchandize,
  And occupie themselves with muche unhonest ware.

At byddinge of his lorde this prieste the seas
    dothe passe, 305
  And that priest haunteth faires, whom no man ought to
    trust,
Another goeth to ploughe as dothe the oxe or asse,
  And thus their order break, accordinge to their lust.

And, like a gentilman, this priest will not be polde,[50]
  An other to be calde a clerke dothe take
    great skorne, 310
The third dothe children chuse, when he his bookes hathe
    sold,
  Amonge they laymen thus the clergie leese their name.

And aftir cam withe wynde of Ethiopps a rowte,[51]
  And from a lymye[52] pitte full blacke and fowle to se,
And in an order longe they raunged rownd about, 315
  And seven tymes they cryed, *Tu autem, Domine.*

Then at the fearful noyse of this huge heydeous crye,
  My guyde beganne to strike and tremble all for feare,
And like a mased corpes for fright nigh dead stood I,
  Until I plainlie sawe the seventhe seale to appeare. 320

48. *fees:* takes a fee from; presumably the fee is all the man's possessions
49. *enormitie:* sins   50. *polde:* polled   51. *rowte:* band   52. *lymye:* lime

I sawe the workes and trade of Abbottes there eche one,
   Of whom their flock to leade to hell not one dothe misse,
In cloister movinge aye, in chamber still as stone,
   But in the chapter howse muche like ague is.

All worldlie pomp these men doe utterlie dispise,   325
   Which maye be proved well by their still silent spirit,
And by their contrite hart, and water from their eyes,
   And by their shavinge vile, and habit like to yt.

But where their garmentes bene bothe fowle and also bare,
   All Venus sport in them with lesse suspect
      maye be,   330
And thoughe uncomelie be the shavinge of their bearde,
   Unto the drinckinge potte their face is much more free.

And thoughe with contrite hart they use muche for to
      weepe,
   Yet laughe they on the cuppe and smilinglie they beck,
And thoughe with silent breathe they can their tunge in
      keepe,   335
   Withe finger they can point, and speke reproche and
      check.[53]

At dyner when they sitte, to which they gone apace,
   Theyr jaws are verie swifte, their teethe muche paine do
      take,
Their throte an open grave, their stomock in like case
   A foming whirlepoole is, eche finger is a cake.   340

And when the Abbat dothe amonge his bretheren suppe,
   Then tossed are the cuppes with quaffinge to and froe,
And then with bothe his handes the wine he holdeth uppe,
   And with a thundringe voice these wordes he doth out
      blowe:

"O how muche glorious is the lordes lamp so bright,   345
   The cuppe in stronge man's hande, that makes men
      druncke I meane.
O Baccus, god of wyne! our covent guyde aright,

---

53. *check:* rebuke

Withe fruict of Daviddes stocke to wash us thoroughlie
   cleane.''

And aftir this the cuppe he takethe from the breade,
   And cryes alowde, "Ho! sires, can yow as well
      as I   350
Drincke this cuppe in his kind[54] that I lift to my heade?''
   They aunswer, "Yea, we can,'' then goe to by and by.

And least that anie one should kepe with him the cuppe
   Till he had druncke but halfe, and so might rise thereby
Amonge them some debate and strife, they drincke all
      uppe,   355
   And thus they plie the potte, and quaffinge quietlie.

And they make a lawe, to which eche one must stand,
   That nothinge shalbe left within the cuppe to spill,
And thus without the rest of bellie or of hand,
   They drawe one vessell out, and then one other fill. 360

Then of a moncke a right demoniacke is made,
   And everie moncke dothe chatte and jangle with his
      brother,
As popingaye or pie,[55] the which are taught this trade,
   By filling of their gorge, to speake one to an other.

Their order to transgresse thei have but small
      remorce,   365
   By fraude and perjurie, by missereport and spite,
By gredines of mynde, withholdinge thinges by force,
   By filling of their pawnches, and fleshlie fowle delight.

Wurse then a moncke there is no feende nor sprite in hell,
   Nothing so covetuouse nor more straunge to be
      knowen,   370
For yf yow give him ought, he maie possesse it well,
   But if you aske him ought, then nothinge is his owne.

And yf he dyne he must no wordes nor talkinge make,
   Least that his tonge doe let his teethe to chewe his
      meate,

54. *in his kind:* properly   55. *popingaye or pie:* parrot or magpie

And if he drinck he must needes sit his draught to
    take,   375
Lest that his foote doe faile, his bellye is so great.

Thus worshippes he the tunnes[56] daunsinge, but all night
    longe
Withe some toofooted beast in bedd he buried is,
By which adventures great, and with sore paines and
    strong,
This man of God deserves to come to heavens
    blisse.   380

And aftir this my guyde fast with his hands me hent,[57]
When I had all perusde and seene things at full,
And with his fingers foure my head in sunder rent,
Dissolvinge in foure partes the compass of my skull.

And then he tooke a strawe that was bothe hard and
    drye,   385
Because I should not se those misteries in vaine,
And in my noddle fast he set in tendirlie,
And all that I has seene he wrote it in my braine.

And then I was caught uppe even to the third skie,
Advaunced in the toppes of clowdes above mans
    sight,   390
Where I a secrete saw, and wonderous misterie,
The which may not be told to any living wight.

Before the highest Judge in counsaill brought was I,
Where many hundred were, and many thowsands eke,
And there the secrets deepe of God I did espie,   395
The which no mynde of man is hable[58] out to seeke.

When these sightes seene had I, I waxt hungrie anon,
The nobles then that were come to that counsaile great
Brought me of poppie bread a loffe to feede uppon,
And drincke of Lethe's floude, my bread therwith to
    eate.   400

56. *tunnes:* tuns (but perhaps a pun on "tunes")
57. *hent:* caught   58. *hable:* able

And when I had myself well fedd with poppie bread,
   And with my wretched lippes this drinck had tasted well,
The counsaile of the Goddes was quite out of my head,
   And of this secret sight not one whit cold I tell.

Then like a Catoe third down from the skie I fell,   405
   No newes to bringe from thence, nor secrets to declare;
But I can shewe you all, and certainlie can tell
   What my fellowe did write upon my noddle bare.

Oh! what tales cold I tell, how strange to heare or se,
   Of things that bene above, and heavenle state and
      trade,   410
If that subtile supper of poppie made to me
   The printinges of my head had not so slippie made.

6

Curia, Corruption, and Council

Introductory Note: One of the most conspicuous and frequently attacked targets of medieval complaint and satire was the life of courts in general and of the papal curia most particularly. From the powerful criticism of St. Bernard, Walter of Chatillon, and John of Salisbury in the twelfth century, through the blunter and less elegant protests of the thirteenth, and down to the elegant, sardonic invective of the humanists in the fourteenth and fifteenth centuries culminating in the work of Erasmus, the failure of the papal curia appears to have been considered one of the chief elements in the failure of other spiritual and temporal institutions as well. The first selection is from the letters of Petrarch, whose long residence near the papal court in Avignon offered the poet and man of letters much occasion for the exercise of his critical pen. The next three selections are from the voluminous literature generated by the problems faced at the Council of Constance (1415–1418) and reflect in histories, tracts, conciliar decrees, and formal recognition of abuses much widespread concern for the integrity of the Church after the crises of the

Avignon papacy (1308–1378), the Great Schism (1378–1417), and the century of war and material disasters that accompanied them. The last two selections illustrate the enduring character of some of the abuses into the sixteenth century.

✤ A. Petrarch on the Avignon Curia

From James Harvey Robinson, The Pre-Reformation Period, *pp. 26–27. Original Latin text in* Petrarchae Opera Omnia, *(Basel, 1581),* Epistolae Sine Titulo V. *On the general problems of the Avignon papacy, see Yves Renouard,* The Avignon Papacy, 1305–1403, *trans. Denis Bethell (London, 1970), a good recent study with extensive bibliography.*

I have a double Parnassus, one in Italy, the other in France, places of refuge, such as they are, for the exiled Muses. I was very happy in my Ausonian [Italian] Helicon *dum fata Deusque sinebant,* as that wretched lover says in Virgil (if indeed we can properly call Dido wretched, rather than the most virtuous and constant of women.) But now I am living in France, in the Babylon of the West. The sun, in its travels sees nothing more hideous than this place on the shores of the wild Rhone, which suggests the hellish streams of Cocytus and Acheron. Here reign the successors of the poor fishermen of Galilee; they have strangely forgotten their origin. I am astounded, as I recall their predecessors, to see these men loaded with gold and clad in purple, boasting of the spoils of princes and nations; to see luxurious palaces and heights crowned with fortifications, instead of a boat turned downwards for shelter. We no longer find the simple nets which were once used to gain a frugal sustenance from the Lake of Galilee, and with which, having labored all night and caught nothing, they took, at day break, a multitude of fishes, in the name of Jesus. One is stupified nowadays to hear the lying tongues, and to see worthless parchments, turned by a leaden seal, into nets which are used, in Christ's name, but by the arts of Belial, to catch hordes of unwary Christians. These fish, too, are dressed and laid on the burning coals of anxiety before they fill the insatiable maw of their captors. Instead of

holy solitude we find a criminal host and crowds of the most infamous satellites: instead of soberness, licentious banquets; instead
of pious pilgrimages, preternatural and foul sloth; instead of the
bare feet of the apostles, the snowy coursers of brigands fly
past us, the horses decked in gold and fed on gold, soon to be
shod with gold, if the Lord does not check this slavish luxury.
In short, we seem to be among the kings of the Persians or
Parthians, before whom we must fall down and worship, and
who can not be approached except presents be offered. O, ye
unkempt and emaciated old men, is it for this you labored? Is
it for this that you have sown the field of the Lord and watered
it with your holy blood? But let us leave the subject.

Commiserate the cruel fate which holds your friend here.
He may merit punishment, but certainly not one like this. Here
I am, at a more advanced age, back in the haunts of my childhood, dragged again by fate among the disagreeable surroundings
of my early days, when I thought I was freed from them. I
have been so depressed and overcome that the heaviness of my
soul has passed into bodily afflictions, so that I am really ill and
can only give voice to sighs and groans. Although many things
offer themselves which I wanted to communicate to you, as both
my stomachs are troubling me, you need look for nothing agree-
able from me to-day. Sweet water cannot come from a bitter
source. Nature has ordered that the sighs of an oppressed heart
shall be distasteful, and the words of an injured soul, harsh.

✥ B. Dietrich Vrie's *History of the Council of Constance*

From Robinson, The Pre-Reformation Period, *p. 28. Latin
original in Hermann von der Hardt,* Magnum Oecumenicum
Constatiense Concilium (*Leipzig, 1697*), *1: 104–6. On the Council
of Constance, see John H. Mundy and K. M. Woody, eds., Louise
Ropes Loomis,* The Council of Constance (*New York, 1961*).

The supreme pontiffs, as I know, are elected through avarice
and simony, and likewise the other bishops are ordained for gold.
These, in turn, will not ordain those below them, the priests,

deacons, subdeacons and acolytes, except a strict agreement be first drawn up. Of this mammon of unrighteousness the bishops, the real rulers, and the chapters, each has his part. The once accepted proverb, "Freely give for freely ye have received," is now most vilely perverted: "Freely I have not received, nor will I freely give, for I have bought my bishopric for a great price, and must indemnify myself impiously for my untoward outlay. I will not ordain you as priest except for money. I purchased the sacrament of ordination when I became a bishop and I propose to sell you the same sacred sign and seal of ordination. By beseeching and by gold, I have gained my office, for beseeching and for gold do I sell you your place. Refuse the amount I demand and you shall not become a priest."

If Simon Magus were now alive he might buy with money not only the Holy Ghost, but God the Father, and Me, the Son of God. But favor is bought from the ungrateful who do not the works of grace, for grace must give freely, but if bought and not given, grace is no longer grace. But why say more? The bishops who take money for ordination become lepers with Gehasi. Those ordained do, by their bribery, condemn themselves to perdition with Simon Magus, to whom Peter said, "Thy money perish with thee."

✤ C. Nicolas of Clemanges' *Downfall of the Church*

From Robinson, The Pre-Reformation Period, pp. 28–30. This was one of several works that criticized explicitly and in great detail the faults of the Church as they appeared to the Fathers of the Council of Constance.

Chap. III. On the Three Vices which have given rise to all the other ills in the Church.

After the great increase of worldly goods, the virtues of our ancestors being quite neglected, boundless avarice and blind ambition invaded the hearts of the churchmen. As a result, they were carried away by the glory of their position and the extent of their power and soon gave way to the degrading effects of luxury. Three most exacting and troublesome masters had now to be satisfied. *Luxury* demands sundry gratifications, wine, sleep, banquets, music, debasing sports, courtesans and the like. *Display* requires fine houses, castles, towers, palaces, rich and varied furniture, expensive clothes, horses, servants and the pomp of luxury. Lastly is *Avarice* which carefully brought together vast treasures to supply the demands of the above mentioned vices or, if these were otherwise provided for, to gratify the eye by the vain contemplation of the coins themselves.

So insatiable are these lords, and so imperious in their demands, that the Golden Age of Saturn, which we hear of in stories, should it now return, would hardly suffice to meet the demands. Since it is impossible, however rich the bishop and ample his revenue, to satisfy these rapacious harpies with that alone, he must cast about for other sources of income.

Chap. IX.   The Institution of Collectors and the Ills they bring with them.

For carrying on these exactions and gathering the gains into the camera or Charybdis, as we may better call it, the popes appoint their *collectors* in every province, those, namely, whom they know to be most skillful in extracting money, owing to peculiar energy, diligence or harshness of temper, those in short who will neither spare nor except but would squeeze gold from a stone. To these the popes grant, moreover, the power of anathematizing anyone, even prelates, and of expelling from the communion of the faithful, everyone who does not, within a fixed period, satisfy their demands for money. What ills these collectors have caused, and the extent to which poor churches and people have been oppressed, are questions best omitted, as we could never hope to do the matter justice. From this source come the laments of the unhappy ministers of the church, which reach our ears, as they faint under the insupportable yoke, yea, perish of hunger. Hence come suspensions from divine service, interdicts from entering a church, and anathemas, a thousand fold intensified in severity. Such things were resorted to in the rarest instances by the fathers, and then only for the most horrible of crimes; for by these penalties, a man is separated from the companionship of the faithful and turned over to Satan. But now-a-days, these inflictions are so fallen in esteem, that they are used for the lightest offence, often for no offense at all, so they no longer bring terror, but are objects of contempt.

To the same cause, is to be ascribed the ruin of numerous churches and monasteries and the levelling with the ground, in so many places, of sacred edifices, while the money which used to go for their restoration, is exhausted in paying these taxes. But it even happens, as some well know, that holy relics in not a few churches, crosses, chalices, feretories and other precious articles go to make up this tribute.

Who does not know how many abbots and other prelates, when they come to die, are, if they prove obnoxious to the papal camera on account of their poverty, refused a dignified funeral and even denied burial, except, perchance, in some field or garden or profane spot, where they are secretly disposed of. Priests, as we all can see, are forced by reason of their scanty means of support, to desert their parishes and their benefices and, in their hunger, seek their bread where they may, performing profane services for laymen. Some rich and hitherto prosperous churches have, indeed, been able to support this burden, but all are now exhausted and can no longer bear to be cheated of their revenue.

❧ D. The Abuses Attacked by the Council of Constance, 1417

From Robinson, The Pre-Reformation Period, *pp. 32–33.*

The holy council of Constance decrees and ordains that the Supreme Pontiff who shall next, by the grace of God, assume office, shall, in conjunction with this holy council, or with the deputies of the several *nations,* reform the church, before the council dissolves, in head and members, as well as the Roman curia, in accordance with justice and the proper organization of the church, in all the respects enumerated below, and which are presented by the *nations* as requiring reform:

The number, character and nationality of the Lords Cardinals.

The Reservations made by the Apostolic See.

The Annates both the *servitia communia* and *servitia minuta*.

The Collation to Benefices and Expectative Favors.

What cases are to be brought before the Roman Curia and what not.

Appeals to the Roman Curia.

The functions of the [Papal] Chancery and Poenitentiary.

Exemptions and Incorporations made during the Schism.

Benefices *in Commendam*.

Confirmation of Elections.

Income during Vacancies.

The non-alienation of the possessions of the Roman Church or other churches.

For what reasons and in what manner shall a Pope be corrected or deposed.

The Extirpation of Heresy.

Dispensations

The means of support of Pope and Cardinals.

Indulgences.

Tenths.

When the above mentioned deputies shall have been appointed by the *nations*, it shall be free to the others, with the permission of the Pope, to return home.

✤ E. Albert of Mainz's Instructions Concerning the Indulgence of 1517

From James Harvey Robinson and Merrick Whitcomb, The Period of the Early Reformation in Germany, *Translations and Reprints from the Original Sources of European History, vol. 2, no. 6 (Philadelphia, 1895), pp. 4–9. Latin original in B. J. Kidd, ed.,* Documents Illustrative of the Continental Reformation *(Oxford, 1911), doc. 6. Although this document, and the one following, date from a century after* Piers Plowman, *they reflect the high degree of professionalism attained by indulgence-promulgators and sellers in the intervening century.*

Here follow the four principal graces and privileges, which are granted by the apostolic bull, of which each may be obtained without the other. In the matter of these four privileges preachers shall take pains to commend each to believers with the greatest care, and, in-so-far as in their power lies, to explain the same.

The first grace is the complete remission of all sins; and nothing greater than this can be named, since man who lives in sin and forfeits the favor of God, obtains complete remission by these means and once more enjoys God's favor: moreover, through this remission of sins the punishment which one is obliged to undergo in Purgatory on account of the affront to the divine Majesty, is all remitted, and the pains of Purgatory completely blotted out. And although nothing is precious enough to be given in exchange for such a grace—since it is the free gift of God and a grace beyond price—yet in order that Christian believers may be the more easily induced to procure the same, we establish the following rules, to wit:

In the first place every one who is contrite in heart, and has made oral confession, or at all events has the intention of confessing at a suitable time, shall visit at least the seven churches indicated for this purpose, that is to say, those in which the papal arms are displayed, and in each church shall say devoutly five Paternosters and five Ave Marias in honor of the five wounds of our Lord Jesus Christ, whereby our salvation is won, or one *Miserere*, which Psalm is particularly well adapted for obtaining forgiveness of sins.

Sick or otherwise incapacitated persons shall visit with the same devotion and prayers the seven altars, which the commissioners and subcommissioners shall have erected in the church where the cross shall be raised, and on which they shall have affixed the papal arms.

Where, however, persons are found so weak that they cannot conveniently come to such a church, then shall their confessor or penitentiary cause an altar to be brought to a convenient place approved by him. And where such persons visit this place and offer up their prayers near the altar or before it, they shall deserve the indulgence as though they had visited the seven churches.

To those, however, who are upon beds of sickness the image of a saint may be sent, before or beside which they may offer up a certain number of prayers, according to the judgment of the confessor, in which case they shall be considered to have done as much as if they had visited the seven churches.

But where a certain one, particularly a woman, requests, on account of some especial cause, that the visitation of the churches and altars be remitted, the penitentiaries may grant the request on proper grounds; but the said visitation shall be replaced with an increased contribution.

Respecting, now, the contribution to the chest, for the building of the said church of the chief of the apostles, the penitentiaries and confessors, after they have explained to those making confession the full remission and privileges, shall ask of them, for how much money or other temporal goods they would conscientiously go without the said most complete remission and privileges; and this shall be done in order that hereafter they may be brought the more easily to contribute. And because the conditions and occupations of men are so manifold and diverse that we cannot consider them individually, and impose specific rates accordingly, we have therefore concluded that the rates should be determined according to the recognized classes of persons.

Kings and Queens and their offspring, archbishops and bishops, and other great rulers as well, provided they seek the places where the cross is raised, or otherwise present themselves, shall pay at least five and twenty Rhenish guilders in gold. Abbots and the great prelates of Cathedral churches, counts, barons, and others of the higher nobility, together with their consorts, shall pay for each letter of indulgence ten such guilders. Other lesser prelates and nobles, as also the rectors of celebrated places, and all others, who, either from permanent incomes or merchandise, or otherwise, enjoy a total yearly revenue of five hundred gold guilders, shall pay six guilders. Other citizens and tradespeople and artisans, who have individual incomes and families of their own, shall pay one such guilder; others of less means only a half. And where it is impossible to adhere rigidly to the schedule above indicated, then we declare that the said kings, bishops, dukes, abbots, prelates, counts, barons, members of the higher nobility and rectors, together with all others above mentioned, shall place or cause to be placed in the chest a sum in accordance with the dictates of sound reason, proportionate to their magnificence or generosity, after they have listened to the advice and council of the subcommissioners and penitentiaries and of their confessors, in order that they may fully obtain the grace and privileges. All other persons are confided to the discretion of the confessors and penitentiaries, who should have ever in view the advancement of this building, and should urge their penitents to a freer contribution, but should let no one go away without some portion of grace, because the happiness of Christian believers is here concerned not less than the interests of the building. And those that have no money, they shall supply their contribution with prayer and fasting; for the Kingdom of Heaven should be open to the poor not less than to the rich.

And although a married woman may not dispose of the husband's goods against his will, yet she shall be able to contribute in this instance against the will of her husband of her dowry or of her own private property, which has come to her in a regular manner. Where she has no such possessions, or is prevented by her husband, she shall then supply such contribution with prayer; and the same we wish to have understood concerning sons who still remain under parental control.

Where, however the said poor wives and sons who still remain under parental control may obtain by entreaty or otherwise from other rich and pious persons the means needed for such payments and contributions, they shall place the sums so acquired in the chest. Where, however, they have absolutely no way of procuring such contributions, then they may obtain through prayer and supplication the said treasures of grace as well for themselves as for the dead.

In all the cases above indicated, however, some room shall be left for the exercise of discretion on the part of the subcommissioners and confessors, who shall have regard to God and their consciences, so that peace of conscience and the welfare of all the above said persons shall be happily secured.

The second signal grace is a confessional letter containing the most extraordinarily comforting and hitherto unheard of privileges, and which also retains its virtue even after our bull expires at the end of eight years, since the bull says: "they shall be participators now and for ever." The meaning of the same, preachers and confessors shall explain and bring unto all possible prominence; for there will be granted in the confessional letter, to those who buy; first, the power to choose a qualified confessor, even a monk from the mendicant orders, who shall absolve them first and foremost, with the consent of the persons involved, from all censures by whomsoever imposed; in the second place, from each and every crime, even the greatest, and as well from those reserved to the apostolic see, once in a lifetime and in the hour of death; third, in those cases which are not reserved, as often as necessary; fourth, the chosen confessor may grant him complete forgiveness of all sins once in life, and at the hour of death, as often as it may seem at hand, although death ensue not; and, fifth, transform all kinds of vows, excepting alone those solemnly taken, into other works of piety (as when one has vowed to perform the journey to the Holy Land, or to visit the holy Apostles at Rome, to make a pilgrimage to St. James at Compostella, to become a monk, or to take a vow of chastity); sixth, the confessor may administer to him the sacrament of the altar at all seasons, except on Easter day, and in the hour of death.

We furthermore ordain that one of these confessional letters shall be given and imparted for the quarter of a Rhenish gold guilder, in order that the poor shall not thereby be shut out from the manifold graces therein contained; it may however happen that nobles and other wealthy persons may, out of devotion and liberality, be disposed to give more. Whatever is given over and above the ordinary fee shall be placed in the chest. In cases where such letters are demanded by colleges or cloisters, whether of men or women, the fee which they shall be obliged to pay must be computed by the subcommissioners according to their number and their property. The same subcommissioners must seal the confessional letters which shall be issued, and sign them with their own hand, setting forth the fee which has been paid for the letter.

It is also our desire that the name of only one person should be written in the confessional letter, except in case of man and wife, who are one in the flesh. To these may also be added the sons and daughters who are still under parental control, and have as yet nothing of their own. And in order that each and every one of the said persons, as well as the poor and those of moderate means, may be able to obtain such confessional letters, we hereby clothe our general subcommissioner with power to fix a certain sum to be paid collectively by the persons whose names are written in a confessional letter, as it may best subserve the interests of the aforesaid church building.

We desire also, that the names of each and every one who buys a letter, or obtains one for any cause without remuneration shall be written by him who issues the same in a special book. And he that issues shall endorse his name upon each letter, in order that an account of the sales may be given later, and that no mistakes may creep in.

We desire, moreover, that the said confessional letters be issued in all places covered by our commission for the sale of indulgences, even where the cross has *not* been raised, during the period of eight years, by those who hold authentic written commissions either from us or from our general subcommissioners

The third most important grace is the participation in all the possessions of the church universal, which consists herein, that contributors toward the said building, together with their deceased relations, who have departed this world in a state of grace, shall from now and for eternity, be partakers in all petitions, intercessions, alms, fastings, prayers, in each and every pilgrimage, even those to the Holy Land; furthermore, in the stations at Rome, in the masses, canonical hours, flagellations, and all other spiritual goods which have been brought forth or which shall be brought forth by the universal, most holy church militant or by any of its members. Believers will become participants in all these things who purchase confessional letters. Preachers and confessors must insist with great perseverance upon these advantages, and persuade believers that they should not neglect to acquire these along with their confessional letter.

We also declare that in order to acquire these two most important graces, it is not necessary to make confession, or to visit the churches and altars, but merely to purchase the confessional letter. . . . .

The fourth distinctive grace is for those souls which are in purgatory, and is the complete remission of all sins, which remission the pope brings to pass through his intercession to the advantage of said souls, in this wise; that the same contribution shall be placed in the chest by a living person as one would make for himself. It is our wish, however, that our subcommissioners should modify the regulations regarding contributions of this kind which are given for the dead, and that they should use their judgment in all other cases, where in their opinion modifications are desirable. It is furthermore not necessary that the persons who place their contributions in the chest for the dead should be contrite in heart and have orally confessed, since this grace is based simply on the state of grace in which the dead departed, and on the contribution of the living, as is evident from the text of the bull. Moreover, preachers shall exert themselves to give this grace the widest publicity, since through the same help will surely come to departed souls, and the construction of the Church of St. Peter will be abundantly promoted at the same time. . . . .

✤ F. The Pardoner Redivivus: Johann Tetzel's Sermon on Indulgences, 1517

From Robinson and Whitcomb, The Period of the Early Reformation in Germany, *pp. 9–10. Latin text in Eusebius Amort,* De origine, progressu, valore ac fructu indulgentiarum *(Augsburg, 1735), pars. 2, section 1, 22, pp. 15–16. On the indulgence controversy generally, see J. M. Todd,* M. Luther *(London, 1964).*

Venerable Sir, I pray you that in your utterances you may be pleased to make use of such words as shall serve to open the eyes of the mind and cause your hearers to consider how great a grace and gift they have had and now have at their very doors. Blessed eyes indeed, which see what they see, because already they possess letters of safe conduct by which they are able to lead their souls through that valley of tears, through that sea of the mad world, where storms and tempests and dangers lie in wait, to the blessed land of Paradise. Know that the life of man upon earth is a constant struggle. We have to fight against the flesh, the world and the devil, who are always seeking to destroy the soul. In sin we are conceived—alas! what bonds of sin encompass us, and how difficult and almost impossible it is to attain to the gate of salvation without divine aid; since He causes us to be saved, not by virtue of the good works which we accomplish, but through His divine mercy; it is necessary then to put on the armor of God.

You may obtain letters of safe conduct from the vicar of our Lord Jesus Christ, by means of which you are able to liberate your soul from the hands of the enemy, and convey it by means of contrition and confession, safe and secure from all pains of Purgatory, into the happy kingdom. For know that in these letters are stamped and engraven all the merits of Christ's passion there laid bare. Consider, that for each and every mortal sin it is necessary to undergo seven years of penitence after confession and contrition, either in this life or in Purgatory.

How many mortal sins are committed in a day, how many in a week, how many in a month, how many in a year, how many in the whole course of life! They are well-nigh numberless and those that commit them must needs suffer endless punishment in the burning pains of Purgatory.

But with these confessional letters you will be able at any time in life to obtain full indulgence for all penalties imposed upon you, in all cases except the four reserved to the Apostolic See. Therefore throughout your whole life, whenever you wish to make confession, you may receive the same remission, except in cases reserved to the Pope, and afterwards, at the hour of death, a full indulgence as to all penalties and sins, and your share of all spiritual blessings that exist in the church militant and all its members.

Do you not know that when it is necessary for anyone to go to Rome, or undertake any other dangerous journey, he takes his money to a broker and gives a certain per cent—five or six or ten—in order that at Rome or elsewhere he may receive again his funds intact, by means of the letter of this same broker? Are you not willing, then, for the fourth part of a florin, to obtain these letters, by virtue of which you may bring, not your money, but your divine and immortal soul safe and sound into the land of Paradise?

Wherefore I counsel, order, and by virtue of my authority as shepherd, I command that they shall receive together with me and other priests, this precious treasure, especially those who were not confessed at the time of the holy Jubilee, that they may be able to obtain the same forever. For the time may come when you may desire, but yet be unable to obtain the least portion of the grace.

Also on the part of SS. D. N. the Pope and of the most holy apostolic See and of the most reverend sir, my legate, to each and every one who shall have profited by the sacred Jubilee and made confession, and to all who may profit by this present brief opportunity, and who shall have lent a helping hand to the construction of the aforesaid house of the Prince of the Apostles, they shall all be participants and sharers in all prayers, suffrages, alms, fasts, supplications, masses, canonical hours, disciplines, pilgrimages, papal stations, benedictions, and all other spiritual goods which now exist or may exist forever in the church militant, and in all of these, not only they themselves, but their relatives, kindred, and benefactors who have passed away; and as they were moved by charity, so God, and SS. Peter and Paul, and all the saints whose bodies rest in Rome, shall guard them in peace in this vale, and conduct them through it to the heavenly kingdom. Give everlasting thanks in the aforesaid names and in mine to the reverend secular priests and prelates, etc.

7

Statutory Reform in England

Introductory Note: Individual churchmen and general councils were not the only sources of ecclesiastical criticism and proposals for reform in the fourteenth and fifteenth centuries. From the quarrel between Philip IV the Fair of France and Boniface VIII between 1298 and 1303, individual rulers drew considerable power over the Church in their own lands into their own hands. The military conflicts of the fourteenth century turned the popes into arbitrators between contending parties and forced the kings of France and England to turn to an increasingly wider mobilization of state resources, including, on occasion, the resources owned by the Church. The Schism of 1378 to 1415 further splintered the unity of the Church and gave yet more power to the kings and other lords temporal. The Statutes of Provisors and Praemunire of 1352 and 1393 forbade the acquisition of "Provisions"—that is, the rights to succeed to ecclesiastical benefices—from Rome, on the one hand, and forbade appeals to the court of Rome, on the other. A good general introduction to the problems of statutory reform in England is May McKisack,

The Fourteenth Century, 1307–1399, The Oxford History of England, vol. 5 (Oxford, 1959), with an extensive bibliography, and W. A. Pantin, *The English Church in the XIV Century* (Cambridge, 1955). A good recent study of related problems is W. R. Jones, "Bishops, Politics, and the Two Laws: The *Gravamina* of the English Clergy, 1327–1399," *Speculum* 41 (1966): 209–45. Both of these statutes were issued several times in several versions, reflecting the continuous concern, much of it expressed in various forms in *Piers Plowman*, with the role of the Church in fourteenth–century English society.

✤ The Statute of Provisors, 1352

The Statutes of Provisors and Praemunire were each reissued several times during the fourteenth century. The following texts are characteristic issuances. Text in Statutes of the Realm, (*London, 1810–22*), *1:323–24. 25 Edw. III, stat. 5, C. 22.*

Because that some do purchase in the court of Rome Provisions to have abbeys and priories in England, in destruction of the realm, and of holy religion; It is accorded, that every man that purchaseth such Provisions of abbeys or priories, that he and his executors and procurators, which do sue and make execution of such Provisions, shall be out of the King's protection; and that a man may do with them as of enemies of our sovereign Lord the King and his realm; and he that offendeth against such Provisors in body or in goods, or in other possessions, shall be excused against all people, and shall never be impeached nor grieved for the same at any man's suit.

✤ The Statute of *Praemunire*, 1393

Both translations of these statutes are from England in the Time of Wycliffe. *Latin text in* Statutes of the Realm, (*London, 1810–22*), *2:84. 16 Rich. II, c. 5.*

Whereas, the Commons of the realm in this present Parliament have showed to our redoubted lord the king, grievously complaining, that whereas the said our lord the king and all his liege people ought of right and of old time were wont to sue in the king's court, to recover their presentments to churches, prebends, and other benefices of Holy Church to the which they had right to present, the cognisance of plea of which suit belongeth only to the king's court of the old right of his crown, used and approved in the time of all his progenitors, kings of England; and when judgment shall be given in the same court upon such a plea and suit, the archbishops, bishops, and other spiritual persons which have institution of such benefices within their jurisdiction be bound, and have made execution of such judgments by the king's commandments, for all the time aforesaid without interruption (for another, a lay person, is not able to make such execution), and also be bound of right to make execution of many other of the king's commandments, of which right the crown of England hath been peaceably seized, as well in the time of our said lord the king that now is, as in the time of all his progenitors till this day.

But now of late divers processes be made by the Holy Father the Pope, and censures of excommunication upon certain bishops of England, because they had made execution of such commandments, to the open disherison of the same crown and destruction of the regalty of our said lord the king, his law, and all his realm, if remedy be not provided. And also it is said and a common clamor is made that the said Holy Father, the Pope, hath ordained and purposed to translate some prelates of the same realm, some out of the realm, and some from one bishopric into another within the same realm, without the king's assent and knowledge, and without the assent of the prelates which are to be so translated, which prelates be much profitable and necessary to our said lord the king, and to all his realm; by which translations, if they should be suffered, the statutes of the realm should be defeated and made void; and his said liege sages of his council, without his assent and against his will carried away and gotten out of his realm and the substance and treasure of the realm should be carried away, and so the realm destitute as well of council as of substance, to the final destruction of the same realm. So the crown of England which hath been so free at all times that it hath had no earthly sovereign, but is immediately subject to God in all things touching the regalty of the same crown, and to none other, should be submitted to the Pope, and the laws and statutes of the realm by him defeated and avoided at his will, in perpetual destruction of the sovereignty of the king our lord, his crown, his regalty, and of all his realm, which God forbid.

And moreover, the Commons aforesaid say, that the things so attempted be clearly against the king's crown and his regalty, used and approved in the time of all his progenitors; wherefore, they and all the liege Commons of the same realm will stand with our said lord the king, and his said crown and his regalty, in the cases aforesaid, and in all other cases attempted against him his crown and his regalty in all points, to live and to die; and moreover, they pray the king and require him, by way of justice, that he would examine all the lords in the Parliament, as well spiritual as temporal severally, and all the estates of the Parliament, how they think of the cases aforesaid, which be so openly against the king's crown, and in derogation of his regalty, and how they will stand in the same cases with our lord the king in upholding the rights of the said crown and regalty.

Wherefore, the lords temporal so demanded have answered every one by himself, that the cases aforesaid be clearly in derogation of the king's crown and of his regalty, as is well known, and hath been of a long time known, and that they will be with the same crown and regalty, in these cases specially, and in all other cases which shall be attempted against the same crown and regalty in all points, with all their power.

And, moreover, it was demanded of the lords spiritual there being, and the procurators of others, being absent, their advice and will in all these cases; which lords, that is to say, the archbishops, bishops, and other prelates, being in the said Parliament severally examined, (making protestations that it is not their intention to say nor to affirm that our Holy Father the Pope may not excommunicate bishops and that he may not make translations of prelates according to the law of Holy Church) answered and said, that if any executions of processes made in the king's court, as before, be made by any, and censures of excommunications be made against any bishops of England, or any other of the king's liege people, for that they have made execution of such commandments, and that if any executions of such translations be made of any prelates of the same realm, which lords be very profitable and necessary to our said lord the king, and to his said realm, or that his sage lieges of his council, without his assent and against his will, be removed and carried out of the realm, so that the substance and treasure of the realm may be consumed, that the same is against the king and his crown, as is contained in the petition before named. And likewise the same procurators, every one by himself examined upon the said matters, have answered and said, in the name and for the lords, as the said bishops have said and answered; and that the said lords spiritual will and ought to stand with the king in these cases loyally in maintenance of his crown, and in all other cases touching his crown and regalty, as they are bound by their allegiance.

Whereupon, our said lord the king, by the assent aforesaid, and at the request of his said Commons, hath ordained and established; that if anyone purchases or pursues or causes to be purchased or pursued in the court of Rome or elsewhere any such translations, processes, and sentences of excommunications, bills, instruments, or any other thing whatsoever which touches the king our lord, against him, his crown and regalty, or his realm, as before is said, and those who bring them within the realm, or receive them, or make thereof notification, or any other execution whatsoever, within the same realm or without; that they, their notaries, procurators, maintainers, abettors, favorers, and counsellors, shall be put out of the protection of our said Lord the king, and their lands and tenants, goods and chattels, shall be forfeited to our lord the king; and that they shall be attached by their bodies, if they may be found, and brought before the king and his council, there to answer to the cases aforesaid, or that process be made against them by *Praemunire facias,* in manner as it is ordained in other statutes of provisors and others who sue in the court of another, in derogation of the regalty of our lord the king.

8

Plague, Population, and the Labor Crisis

Introductory Note: Social and ecclesiastical abuses drew, perhaps, the heaviest fire of preachers and satirists, but the fourteenth century faced severe material crises as well, from the run of famine and drought after the 1280s to the financial collapses of the 1330s and 1340s, the Black Death after 1348, and the spreading frequency of wars after the mid century. The texts given below reflect the various estimations of the impact of the Black Death after 1348. They are all taken from *England in the Time of Wycliffe*. The *Statute of Laborers* of 1351 is characteristic of many attempts, in England and on the Continent, to hold down the escalating price of labor in a depopulated, labor-intensive world. A good general introduction to the Black Death is Philip Ziegler, *The Black Death* (New York, 1969), and to the conditions of labor, see Michel Mollat and Philippe Wolff, *The Popular Revolutions of the Late Middle Ages* (London, 1973).

✤ A. Plague

From Thomas Walsingham, Historia Anglicana, *ed. Henry Thomas Riley, vol. 1, Rolls Series, vol. 28 (London, 1863–64).*

In the year of grace 1349, which was the twenty-third year of King Edward, the Third since the Conquest, a great mortality of mankind advanced over the world; beginning in the regions of the North and East, and ending with so great a destruction that scarcely half of the people remained. Then towns once full of men became destitute of inhabitants; and so violently did the pestilence increase that the living were scarce able to bury the dead. Indeed, in certain houses of men of religion, scarcely two out of twenty men survived. It was estimated by many that hardly a tenth part of mankind had been left alive. A murrain among animals followed immediately upon this pestilence; then rents ceased; then the land, because of the lack of tenants, who were nowhere to be found, remained uncultivated. So great misery followed from these evils that the world was never afterward able to return to its former state.

From The Chronicle of Robert of Avesbury, *Rolls Series, vol. 93 (London, 1889), pp. 406–7.*

The pestilence which had first broken out in the land occupied by the Saracens became so much stronger that, sparing no dominion, it visited with the scourge of sudden death the various parts of all the kingdoms, extending from that land to the northward, including even Scotland, destroying the greater part of the people. For it began in England in Dorsetshire, about the feast of St. Peter, called Ad Vincula, in the year of the Lord 1348, and immediately advancing from place to place it attacked men without warning and for the most part those who were healthy. Very many of those who were attacked in the morning it carried out of human affairs before noon. And no one whom it willed to die did it permit to live longer than three or four days. There was moreover no choice of persons, with the exception, at least, of a few rich people. In the same day twenty, forty or sixty corpses, and indeed many times as many

more bodies of those who had died, were delivered to church
burial in the same pit at the same time. And about the feast
of All Saints, reaching London, it deprived many of their life
daily, and increased to so great an extent that from the feast
of the Purification till after Easter there were more than two
hundred bodies of those who had died buried daily in the ceme-
tery which had been then recently made near Smithfield, besides
the bodies which were in other graveyards of the same city.
The grace of the Holy Spirit finally intervening, that is to say
about the feast of Whitsunday, it ceased at London, proceeding
continuously northward. In these parts also it ceased about the
feast of St. Michael, in the year of the Lord 1349.

❧ B. The King's Proclamation Concerning
Laborers, 1351

Text in Statutes of the Realm (*London, 1810*), *1:307–8.*

The King to the sheriff of Kent, greeting: Because a great
part of the people, and especially of workmen and servants, have
lately died in the pestilence, many seeing the necessity of
masters and great scarcity of servants, will not serve unless they
may receive excessive wages, and others preferring to beg in
idleness rather than by labor to get their living; we, considering
the grievous incommodities which of the lack especially of
ploughmen and such laborers may hereafter come, have upon
deliberation and treaty with the prelates and the nobles and
learned men assisting us, with their unanimous counsel ordained:
That every man and woman of our realm of England, of
what condition he be, free or bond, able in body, and within
the age of sixty years, not living in merchandize, nor exercising
any craft, nor having of his own whereof he may live, nor land
of his own about whose tillage he may occupy himself, and not
serving any other; if he be required to serve in suitable service,
his estate considered, he shall be bound to serve him which shall
so require him; and take only the wages, livery, meed, or salary
which were accustomed to be given in the places where he oweth
to serve, the twentieth year of our reign of England, or five

or six other common years next before. Provided always, that the lords be preferred before others in their bondmen or their land tenants, so in their service to be retained; so that, nevertheless, the said lords shall retain no more than be necessary for them. And if any such man or woman being so required to serve will not do the same, and that be proved by two true men before the sheriff, bailiff, lord, or constable of the town where the same shall happen to be done, he shall immediately be taken by them or any of them, and committed to the next gaol, there to remain under strait keeping, till he find surety to serve in the form aforesaid.

If any reaper, mower, or other workman or servant, of what estate or condition that he be, retained in any man's service, do depart from the said service without reasonable cause or license, before the term agreed, he shall have pain of imprisonment; and no one, under the same penalty, shall presume to receive or retain such a one in his service.

No one, moreover, shall pay or promise to pay to any one more wages, liveries, meed, or salary than was accustomed, as is before said; nor shall any one in any other manner demand or receive them, upon pain of doubling of that shall have been so paid, promised, required or received, to him who thereof shall feel himself aggrieved; and if none such will sue, then the same shall be applied to any of the people that will sue; and such suit shall be in the court of the lord of the place where such case shall happen.

And if lords of towns or manors presume in any point to come against this present ordinance, either by them or by their servants, then suit shall be made against them in the form aforesaid, in the counties, wapentakes, and trithings, or such other courts of ours, for the penalty of treble that so paid or promised by them or their servants. And if any before this present ordinance hath covenanted with any so to serve for more wages, he shall not be bound, by reason of the said covenant, to pay more than at another time was wont to be paid to such a person; nor, under the same penalty, shall presume to pay more.

Item. Saddlers, skinners, white tawers, cordwainers, tailors, smiths, carpenters, masons, tilers, shipwrights, carters, and all other artificers and workmen shall not take for their labor and workmanship above the same that was wont to be paid to such persons the said twentieth year, and other common years next preceding, as before is said, in the place where they shall heppen to work; and if any man take more he shall be committed to the next gaol, in manner as before is said.

Item. That butchers, fishmongers, hostelers, brewers, bakers, poulterers, and all other sellers of all manner of victuals, shall be bound to sell the same victuals for a reasonable price, having respect to the price that such victuals be sold at in the places adjoining, so that the same sellers have moderate gains, and not excessive, reasonably to be required according to the distance of the place from whence the said victuals be carried; and if any sell such victuals in any other manner, and thereof be convict, in the manner and form aforesaid, he shall pay the double of the same that he so received to the party injured, or in default of him, to any other that will sue in this behalf. And the mayors and bailiffs of cities, boroughs, merchant towns, and others, and of the ports and maritime places, shall have power to inquire of all and singular, which shall in any thing offend against this, and to levy the said penalty to the use of them at whose suit such offenders shall be convict. And in case that the same mayors and bailiffs be negligent in doing execution of the premises, and thereof be convict before our justices, by us to be assigned, then the same mayors and bailiffs shall be compelled by the same justices to pay the treble of the thing so sold to the party injured, or to any other, in default of him, that will sue; and nevertheless toward us they shall be grievously punished.

And because that many strong beggars, as long as they may live by begging, do refuse to labor, giving themselves to idleness and vice, and sometimes to theft and other abominations; none upon the said pain of imprisonment, shall, under the color of pity or alms, give anything to such, which may labor, or presume to favor them in their idleness, so that thereby they may be compelled to labor for their necessary living.

9

The Peasants'
Rebellion of 1381

Introductory Note: The growing restiveness of all classes of English society after the impact of the Black Death and the first rounds of the Hundred Years War is reflected in the following documents. The first selection is the Statute of 1377 against peasant excesses, one of the stimuli of the uprising of 1381. The second selection is John Ball's famous Letter to the Commons of Essex. The third, fourth, and fifth selections deal with the royal attempts to put down the lower social ranks in the rebellion and the king's pardon to those lords who violated the law in repressing the uprisings. A convenient collection of materials may be found in *The Peasants' Revolt*, ed., Douglas Hill (London, n.d.). See also Mollat and Wolff, *The Popular Revolutions of the Late Middle Ages* (London, 1973), R. H. Hilton and H. Fagan, *The English Rising of 1381* (London, 1950), and R. H. Hilton, *Bond Men Made Free* (New York, 1973).

✤ A. The Law Against Excesses of the Villains

Statutes of the Realm, *2:2–3. Eng. trans.*, England in the Age of Wycliffe.

At the grievous complaint of the lords and commons of the realm, as well men of Holy Church as other, made in this Parliament, of that in many signories and parts of the realm of England, the villains and land tenants in villainage, who owe services and customs to their said lords, have now late withdrawn and do daily withdraw their services and customs due to their said lords, by comfort and procurement of other their counsellors, maintainers and abettors in the country, which have taken hire and profit of the said villains and land tenants by color of certain exemplifications made out of the book of Domesday of the manors and towns where they have been dwelling, and by virtue of the same exemplifications and their evil interpretations of the same, they affirm them to be quit and utterly discharged of all manner serfage, due as well of their body as of their said tenures, and will not suffer any distress or other justice to be made upon them; but do menace the ministers of their lords of life and member, and, which is more, gather themselves together in great routs, and agree by such confederacy, that every one shall aid other to resist their lords with strong hand, and much other harm they do in sundry ways, to the great damage of their said lords and evil example to other to begin such riots; so that if due remedy be not the rather provided upon the same rebels, greater mischief, which God prohibit, may thereof spring through the realm. It is ordained and established that the lords which feel themselves grieved, shall have special commission under the Great Seal to the Justices of Peace, or to other sufficient persons, to inquire of all such rebels, and of their offences, and their counsellors, procurers, maintainers and abettors, and to imprison all those that shall be thereof indicted before them, as well for the time past as for the time to come without delivering them out of prison by mainprise, bail or otherwise, without assent of their lords, till they be attainted or acquitted thereof; and that the same justices have power to hear and determine as well at the king's suit as at the suit of the party. . . .

And as to the said exemplifications, made and purchased as afore is said, which were caused to come in the Parliament, it is declared in the said Parliament that the same may not nor ought to avail, or hold place to the said villains or land tenants, as to the franchise of their bodies; nor to change the condition of their tenure and customs of old time due; nor to do prejudice to the said lords, to have their services and customs as they were wont of old time; and it is ordained that upon this declaration the said lords shall have letters patents under the Great Seal, as many and such as they shall need, if they the same require.

❧ B. The Letter of John Ball to the Commons of Essex

Text in Thomas Walsingham, Historia Anglicana, *Rolls Series, vol. 28, (London, 1863–64), 2:33–34.*

John Schep, som tyme Seynt Marie prest of Yorke, and now of Colchestre, greteth welle Johan Nameles, and Johan the Mullere, and Johan Cartere, and biddeth hem that thei ware of gyle in borugh, and stondeth togiddir in Goddis name, and biddeth Peres Ploughman go to his werke, and chastise welle Hobbe the robber, and taketh with you Johan Trewman, and alle his felaws, and no mo, and loke scharpe you to on heved, and no mo.

> Johan the Muller hath ygrownde smal, smal, smal;
> The Kyngis sone of hevene shalle pay for alle.
> Be ware or ye be wo,
> Knoweth your frende fro youre foo,
> Haveth ynowe, and seythe "Hoo;"
> And do welle and bettre, and fleth synne,
> And seketh pees, and holde therynne.
> And so biddeth Johan Trewman and alle his felawes.

✤ C. The Charter of Manumission and Pardon to the Rebels from Hertfordshire

Text in Walsingham, Historia Anglicana, *1:467*.

Richard, by the grace of God, King of England and France, and Lord of Ireland, to all his bailiffs and faithful ones, to whom these present letters shall come, greeting. Know that of our special grace, we have manumitted all of our lieges and each of our subjects and others of the County of Hertford; and them and each of them have made free from all bondage, and by these presents make them quit. And moreover we pardon our same lieges and subjects for all kinds of felonies, treasons, transgressions and extortions, however done or perpetrated by them or any of them, and also outlawry, if any shall have been promulgated on this account against them or any of them; and our most complete peace to them and each of them we concede in these matters. In testimony of which thing we have caused these our letters to be made patent. Witness, myself, at London, on the fifteenth day of June, in the fourth year of our reign.

✤ D. The Withdrawal of Manumissions

Text in Statutes of the Realm, *2:20. 5 Rich. II, stat. 1, c. 6*

It is ordained that all manner of manumissions, obligations, releases, and other bonds made by compulsion, duress and threat, in the time of this last rumor and riot against the laws of the land and good faith shall be wholly quashed, annulled and holden for void; and they which have caused to be made or do yet withhold such manumissions, obligations, releases, bonds and other deeds, so made by duress, shall be sent before the king and his council, there to answer of their deed; and further, shall be constrained to make delivery and restitution of the said deeds to them that made the same against their good will, with the copies of the same, if perchance they have thereof made any before in order to use or renew the effect of the same another time, if they may. And likewise, it is accorded that all entries made in lands or tenements, and also all feoffments made in the time of the same rumor by compulsion and menace, or otherwise with force of people, against the law, shall be void and holden for none. And the king straitly forbiddeth to all manner of people, upon pain of as much as they are able to forfeit to him in body and goods, that none from henceforth make nor begin again, in any manner, such riot and rumor, nor other like them. And if any do the same, and this be duly proved, it shall be done concerning him as of a traitor to the king and to his said realm.

✤ E. The Pardon of the King to the Lords

Text in Statutes of the Realm, *2:20. 5 Rich. II, stat. 1, c. 5*

Our sovereign lord the King, perceiving that many lords and gentlemen of his realm, and other with them in the rumor and insurrection of villains, and of other offenders, which now of late did traitorously rise by assemblies in outragious numbers in divers parts of the realm, against God, good faith, and reason, and against the dignity of our sovereign lord the King and his crown, and the laws of his land, made divers punishments upon the said villains and other traitors, without due process of the law, and otherwise than the laws and usages of the realm required, although they did it of no malice prepense, but only to appease and cease the apparent mischief, and considering the great diligence and loyalty of the lords and gentlemen in this behalf, which were not learned of the said laws and usages, and though at that time they had been learned, a man might not upon those punishments have tarried the process of the law, and that this they did with good intent, of their advice and of their good discretions, and willing therefore to do them grace, according as they have the same greatly deserved, of the assent aforesaid hath pardoned and released to the said lords and gentlemen, and all other being in their aid at the same deed, and to every of them, as much as to him thereof pertaineth, or to him and to his heirs may pertain; so that, hereafter for whatsoever thing that was done by them upon the said punishments in resistance, they shall never be impeached nor grieved in body, goods, nor their heritages and possessions, in any way, by our sovereign lord the King, his heirs or ministers, nor none other in time to come, but utterly shall be thereof quit for ever by this grant and statute without having thereof other special charter or pardon.

10

On the Times

Introductory Note: This denunciation of contemporary abuses reflects, in its alternating Middle English and doggerel Latin lines, that half-learned world reflected in the Prologue of *Piers Plowman* and in the macaronic Latin-English lines that occur elsewhere in the poem. The poem was originally edited by Thomas Wright in his *Political Poems and Songs Relating to English History composed during the Period from the Accession of Edward III to that of Richard II*, Rolls Series, vol. 14 (London, 1859), 1:224–26, The manuscripts used here are: British Museum Ms. Harley 941 fol. 21v; British Museum Ms. Harley 536 fol. 34r; Trinity College Dublin Ms. E. 5. 10; Oxford, Bodleian Library Ms. Bodley 11951 folio 59a (only first four lines). Wright used the Trinity Ms. as a base text. This edition uses Harley 536 with variants from the other Mss. Lines 95–100 use the image of belling the cat, which Langland uses in the *Prologue* of the B-Text. (Compare Bozon's application of the fable to priests and parishioners, below, chapter 17.) "On the Rebellion of Jack Straw," is also from Wright, *Political Poems and Songs*, 1:270–78, and employs the same use of alternating English and Latin lines in suggesting some of the popular doggeral propaganda that the political crises of Richard II's reign called forth.

✤ A. On The Times

Syng y wolde, but, alas!
descendunt prospera grata;
Englond sum tyme was
regnorum gemma vocata;
Of manhod the flowre   5
ibi quondam floruit omnis;
Now gon ys that tour
traduntur talia somnis.
Lechery, slouthe and pryde,
hec sunt quibus Anglia paret;   10
Sith trouthe[1] ys set asyde,
dic qualiter Anglia staret.
Whiche owre frendis were,
nostri fient inimici,
With bowe, scheld and spere   15
poterunt—eu!—talia dici.
Ofte tymes have we herd[2]
mala nobis esse futura,
But ever desired we
a nobis commercia plura.   20
Lo! within owre lond
insurgunt undique guerre.
But God put to his hond,
fiet destructio terre.
On water and on lond,   25
que quondam nos timuerunt,
Now many a thowsand
nos parvo per mare querunt.
The dred of God is went,
humanus sed timor astat.   30
Ho seyt[3] truth is schent

1. *Sith trouthe:* Since truth   2. *herd:* heard   3. *Ho seyt:* whoever says

regnum violentia vastat;
Rowners[4] and flatreres
hi regno sunt nocituri;
Wolde God swoch claterers   35
sua subdant colla securi.
Englond, awake now—
consurgunt jugiter hostes,
And good heede take thow
fac hostia, dirige postes.   40
The riche make mery,
sed vulgus collachrimatur;
The pepul ys weri,[5]
quia firme depopulatur.
The chyrche is grevyd,   45
quia spiritualia cadunt.
Sume bethe myschevyd[6]
plus damni crescere credunt.
Englond goith to noght
plus fecit homo vitiosus   50
To lust man is broght,
nimis est homo deliciosus.
Goddes halydayys[7] ar noght,
non observantur honeste.
For unthrifty[8] pley is worght,   55
in eis regnat manifeste,
Unthrifte and wombe joye
steriles et luxuriose,
Gentyls, gromys,[9] and boyys,
socii sunt atque gulosi.   60
Sojettys[10] and sovereynys
uno quasi fine trahuntur.
Put thei be to peyne[11]
in eos quicunque loquuntur.
At Westmyster halle   65
legis sunt valde scientes;

4. *Rowners:* whisperers   5. *ys weri:* are weary
6. *Sume bethe myschevyd:* Are brought to misfortune
7. *halydayys:* holy days   8. *unthrifty:* profligate
9. *gromys:* grooms   10. *sojettys:* subjects   11. *peyne:* punishment

Neverthelesse for hem alle,
ibi vincuntur jura potentes.
That never herd the caas,
juramento tunc mediabunt,   70
Than the mater wolle thei face
et justum damnificabunt,
And an obligacion
de jure satis valitura.
Thorgh (a fals) cavelacion,[12]   75
erit effectu caritura.
His owyn caas many a man
nunc judicat et moderatur.
Law helpyth noght hem
ergo eu! lex evacuatur.   80
Manslaughter and thefte
crucis ad votum redimuntur;
Ware of evel spon wefte[13]
quia pravos prava sequuntur.
Jurrours[14] with peyntyd slewys,[15]   85
inopes famuli dominorum.
This hurtyth and grevyth
novit Deus ipse deorum.
Gret hurt to this lond
est usurpata potestas;   90
Therfor put to ys hond
regis metuenda majestas.
For harme that mow falle,
nonnulla statuta parantur;
The kyng knowyth not alle,   95
non sunt qui vera loquuntur.
He and he seyd wel,
et sermo placere videtur;
The cattys nec[16] to the belle
hic et hic ligare veretur.   100

12. *cavelacion:* legal quibble
13. *Ware of evel spon wefte:* Beware of ill-spun wool
14. *Jurrours:* Jurors   15. *pentyd slewys:* brightly-colored sleeves
16. *cattys nec:* cat's neck (compare Langland's prologue)

Qwat[17] is the cause of this?
vere violentia legis.
Amende that is amys
poterit clementia regis.
Now without a jacke[18] 105
pauci metuunt remanere;
Sum hath hym on here[19] bak,
sed bursa mallet habere.
Good Jake, qwere[20] is Jon?
ubi gratia nunc requiescit? 110
Jake, now grace is gon,
ad regna remota recessit;
Jake nobil with hym ys
iter in simul arripuerunt.
Of bothe ys gret mys,[21] 115
illos multi modo querunt.
Galauntes,[22] Purs Penyles
per vicos ecce vagantur.
Yf yt be as I gesse,
male solvent quod metuantur. 120
On with another man
satagit committere guerram.
Now is he here, and now is he gon,
destruxit ut advena terram.
Fresshest of the newe towch, 125
incedunt ridiculose,
Lityle or nought in her powch,
pascuntur deliciose.
Brodder than ever God made
humeris sunt arte tumentes; 130
Narugh[23] they be, thou3 they seme brode,
nova sunt; factio gentis
They bere a newe fascion,
humeris in pectore tergo;
Goddes plasmacion[24] 135
non illis complacet ergo.

17. *Qwat:* what   18. *jacke:* coat of mail   19. *here:* their
20. *qwere:* where   21. *mys:* loss   22. *Galauntes:* Gallants
23. *Narugh:* Narrow   24. *plasmacion:* formation

Wyde coleres[25] and hye,
  gladio sunt colla parata—
Ware[26] the prophecye
  contra tales recitata.   140
Long sporys[27] on her[28] helys,
  et rostra fovent ocrearum.
They thynke it doth welle;
  non sit regula Sarum.
A strecte[29] bende hath the hose,   145
  laqueantur a corpore crura.
They may noght, I suppose
  curvare genu sine cura:
Qwen oder (men) knelys[30]
  pia Christo vota ferentes,   150
Thei stond onn here helis,[31]
  set non curvare valentes;
For hortyng[32] of here hose
  non inclinare laborant
I trow, for here long toos[33]   155
  dum stant ferialiter orant.
Many men thei let
  et turbant ad sacra stando;
Crystes curse they get,
  nisi Deus instat aliquando.   160
Women, lo! with wantounly brestes
  procedunt arte profana;
Precher ne pristes[34]
  possunt hec pellere vana.
With poyntys[35] ful strong   165
  caligas de more sigillant
Now shorte and now longe
  ut ventus ecce! vacillant.
Now knokelyd[36] elbowys
  manice laqueant lacerate   170

25. *coleres:* collars   26. *Ware:* Beware   27. *sporys:* spurs
28. *her:* their (cf. footnote 19)   29. *strecte:* straight
30. *Qwen oder (men) knelys:* When other men kneel
31. *onn here helis:* on their heels   32. *hortyng:* hurting harming
33. *toos:* toes   34. *prists:* priests   35. *poynts:* laces   36. *knokelyd:* knuckled

In frost and (in) snowes,
ut aves spectant laqueate.
Qwhan[37] frost awakys,
et stringunt frigore gentes,
Than ther teth quakis,[38]   175
sed se quasi concutientes.
Qwan men rest takyn,
noctis somno recreati,
Swoch[39] felawys wakyn
ad damna patrata patrati   180
Ful oft tymes iwys[40]
gelido fervent in amore,
Ther special whan thei kus[41]
distillat nasus in ore.
Huf[42] a galaunt thee atowche,   185
unguentum stillat amoris.
I wolde fil were here[43] pouche
tanti dulcedine roris!
Lo! this for a gret nede,
sua miscent ora libenter.   190
Ho so ever[44] take hede
manet liquor irreverenter.
"Viva sa belle!" thei cry,
fragrantia vina bibentes,
Thei drynke tyl they (be) dry,[45]   195
lingua sensusque carentes.
Thei cry, "Fyl the bowles!"
"Bonus est liquor, hic maneamus!
For alle Crystone sowllys,[46]
dum durant vasa, bibamus!"   200
Armys, sidus, and blode[47]
horum quidam recitabit;
Yit whan he ys most wode,[48]
tunc blandus sermo donabit

---

37. *Qwhan:* When   38. *quakis:* shake   39. *Swoch:* such
40. *iwys:* certainly   41. *kus:* kiss   42. *Huf:* If   43. *here:* their
44. *Ho so ever:* Who so ever   45. *dry:* stupefied   46. *sowllys:* souls
47. *Armys, sidus, and blode:* Arms, sides, and blood (or bones) of Christ–an oath
48. *wode:* mud

Peraventure[49] at an houre   205
   poscunt hi tempora plausis
A cowntur-tenur[50] (at Newgat)
   cantabit carcere clausis
Of the chyrche that I write,
   non forte placet sibi psalmus   210
Now sey I for this dispite
   Sic me Deus adjuvat almus,
Alas and welaway!
   decus ecclesiam tenebrascit;
Lyght wol fayle, I dar say   215
   Sanctus nunc Spiritus assit.
Symon, that fals man
   decus nocet ecclesiarum;
Moche sorow he began
   virus diffudit amarum.   220
And than fals avarise
   satis ecclesiam laqueasti;
With many evyl vice
   Christi sponsam violasti.
Here myght I more sey,   225
   cum ordo vetat seriarum;
Of swche more se ȝe may[51]
   in libris ecclesiarum.
The lanterne of lyghtte
   non fulget luce serena   230
Yt is not alle aryght
   populus bibit ecce vena.
Oure kynge and oure lond
   servet, regat et teneatur;
God that with ys hond   235
   celum, terram moderatur.
In age as he growyt[52]
   sua crescit gratia fructu;
Ful litle hee knowith
   quanto dolet Anglia luctu.   240

---

49. *Peraventure:* By chance   50. *cowntur-tenur:* counter tenor
51. *se ȝe may:* you may see   52. *growyt:* grows

O rex, si rex es, rege te, vel eris sine re rex
Nomen habes sine re, nisi te recteque regas rex.

Explicit autem scriptum. Nunc finem feci, da mihi quod
   merui.

✤ B. On The Rebellion of Jack Straw (1381)

Corpus Christi College Cambridge Ms. 369
Oxford, Bodleian Library Ms. Digby 196, fol. 20v. This text follows
Digby, with additional stanzas (in parenthesis) from CCCC 369.

Previously edited by Thomas Wright, Political Poems and Songs
Relating to English History composed during the Period from the
Accession of Edward III to that of Richard III, *Rolls Series, vol. 14*
(London 1859), 1: 224–26.

Tax hath tened[1] us alle,
   probat hoc mors tot validorum;
The kyng therof hade smalle,[2]
   fuit in manibus cupidorum.
Hit hade ful harde honsalle,[3]   5
   dans causam fine dolorum.
Vengeaunce nede most falle,
   propter peccata malorum.

In Kent this kare began,
   mox infestando potentes,   10
On rowte[4] the rybawdus[5] they ran,
   sua turpida arma ferentes;
Fole[6] they dred no mon,
   regni regem neque gentes,
Churles were here chevetan,[7]   15
   sue iure fere superantes.

(Thus hor wayes thay wente,
   pravis pravos emulantes,
To London fro Kent
   sunt predia depopulantes;   20

1. *tened:* ruined   2. *smalle:* little   3. *honsalle:* fortune
4. *rowte:* crowds   5. *rybawdus:* robbers   6. *Fole:* Fools
7. *chevetan:* chieftains

Ther was an uvel covent,[8]
australi parte vagantes;
Sythenne[9] they sone were schent,[10]
qui tunc fuerant superantes.

(Bondus they blwun bost,[11]   25
nolentes lege domari,
Nede they fre be most,[12]
vel nollent pacificari;
Charters were endost,[13]
hos libertate morari;   30
Ther hor fredam thay lost,
digni pro cede negari.)

Laddes[14] lowde they lought,[15]
clamantes voce sonora,
The bisschop wan[16] thay sloge,[17]   35
et corpora plura decora;
Maners[18] down thay drowge,[19]
in regno non meliora;
Harmes thay dud ynowght[20]
habuerunt libera lora.   40

(Marginal note: sunt tria sua termina nota)

Jak Strawe made yt stowte[21]
cum profusa comitiva,
And seyd al schuld hem lowte[22]
Anglorum corpora viva.
Sadly can they schowte,   45
pulsa pietatis oliva,
The wycche[23] were wont to lowte,
aratrum traducere stiva.

Hales, that dowghty kny3ght,
quo splenduit Anglia tota,   50

8. *covent:* assemblage   9. *Sythenne:* Afterwards   10. *schent:* destroyed
11. *Bondus they blwun bost:* Peasants make their boasts
12. *Nede they fre be most:* They must be free   13. *endost:* signed
14. *Laddes:* Lads   15. *lought:* laughed   16. *wan:* when   17. *sloge:* slew
18. *Maners:* Manors   19. *drowge:* pulled down   20. *ynowght:* enough
21. *stowte:* bold   22. *lowte:* bow to   23. *The wycche:* Those who

Dolefully was he dy3ght,[24]
cum stultis pace remota,
There he my3ght not fyght,
nec Christo solvere vota

Savoy semely[25] sette, 55
heu! funditus igne cadebat,
Arcadon there they bett,[26]
et eos virtute premebat,
Deth was ther dewe dett,[27]
qui captum quisque f(e)rebat. 60

Owre kyng myght have no rest,
alii latuere caverna,
To ride he was ful prest,[28]
recolendo gesta paterna
Jak Straw down they cast 65
Smythfeld virtute superna.
God, as thou may best,
regem defenda, guberna.

(*Vulpes cum cauda caneat, cum cantat alauda,*
Ne rapide pecus voculus capiatur et equus.) 70

24. *dy3ght:* treated   25. *semely:* beautifully   26. *bett:* beat
27. *dewe dett:* due reward   28. *prest:* pressed

11

The Sloane Satires

Introductory Note: British Museum Ms. Sloane 2593 is a small, un-distinguished-looking, fifteenth-century manuscript containing a miscellany of lyrics. Many of them are religious; it contains, for instance, the unique text of "I syng of a maydyn" (fol. 10v). There are love-songs and a number of satirical poems, all jumbled together and crowded onto the page in no particular order; nevertheless occasionally poems with similar refrains or stanza-patterns, though usually with different subjects, are grouped together. One might hazard a guess that they could be sung to the same tune, but there is no music in the manuscript itself.

The first two of the lyrics given here—the short allegorical treatment of Guile, and the lightheartedly lecherous chapman's song —can be found in Richard Greene, *The Early English Carols* (Oxford, 1935). The third, a delightful allegory on Sir Penny, repeats in the vernacular a poetic satire on the powers of Nummus which had circulated in Latin since the twelfth century, and was still current in the fifteenth. Latin and English texts can also be found in Thomas Wright,

The Latin Poems Commonly Attributed to Walter Map, Camden Society, 1st series. (London, 1841). These satires may be said to echo some of the personifications of the sins, as in *Passus* V, as well as the description of Haukyn the Active Man in *Passus* XIII.

✤ A. "Now go gyle . . ."

London, British Museum Ms. Sloane 2593, fols. 5v–6r.

Now go gyle,[1] gyle gyle now go gile, gyle go

Gyle and gold togeder arn met,
Coveytyse[2] be hym is set;
now haȝt gyle leyd[3] his net
    to gyle[4] bothe frynd and fo.   5

Þer is non wman worȝt a scholle
but he cun plete wit wryte or bylle[5]
his neybowris for to spylle,[6]
    and oþere men to werkyn wo.

Coweytise in herte is lent,[7]   10
Ryȝht and Resoun away is went;
Man, be war þu be not schent—[8]
    Gyle wil þi herte slo[9]

Now haȝt gyle get hym gre[10]
boþe in town and in cete;   15
Gyle goth wit gret mene[11]
    wit men of lawe and oþere mo.

Trewþe, hevene mot[12] he wynne;
Gyle xal in helle brenne.
he þat made al man kynde   20
    amend hem þat mys han do.[13]

1. *gyle:* guile   2. *Coveytyse:* Covetousness, greed
3. *haȝt . . . leyd:* has laid   4. *gyle:* deceive
5. *but he cun plete wit wryte or bylle:* but he can plead with writ or petition
6. *spylle:* harm   7. *lent:* housed   8. *schent:* destroyed, cursed
9. *slo:* slay   10. *gre:* favor
11. *mene:* entourage (rhyme indicates "menie")   12. *mot:* must
13. *mys han do:* has done misdeeds

✤ B. "We ben chapmen . . ."

British Museum Ms. Sloane 2593, fols. 26v–27r.

We ben chapmen[1] lyght of fote, the fowle weyis for to fle.

We bern a bowtyn[2] non cattis skynnys,
Pursis, perlis, sylver pynnis,
smale wympele[3] for ladyis chynnys—
    damsele, bey sum ware of me!   5

I have a poket for the nonys,
þerine ben tweyne[4] precyous stonys;
Damsele, hadde ye asayid[5] hem onys,
    ye xuld þe rathere gon wiþ me!

I have a relyf[6] of godis sonde;   10
Withoutyn fyt[7] it can stonde;
It can smytyn,[8] and haȝt[9] non honde—
    ryd[10] your self quat[11] it may be!

I have a powder for to selle;
quat it is can I not telle.   15
It makit maydenys wombys to swelle—
    therof I have quantyte.[12]

✤ C. "Go bet peny . . ."

British Museum Ms. Sloane 2593, fol. 26b.

Go bet[1] peny, go bet, go! For thu mat makyn bothe
    frynd and fo

Peny is an hardy knyȝt,
Peny is mekyl[2] of myȝt;
Peny of wrong he makyt right
    In every cuntre qwer[3] he goo.   5

---

1. *chapmen:* merchants   2. *bern a bowtyn:* bear about
3. *wympele:* wimple (kerchief)   4. *ben tweyne:* are to
5. *a sayid:* tried, examined   6. *relyf:* relief, remedy   7. *fyt:* difficulty
8. *smytyn:* smite, strike   9. *haȝt:* has   10. *ryd:* ask   11. *quat:* what
12. *quantyte:* quantity

1. *bet:* better   2. *mekyl:* great   3. *qwer:* where

Thow[4] I have a man islawe,[5]
and forfetyd the kyngis lawe,
I xal[6] fyndyn a man of lawe
    Wyl takyn my peny and let me goo.

And if I have to done fer or ner,   10
and peny be myn massanger[7]
þan am I non thing in dwer
    my cause xal be wel idoo.[8]

If I have pens[9] bothe good and fyn,
men wyl byddyn me to þe wyn;   15
þat[10] I have xal be thi(n)—
    sekyrly[11] thei wil seyn so.

And quan[12] I have non in myn purs,
peny bet ne peny wers,
of me thei holdyn but lytil fors—[13]   20
    he was a man, let hym go.

4. *Thow:* Though   5. *islawe:* slain   6. *xal:* shall
7. *massanger:* messenger   8. *idoo:* done   9. *pens:* pence   10. *þat:* what
11. *sekyrly:* certainly   12. *quan:* when   13. *fors:* importance

12

Against the Friars

Introductory Note: The great sweep of evangelistic, pastoral enthusiasm that swept the late twelfth and thirteenth centuries produced the two new Orders (the Order of Friars Minor and the Order of Preachers) popularly known as the Franciscans and Dominicans. By the late fourteenth century, however, the vast prestige and power of the orders had drastically declined, and this decline is nowhere more visible than in the vicious satires written against their members. Chaucer's Friar is but one of a long line of Franciscan butts of complaint and proposals for reform that the orders faced in the fourteenth and fifteenth centuries. The two following poems both refer to the Franciscans, but the Dominicans had their share of criticism as well, and both Popes and Councils expressed repeated concern for the reform of all religious orders. G. G. Coulton's *Five Centuries of Religion*, 4 vols. (Cambridge, England, 1927–50) gives perhaps the most detailed and picturesque account of anti-order feeling between the twelfth and the sixteenth centuries. The figures of the friars in *Piers Plowman* especially in *Passus* XX, are also in the tradition of anti-religious criticism and satire. Both selections are from Ms. Cotton. Cleopatra B. ii. fol. 62.

✠ A. Song Against the Friars

Previously edited by Thomas Wright, Political Poems and Songs Relating to English History composed during the Period from the Accession of Edward III to that of Richard III, *Rolls Series, vol. 14, (London, 1859), 1: 224–26.*

Preste, ne monke, ne ʒit chanoun,[1]
Ne no man of religioun,
Gyfen hem so to devocioun,
    As done thes holy frers.
For summe gyven ham[2] to chyvalry,   5
Somme to riote[3] and ribaudery;
Bot ffrers gyven ham to grete study.
    And to grete prayers,
  Who so kepes thair reule al,
    bothe in worde and dede;   10
  I am ful siker[4] that he shal
    have heven blis to mede.[5]

Men may se by thair contynaunce,
That thai are men of grete penaunce,
And also that thair sustynaunce   15
    Simple is and wayke.[6]
I have lyved now fourty ʒers,
And fatter men about the neres[7]
ʒit sawe I never then are these frers,
  In contreys ther[8] thai rayke.[9]   20
Meteles[10] so megre are thai made,
  and penaunce so puttes ham doun,
  That ichone is an hors-lade,[11]
    when he shal trusse of[12] toun.

Allas! that ever it shuld be so,   25
  Suche clerkes as thai about shuld go,

---

1. ʒit *chanoun:* yet canon   2. *ham:* themselves   3. *riote:* extravagance
4. *siker:* certain   5. *to mede:* as a reward   6. *wayke:* weak
7. *neres:* kidneys   8. *ther:* where   9. *rayke:* wander
10. *Meteles:* Meatless   11. *hors-lade:* horse-load   12. *trusse of:* depart from

Fro toun to toun by two and two,
    To seke thair sustynaunce.
By God that al this world wan,
He that that ordre first bygan,   30
Me thynk certes it was a man
Of simple ordynaunce.[13]
For thai have noght to lyve by,
    thai wandren here and there,
And dele with dyvers marcerye,[14]   35
    right as thai pedlers were.

Thai dele with purses, pynnes, and knyves,
With gyrdles, gloves, for wenches and wyves;
Bot ever bacward the husband thryves
    Ther thai are haunted[15] tille.   40
For when the gode man is fro[16] hame,
And the frere comes to oure dame,
He spares nauther for synne ne shame,
    That he ne dos his wille.
ȝif thai no helpe of houswyves had,   45
    when husbandes are not inne,
The freres welfare were ful bad,
    for thai shuld brewe ful thynne.

Somme frers beren pelure[17] aboute.
For grete ladys and wenches stoute,   50
To reverce[18] with thair clothes withoute;
    Al after that thai ere.[19]
For somme vaire, and somme gryse,[20]
For somme bugee, and for somme byse,
And also many a dyvers spyse,[21]   55
    In bagges about thai bere.
  Al that for women is plesand
    ful redy certes have thai;

---

13. *ordynaunce:* provision
14. *marcerye:* mercury, cloth (but here perhaps a pun on "mercy")
15. *haunted:* accustomed to be   16. *fro:* from   17. *pelure:* fine fur
18. *reverce:* adorn   19. *ere:* are
20. *somme vaire, and somme gryse:* squirrel fur, grey fur   21. *spyse:* spice

Bot lytel gyfe thai the husband,
    that for al shal pay.   60

Trantes²² thai can, and many a jape;
For somme can with a pound of sape²³
Get him a kyrtelle²⁴ and a cape,
    And som what els therto.
Wherto shuld I othes swere?   65
Ther is no pedler that pak can bere,
That half so dere can selle his gere,²⁵
    Then a frer can do.
For if he gife a wyfe a knyfe
    that cost bot penys two,   70
Worthe ten knyves, so mot I thryfe,
    he wyl have er he go.

Iche man that here shal lede his life,
That has a faire doghter or a wyfe,
Be war that no frer ham shryfe,²⁶
    (Nauther loude ne still.)   75
Thof²⁷ women seme of hert ful stable,
With faire byhest²⁸ and with fable
Thai can make thair hertes chaungeable,
    And thair likynges fulfille.   80
Be war ay with the lymitour,²⁹
    and with his felawe bathe,³⁰
And³¹ thai make maystries³² in thi hour,
    it shal turne the to scathe.³³

Were I a man that hous helde,   85
If any woman with me dwelde,
Ther is no frer, bot he were gelde,³⁴
    Shuld com within my wones.³⁵
For may he til a woman wynne,
In priveyte, he wyl not blynne,³⁶   90

22. *Trantes:* Tricks   23. *sape:* soap   24. *kyrtelle:* kirtle
25. *gere:* merchandise   26. *ham shryfe:* them shrive   27. *Thof:* Though
28. *byhest:* promises   29. *lymitour:* licensed friar   30. *bathe:* both
31. *And:* If   32. *maystries:* conquests
33. *turne the to scathe:* result in your harm   34. *gelde:* gelded
35. *wones:* dwelling   36. *blynne:* cease

Er he a childe put hir withinne,
        And perchaunce two at ones.
Thof[37] he loure under his hode,
        with semblaunt quaynte and mylde,
If thou him trust, or dos him gode,   95
        by God, thou ert bygyld.[38]

Thai say that thai distroye synne,
And thai mayntene men moste therinne;
For had a man slayn al his kynne,
        Go shryve him[39] at a frere,   100
And for lesse than a payre of shone[40]
He wyl assoil him clene and sone,
And say the synne that he has done
        His saule shal never dere.[41]
It semes sothe that men sayne of hayme[42]   105
        in many dyvers londe,
That that caytyfe[43] cursed Cayme[44]
        first this order fonde.

Nou se the sothe whedre it be swa,
That frer Carmes[45] come of a k.,
The frer Austynes[46] come of a.,   110
        Frer Jacobynes[47] of i.,
Of m. comen the frer Menours;[48]
Thus grounded Caym thes four ordours,
That fillen the world ful of errours,   115
        And of ypocrisy.[49]
Alle wyckednes that men can telle
        regnes ham among;
Ther shal no saule have rowme in helle,
        of frers ther is suche throng.   120

Thai travele ȝerne and bysily,
        To brynge doun the clergye;

37. *Thof:* Though   38. *bygyld:* beguiled
39. *Go shryue him:* And were to go   40. *shone:* shoes   41. *dere:* harm
42. *hayme:* them   43. *caytyfe:* wretch   44. *Cayme:* Cain
45. *Carmes:* Carmelites   46. *Austynes:* Augustinians
47. *Jacobynes:* Dominicans   48. *Menours:* Franciscans
49. *ypocrisy:* hypocrisy

Thai speken therof ay vilany,
　　And therof thai done wrong.
Whoso lyves oght many ʒers,　　　125
Shal se that it shal falle of[50] frers,
As it dyd of the templers,
　　That wonned[51] here us among.
For thai held no religioun,
　　bot lyved after lykyng,[52]　　　130
Thai were distroyed and broght adoun.
　　thurgh ordynance of the kyng.

Thes frers haunten[53] a dredful thing,
That never shal come to gode endyng;
O frer for eght or nyen shal syng,　　　135
　　For ten or for elleven.
And when his terme is fully gone,
Conscience then has he none,
That he ne dar take of ychone
　　Markes sixe or seven.　　　140
Suche annuels[54] has made thes frers,
　　so wely and so gay,
That ther may no possessioners
　　mayntene thair array.

Tham felle to lyve al on purchace,　　　145
Of almes geten fro place to place,
And for alle that tham holpen has,
　　Shuld thai pray and syng.
Bot now this londe so neghe soght is,
That unnethe[55] may prestes seculers　　　150
Gete any service for[56] thes frers,
　　That is wondre thing.
This is a quaynt[57] custome
　　ordeyned ham among,
That frers shal annuel prestes bycome,　　　155
　　and so gates[58] selle ther song.

50. *falle of:* happen to　　51. *wonned:* dwelt　　52. *lykyng:* pleasure
53. *haunten:* usually practice
54. *annuels:* payment for singing anniversary masses for the dead
55. *unnethe:* with difficulty　　56. *for:* because of　　57. *quaynt:* curious
58. *gates:* in that manner

Ful wysely can thai preche and say;
Bot as thai preche no thing do thai.
I was a frere ful many a day,
    Therefor the sothe I wate.[59]   160
Bot when I sawe that thair lyvyng
Acordyd not to thair preching,
Of I cast my frer clothing,
    And wyghtly went my gate.[60]
Other leve ne toke I none,   165
    fro ham when I went,
Bot toke ham to the devel ychone,[61]
    the priour and the covent.

Out of the ordre thof[62] I be gone,
Apostota[63] ne am I none,   170
Of twelve monethes me wanted one,
    And odde days nyen or ten.
Away to wende I made me boun;
Or tyme come of professioun,[64]
I went my way thurghout the toun,   175
    In syght of many men.
Lord God, that with paynes ille
    mankynde boght so dere,
Let never man after me have wille
    for to make him[65] frere.

✤ B. On the Minorite Friars

Of thes frer mynours me thenkes moch wonder,
    That waxen are thus hauteyn,[1] that som tyme weren
        under;
Among men of holy chirch thai maken mochel[2] blonder;
Now he that sytes us above make ham sone to sonder![3]

---

59. *wate:* know   60. *wyghtly went my gate:* quickly went my way
61. *ychone:* commended each one   62. *thof:* though   63. *Apostota:* Apostate
64. *professioun:* profession of vows   65. *him:* himself

1. *waxen . . . hauteyn:* are grown . . . haughty   2. *mochel:* great, much
3. *sonder:* come apart

With an O and an I, thai praysen not seynt
    Poule, 5
Thai lyen on seyn[t] Fraunceys, by my fader soule.

First thai gabben on[4] God, that alle men may se,
When thai hangen him on hegh on a grene tre,
With leves and with blossemes that bright are of ble;
That was never Goddes son, by my leute.[5] 10
    With an O and an I, men wenen that thai wede,
    To carpe so of clergy, thai can not[6] thair crede.

Thai have done[7] him on a croys[8] fer up in the skye,
And festned on hym wyenges, as he shuld flie.
This fals feyned byleve shal thai soure[9] bye, 15
On that lovelych Lord so for to lye.
    With an O and an I, one sayd ful stille.
    Armachan distroy ham, if it is Goddes wille.

Ther comes one out of the skye in a grey goun,
As it were an hog-hyerd hyand[10] to toun; 20
Thai have mo goddes than we, I say by Mahoun,[11]
Alle men under ham, that ever beres croun.
    With an O and an I, why shuld thai not be shent?[12]
    Ther wantes noght bot a fyre that thai nere alle
    brent.

Went I forther on my way in that same tyde; 25
Ther I sawe a frere blede in myddes of his syde;[13]
Bothe in hondes and in fete had he woundes wyde
To serve to that same frer, the pope mot abyde.
    With an O and an I, I wonder of thes dedes,
    To se a pope holde a dische whyl the frer bledes. 30

A cart was made al of fyre, as it shuld be:
A gray frer I sawe therinne, that best lyked me.
Wele I wote[14] thai shal be brent,[15] by my leauté;

4. *gabben on:* talk to   5. *leute:* loyalty faith   6. *can not:* do not know
7. *done:* put   8. *croys:* cross   9. *soure:* bitterly
10. *hog-hyerd hyand:* swineherd going   11. *Mahoun:* Mohamed
12. *shent:* put to shame   13. St. Francis, who received the stigmata.
14. *wote:* know   15. *brent:* burned

God graunt me that grace that I may it se.
With an O and an I, brent be thai alle!   35
And alle that helpes therto faire mot byfalle.[16]

Thai preche alle of povert,[17] bot that love thai noght;
For gode mete[18] to thir mouthe the toun is thurgh soght.
Wyde are thair wonnynges,[19] and wonderfully wroght;
Murdre and horedome[20] ful dere has it boght.   40
  With an O and an I, for six pens er thai fayle,
  Sle[21] thi fadre, and jape[22] thi modre, and thai wyl
      the asseile.[23]

16. *faire mot byfalle:* fairly must befall   17. *povert:* poverty
18. *gode mete:* good meat   19. *wonnynges:* dwellings
20. *horedome:* whoredom   21. *Sle:* kill   22. *jape:* cheat, mock
23. *asseile:* cleanse from sin

PART III:

The Voice of the Preacher and the Heretic

Since the publication in 1926 of G. R. Owst's *Preaching in Medieval England*, scholarly editions and studies of fourteenth-century sermon collections have helped to cast much light upon both devotional strains and the ecclesiastical perception of some social conditions in the century of *Piers Plowman*. Although few scholars attribute to the sermons of the late fourteenth century quite the same fundamental role in influencing the shape of *Piers Plowman* that Owst did, no one denies their importance in reflecting the tensions that the poem itself also reflects. Besides *Preaching in Medieval England*, Owst's *Literature and Pulpit in Medieval England* (Cambridge, 1933) explores in detail the relation between sermon literature and other literary genres of the fourteenth century. Th.-M. Charland, *Artes Praedicandi* (Paris-Ottawa, 1936) explores the rhetoric and structure of thirteenth- and fourteenth-century sermons. Three major collections of English sermons of this period are Theodor Erbe, ed.,

Mirk's Festial: A Collection of Homilies by Johannes Mirkus (*John Mirk*), Early English Text Society, Extra Series, vol. 96 (London, 1905); Woodburn O. Ross, ed., *Middle English Sermons Edited from British Museum Ms. Royal 18 B. xxiii*, Early English Text Society, Extra Series, vol. 209 (London, 1940 [for 1938]); Sister Mary Aquinas Devlin, O. P., Ph.D., *The Sermons of Thomas Brinton, Bishop of Rochester (1373–1389)*, Camden Society, Third Series, vols. 85–86 (London, 1954). Thomas Wimbledon's famous sermon preached at Paul's Cross in 1388 has been edited by Nancy H. Owen, "Thomas Wimbledon's Sermon: 'Redde racionem villacionis tue,' " *Medieval Studies* 28 (1966):176–97. Most of the works cited above contain extensive introductory and bibliographical materials. Among the best short studies is William J. Brandt, "Church and Society in the Late Fourteenth Century: A Contemporary View," *Medievalia et Humanistica* 13 (1960): 56–67. The following selection is generally indicative of some of the kinds of social criticism that the sermon literature contains, but it should not be considered "typical" either of sermon literature *in extenso* or of commonplace fourteenth-century attitudes.

A good study of the shaping of the English parish and the literature of instructions for priests is John Godfrey, *The English Parish, 600–1300*, Society for the Propagation of Christian Knowledge, (London, 1969), with a good bibliography. A good description of a later collection of similar materials that bridge the gap between sermons and moral theology treatises is G. R. Owst, *The Destructorium Viciorum of Alexander Carpenter*, Society for the Propagation of Christian Knowledge, (London, 1952). There is no modern edition of the great work of John Bromyard, the *Summa Predicantium*, a vast handbook of preaching topics. We have used the edition of Venice, 1586. On the date of this work and the literature, see Leonard E. Boyle, O. P., "The Date of the *Summa Predicantium* of John Bromyard," *Speculum* 48 (1973): 533–37.

G. R. Owst, in "The 'Angel' and the 'Goliardeys' of Langland's Prologue," *Modern Language Review* 20 (1925):270–79 argued that the angel mentioned by Langland as admonishing the king was, in fact, Bishop Thomas Brinton, and that the angel's sermon is the sermon printed here, delivered on 17 July, 1377, on the day after Richard II's coronation. The *Prologue* is not, however, the only occasion for sermonizing in *Piers Plowman*, and *Passus* V, VII, XI, and XIII all echo references to sermon discourse that strongly suggest that Langland, although not constructing a sermon himself, knew well the place that sermons had in the minds and lives of himself and his audience and freely used references that he knew would be quickly and clearly understood.

John Wyclif, perhaps the greatest fourteenth-century English critic of both abuses and doctrine, is the subject of a vast literature, perhaps the best introductory examples of which are G. Lechler, *John Wycliffe and His English Precursors*, trans. P. Lorimer, 2 vols. (London, 1884) and H. B. Workman, *John Wyclif*, 2 vols. (Oxford, 1926). K. B. McFarlane, *John Wycliffe and the Beginnings of English Non-Conformity* (London, 1952) and J. A. Robson, *Wyclif and the Oxford Schools* (Cambridge, 1966) offer more recent views. On Wyclif and late medieval heresy in general, see Gordon Leff, "Heresy and the Decline of the Medieval Church," *Past and Present* 20 (1961):36–51, and Leff's *Heresy in the Later Middle Ages*, 2 vols. (New York, 1967), esp. 2: pp. 494–605.

13

Thomas Brinton, Sermon 44, *Simul in unum, dives et pauper,* 1377

Introductory Note: The Latin text is in Sister Mary Aquinas Devlin, O.P., ed., *The Sermons of Thomas Brinton, Bishop of Rochester (1373–1389),* Camden Society, Third Series, vol. 85 (London, 1954), pp. 194–200. This is probably the sermon preached by Brinton on 17 July, 1377, in a procession on the day after the coronation of Richard II. Although the sermon is extraordinarily explicit in its denunciation of social abuses, it is not wholly uncharacteristic of much of the sermon literature of social criticism.

 Simul in unum, dives et pauper

Rich and poor, alike in one. The Book of Psalms 48 [49:2]

Just as different streams flow out of a single sea, diverse beams from a single light, different lines from a single point, and many works from a single craftsman, so from one God comes forth all, not out of His substance, but because all is made by

His will and power, the apostle [Paul] saying, in the First Epistle to the Corinthians 12, *There are divisions of work, but all of them, in all men, are the work of the one Lord.* When, therefore, it is time for preaching, let the preaching be chiefly of God, since *The Lord will give the spirit to the preachers* [Psalms 47:12], as in the Psalms. It is fitting that we honor God with a single mouth; let us pray with one spirit for the king and for the peace of the kingdom, saying devoutly an 'Our Father' and a 'Hail Mary.'

Rich and poor alike, and so forth, as above. It is the law that all Christians, rich as well as poor, without distinction of persons, in the sign of purity are from one father, Adam in the flesh and Christ in the spirit, as Christ says in Matthew 23: *Indeed you have one celestial father, who is in heaven.* All are redeemed by one blood, that is, the blood of the savior. All are founded in one faith, and all are regenerated by one Baptism, as the apostle says, *One God, one faith, one baptism* [Ephesians 4:5]. All are fed by one bread, that is, the Eucharist, since the apostle says *We all share of one bread and of one cup* [1 Corinthians 10, 16–17]. All of us are gathered into one flock, that is, the Church, since *One is the flock and one the shepherd,* John 10. All seeking a single beatitude, since, according to the apostle, *It is permitted that all may race; one, however, shall receive the prize* [1 Corinthians 9:24].

It is the law that in these and in many other ways the rich and the poor are alike and equal, and since this is our theme today, we say that in two senses rich and poor ought to be alike as one, that is in supporting each other and in praying each for his neighbor. Of the first of these senses, St. Augustine speaks in a certain sermon: [Augustine, *Sermones de Diversis,* 347; *Patrologia Latina,* vol. 39, col. 1651] Although the rich and the poor appear to be contraries, this is necessary. For if all were poor, no one would be able to support another. If all were rich, no one would labor, and thus the world would collapse. Thus, the rich exist on account of the poor and the poor on account of the rich. The rich must offer alms, and the poor must pray. For anyone who accepts charity from the rich is obliged to pray for them, and even if they did not, the act of charity would itself be a prayer, as scripture says, *Conceal charity in the bosom of a poor man, and the act itself will pray for you* [Ecclesiasticus 29:15]. And this almsgiving is of the greater merit and virtue when it is done in health and in life. What is meant by charity is gold, siver, and lead, as the angel showed who walked with the pilgrim [*Jacques de Vitry*, no. 109], as it is shown in the lives of the fathers.

The catholic doctors all agree on that saying of the Gospels, *the poor you will always have with you*, and so forth, and they set down the reasons why God permits the poor to remain among us, even though He is able to provide enough for all. First, just as a mother provides enough for her child when she gives enough to the nurse so that the nurse and the infant both may be nourished, so God provides enough for the poor in giving so much to the rich. Truly, both they and the poor may eat and drink, God saying in Deuteronomy 15, *Today I command you to open your hand to the poor and the wretched who are your fellows in your own land*, for a hand opened in charity to the poor will not corporally perish.

This is proved by Bede in his *Ecclesiastical History of the English People* [III, 6] where he speaks of King Oswald who, after giving much in charity to the poor, gave a silver dish to a poor man while he was sitting at table. Bishop Aidan seeing this and sitting next to the king, took his hand and said, "This hand will never putrefy." What more need be said? After the king's martyrdom the hand with its arm remains intact even today as a sign of the alms the king offered to the poor. Secondly, the poor exist so that God may test the love of the rich. Therefore He willed that the poor should remain in want so that by them God might see which of the rich were His friends and which His enemies. Thirdly, for increasing the merit of the poor, for the patient poor deserve much from God. An example of this is that of the poor man Lazarus, borne by angels to Abraham's bosom, singing the Psalm [9:19], *The patience of the poor will not perish* [unheeded] *in the end*. As evidence for this it is to be known that there is the poverty of honesty and that of necessity. First, involuntary paupers sustain their poverty who might, if they were able, freely obtain riches themselves. Truly it is sometimes lawful for such out of impatience to accuse God of iniquity, their neighbor of miserliness, and they may be prone to complaining, to laziness, to mendacity, and even to thievery, and therefore we ought to nourish and feed these for two reasons. First on account of the likeness of their and our natures. For every creature should naturally love that which is like himself, and so great is the likeness between the rich and the poor that *there is one entrance for all into life*, The Wisdom of Solomon 7. For God did not from the beginning create one man of gold or silver from whom were propagated all the rich and the gentle, and another of mud from whom descend the poor and the ragged who, with Adam, dig in the earth with a spade. Indeed, even in death are rich and poor alike, for, just as chess pieces at the end of their play are thrown back into the box from which they were first taken, so the rich and the poor, having reigned in this present life, are grasped by death and returned to the earth from which they were first created. And thus, *Rich and poor, alike in one.* How many times have we aided these involuntary paupers, for we ought to help them not out of patience, but out of nature, the Psalm [40:2] saying, *Blessed is he who takes heed of the poor and the wretched*, and so forth. Secondly, we ought to do good things for them in expectation of a reward from God. An example is that of Martin, at the time a catechumen, who gave a part of his cloak to Christ because he aided a poor man on account of Christ. Truly Christ said to Martin, "Whatever you do for one of the least of mine," and so forth. And hence I preach against this and against all ingratitudes of the rich who, even when they offer some modicum to the poor will first insult them with harsh words and condemn them, for it would be better for the poor to be without alms than to receive them with such opprobrium. Against these it is said in Ecclesiasticus 10, that *The glory of the honest rich is that they do not spite the poor.* I preach too against those hard, rich, and middling people who for all the world are ready to give precious gifts to the rich who are not wretched, and yet for God will give to the poor no food that is not already foetid, nor clothing that is not already worm-eaten. To them, indeed, the Epistle of St. James 5, speaks these words: *Wail, O ye rich, in the wretched-*

ness that shall come upon you. For your wealth has turned to decay and your clothing is eaten by worms. He has spat out your gold and silver and their decay shall be witness against you. Thus it is said. Just as the flight of the thief brought before the judge is evidence against him of the wicked deeds on whose account he is condemned, so hidden riches speak out as evidence against those who conceal them, both at death and at the final judgement. I therefore preach against the injustice of those rich people who sympathize less with their brothers the poor in Christ than do the Jews and Saracens. It is proven. The Princes of the Jews collect from the rich those things by which the poor may be nourished. Christian princes, however, collect from the poor so that the rich in their pride may be maintained. Among Christians it is never heard that a tenth from the Church or from a tax on the people should be asked for the poor dying of hunger, but for the rich and the princes, as much as from the Church and the people, it is indeed asked. Even the Saracens are daily scandalized that we treat those poor whom we call the servants of Christ so shamefully and with such a lack of compassion. This is shown in the history of Charlemagne, who, when fighting with the Saracens, was approached by a certain great prince bearing a flag of truce and wishing to speak about Christianity. The prince sat next to the king and observed the order of ministers closely, trying to determine which they might be who ate upon the earth as paupers. The king answered, "These are they who are the servants we feed for the love of Christ our Lord." The prince responded, "Thy servants are richly dressed, and they eat and drink well; the servants of your Christ, however, are left naked and starving. I do not wish to be of that sect which in such a way honors its God." And thus he departed with great indignation. Not thus, my dear children, should things be done, but because in the poor Christ is filled, given drink, clothed, visited, and sheltered. From a certain love of Christ and justice, the rich should humbly assist the poor, the poor serve the rich faithfully and pray for them diligently, so that from this mutual assistance they may indeed be *Rich and poor, alike in one.*

[Besides this poverty of necessity, there is a second,] the

poverty of honesty, which they have as a precious treasure who are voluntarily poor on account of Christ, those soldiers of God accepted into religion under obedience, continence, and voluntary poverty, saying with scripture, *Neither riches nor poverty will you give to me* [Proverbs 30:8], and so forth. These are poor voluntarily and honestly, for through their cares and labors they have quiet and enough. As in Isaiah 14, *For the poor shall have rest in honor,* and in place of anxiety and wretchedness, they shall have gentleness of the spirit. What is more sweet, then, than to serve Christ daily, as do the angels? To that end the Psalmist says, *Thou hast prepared for the poor in Thy gentleness, O God.* For the usefullness of this world, they have the honor of judgements, as in Job 36: *For judgement shall be given to the poor.* And this is what Christ promised in Matthew 19, with the words: *You who leave everything and follow me shall sit with the Son of Man,* etcetera. Surely this prospect of judgement by the poor in religion should strike fear into the hearts of the rich and the great temporal lords, who, although their holy and just predecessors were the founders and protectors of monasteries for these poor in Christ, are led by wicked counsels and seek rather how they may be able to hurl into confusion these places dedicated unto God. And of this, where shall there be an end? Certainly, although God may for a time permit His poor to suffer from injustice, at the end, however, *God will rise up against the wretchedness and misery of the poor,* and bring such injuries swiftly to justice. One may read of a certain abbot, who, on account of an injury done to him by a certain temporal lord for which he was unable to obtain justice in any court, saw his monastery oppressed in defending the cause of the Church. He spoke to the lord in these words: "Let us both plead before that Judge who will consider again that which has been badly judged and will do justice to those patiently suffering injury." Having said this, the abbot fell ill and died within two days. The temporal lord, hearing this of the abbot and being advised of his death, called together his servants and said "Woe is me, for now I must die, so now I must respond to that tribunal of Christ concerning the issue pending between me and the abbot." And this happened. At the funeral service for the lord there were many prelates and great lords together. In the midst of the service, the dead man raised his head and said: "I am called before the most terrible judgement!" Then he said: "I am accused of many crimes, and especially those which I inflicted upon the poor of the monastery!" Third, he said: "By the perpetual just judgement of God, I am damned!" And he added: "If I had not been mighty among the mighty of this world, I would not be among the number of the damned." Hearing these words, the prelates and lords were struck with such horror that they ran and hid themselves in the forest, and afterwards they began the Carthusian Order in Burgundy. Not thus, O Lord, but since *It is better to walk in simplicity as a pauper than to walk in depraved ways as a rich man*, Proverbs 20. If the rich man does not give of his own wealth, he will surely burn in Hell, as is shown in Luke 16, where the rich man is plucked by many pincers by devils when he has stolen by violence the goods of others and especially the goods of Christ's poor. I advise lords and other wealthy people to maintain the clerics and the poor in Christ in their pristine liberty, and that churchmen and rectors and religious support lords and the rich by their sanctity, since *Chrysostom on Matthew* says: "As long as there are holy and faithful people in the world, so long will the world stand. And when the holy take leave of the world, the world will fall, since with death poverty will cruelly come to take all, *Rich and poor alike*." Behold the proof of how the rich and poor ought to be alike, keeping one another by aiding.

I have said that *Rich and poor ought to be alike in one* in praying for their neighbors. Just as a weight appears to be lighter when it is shared and carried by many people, so God shall hear prayers if rich and poor, old and young, religious and secular clergy come together in prayer, the apostle saying: "*Ye shall be of one spirit in prayers*" [Acts 1:14], because the truth is to be found in the concord of many [*Decretum Gratiani*, C. 23, q. 5, c. 20], 33 q. *ultima*, c. ii. Indeed, if there is held a procession for the peace of the kingdom, the lords and rich merchants who lose more through great wars than do the poor and the middling people should walk to pray for peace more fervently and devoutly than they. If there should be a procession in the city for whatever imminent tribulation, if on account of sin good weather changes to rainy, times of peace to times of war, fertile earth to sterile earth, if animals die, bodies sicken, and spirits decline, let these and other like things be attributed to the dominance of Saturn or other planets by some; I, however, impute these totally to our sins, for according to the scripture, *We suffer these things by reason of sin* [Genesis 42:21]. So that if we serve our lord God, so will His creatures and elements serve us. But the sins of the rich and the powerful are greater than those of the middling and poor. Where the middling people live in community honestly of their own, the magnates live off the work of others, so that by violence and rapine, exactions and extortions, forged documents and excessive spending, it comes about that those who ought to be rich are poor, so that whoever wishes might say with Revelation 3, [17]: *You say, "I am rich and desire nothing," but you do not know that you are a pauper, wretched, blind, and naked.* Truly wrote Aristotle to Alexander [the Great] in the *Secret of Secrets* that the kingdom of the Chaldeans was destroyed precisely because the expenses of the king and his lords exceeded their income, and because their subjects appealed of this to the Lord, the Lord heard them and destroyed the kingdom. Such is the rule of justice or equity when the greatest unity is defective; when ecclesiastics and religious and a few middling and poor people attend processions against imminent tribulations, when they are less responsible for them, and the rich and the powerful, who are their cause, come not at all, nor pray, nor do penance for their sins, but carry right on lasciviously in their chambers and in other comforts just as much as they like. Surely the burden of penitence should not be thus so unequally divided, but, humbly praying to God for mercy, there should be *Rich and poor alike, as one.* But someone may perhaps say, "The good Bishop of Rochester intends to show by his sermon that kings and lords are obliged to attend processions, even though such a thing has never been heard of before." We answer that it is not our intention to compel anyone to march in a procession, but rather to persuade people to devotion. Does it not appear abominable and greatly reprehensible that if, in the city of London, there should be a duel held tomorrow, prohibited though they are by divine law, there would quickly congregate the rich and the powerful so thickly that there would be scarcely a single place remaining? But if London orders a procession to pray for the king or the peace of the kingdom or whatever other necessity, even if the bishop be there present with his clergy, there would be scarcely a hundred people to follow. Concluding that the presence of the king, of the prince, or of other great lords would greatly please God and would be commendable and honorable in the world, this is first proved by the king of Nineveh, and the King David, who, seeing the tribulation of his people, recognized his own sin as the cause, saying *I am he who has sinned* [2 Kings, 24]; *I am he who has done evil. What have these done, who are only sheep?* And thus were the tribulations quieted.

I dare to say assertively that if a person of such great dignity, showing his bodily presence in processions, should give so great an example of humility, he would be held in the greatest reverence by his people and by the whole world, all the days of his life. But if we wish our prayers to be heard, there are two things required. First, we who ought to pray should be clean in conscience. For God heareth not sinners, saying in the psalm: *For if I show iniquity in my heart, God will not hear me* [Psalms 65:18]. Second, that those for whom we ought to pray should effectively conform their lives to our deeds, saying with Augustine [*Sermon 70; Patrologia Latina*, vol. 38, col. 923]: God can create you without you, but He cannot justify you by Himself without you. A life of evils impedes those who pray, so that God does not hear them. Here is an *exemplum*. A thief, who heard of the fame of a certain holy hermit, swore to him that he would cut off his head unless the hermit converted him by his prayers within a year. When the hermit failed to do this, and the thief was about to decapitate him, the hermit asked the thief, before he killed him, to help him raise a stone and carry it outside the house, thus wishing to redeem himself from death. When the thief tried to move the stone away, the hermit kept pulling it back. The thief then said to the hermit, "I cannot move the stone because of what you are doing." "Nor can I convert you," said the hermit, "because of your evil." Nor should this be wondered at, since scripture says in Ecclesiasticus 34: *One building and one tearing down, what do these produce, if not labor? One praying and one cursing, whose voice shall God hear?* Not thus, but if the great and the temporal lords want the leaders of the clergy to pray for them, they must first correct themselves, so that before God they are examples of true humility and confession, and to their neighbors examples of equity and fair restitution, since *The sin is not forgiven unless the offerings are restored,* so that scripture shall be fulfilled by the rich, the middling, and the poor meeting together with one spirit in prayer; *Israel came together to the city, as one man, one spirit, and one counsel,* Judges 20. Therefore, since the work of a sermon is not completed without a brief conclusion, since the whole sermon is as it were a conclusion, I conclude by saying that there are three kinds of riches. One kind is temporal riches, of which the psalm says [61:11]: *If wealth increases, do not set your heart upon it.* Another kind of wealth is spiritual, such as graces and virtues, of which Isaiah 33 says: *The riches of salvation are wisdom and knowledge.* The third kind of wealth is heavenly and eternal, of which in the psalm [111:31] *Glory and riches in his house,* and so forth. *He who is rich in those who call upon him,* shall give you grace as you give the first kind of riches to the worthy poor, the second shall thus be well preserved, and to the third kind you may aspire in your heart as, *alike as one, the rich man and the poor man* shall dwell eternally together, saying with the psalm [132:1] *Behold how good and joyful it is to live in one, as brothers.*

14

The Heretic

Introductory Note: Few men dominate the thought of their age as did John Wycliffe, a learned, articulate reformer in and out of Oxford whose views on the morals of the clergy and the need for new springs of devotion in lay life, doctrinal originalities, and support of the translation of the Bible into the Vernacular stirred great waves of support and criticism in England and on the Continent. By the first quarter of the fifteenth century, Wycliffe was regarded universally as the heresiarch *par excellence*, a terrible example of the sort of critic that rises up in an age of abuse and tepid reform. In many respects, of course, Wycliffe's criticisms were similar to those of many critics, and although he was heterodox doctrinally, he was supported by powerful figures in England throughout his life. The following selections, all from *England in the Age of Wycliffe*, describe Wycliffe's relation to the power of Rome. The first selection is a list of alleged errors propounded by Wycliffe, ten of them as heretical and fourteen as erroneous. The second and third documents consist of an exchange of letters between Pope

Gregory XI and Wycliffe. The last selection is the text of the Statute, commonly called *de haeretico comburendo,* of 1401, directed against Wycliffites and Lollards, the first statutory authority in English history that inflicted the death penalty for heresy.

✤ A. Wycliffite Conclusions Condemned by Rome

Text in Fasciculi Zizaniorum, *Rolls Series, vol. 5 (London, 1858), pp. 277–82.*

I—That the material substance of bread and of wine remains, after the consecration, in the sacrament of the altar.

II—That the accidents do not remain without the subject, after the consecration, in the same sacrament.

III—That Christ is not in the sacrament of the altar identically, truly, and really in his proper corporal presence.

IV—That if a bishop or priest lives in mortal sin he does not ordain, or consecrate, or baptize.

V—That if a man has been truly repentant, all external confession is superfluous to him or useless.

VI—Continually to assert that it is not founded in the gospel that Christ instituted the mass.

VII—That God ought to be obedient to the devil.

VIII—That if the Pope is foreordained to destruction and a wicked man, and therefore a member of the devil, no power has been given to him over the faithful of Christ by anyone, unless perhaps by the Emperor.

IX—That since Urban the Sixth, no one is to be acknowledged as Pope; but all are to live, in the way of the Greeks, under their own laws.

X—To assert that it is against sacred scripture that men of the church should have temporal possessions.

XI—That no prelate ought to excommunicate any one unless he first knows that the man is excommunicated by God.

XII—That a person thus excommunicating is thereby a heretic or excommunicate.

XIII—That a prelate excommunicating a clerk who has appealed to the king, or to a council of the kingdom, on that very account is a traitor to God, the king and the kingdom.

XIV—That those who neglect to preach, or to hear the

word of God, or the gospel that is preached, because of the excommunication of men, are excommunicate, and in the day of judgment will be considered as traitors to God.

XV—To assert that it is allowed to anyone, whether a deacon or a priest, to preach the word of God, without the authority of the apostolic see, or of a Catholic bishop, or of some other which is sufficiently acknowledged.

XVI—To assert that no one is a civil lord, no one is a bishop, no one is a prelate, so long as he is in mortal sin.

XVII—That temporal lords may, at their own judgment, take away temporal goods from churchmen who are habitually delinquent; or that the people may, at their own judgment, correct delinquent lords.

XVIII—That tithes are purely charity, and that parishioners may, on account of the sins of their curates, detain these and confer them on others at their will.

XIX—That special prayers applied to one person by prelates or religious persons, are of no more value to the same person than general prayers for others in a like position are to him.

XX—That the very fact that anyone enters upon any private religion whatever, renders him more unfitted and more incapable of observing the commandments of God.

XXI—That saints who have instituted any private religions whatever, as well of those having possessions as of mendicants, have sinned in thus instituting them.

XXII—That religious persons living in private religions are not of the Christian religion.

XXIII—That friars should be required to gain their living by the labor of their hands and not by mendicancy.

XXIV—That a person giving alms to friars, or to a preaching friar, is excommunicate; also the one receiving.

✠ B. The Bull of Pope Gregory XI Against John Wycliffe

Text in Fasciculi Zizaniorium, *pp. 242–44.*

Gregory, bishop, servant of the servants of God, to his beloved sons the Chancellor and University of Oxford, in the diocese of Lincoln, grace and apostolic benediction.

We are compelled to wonder and grieve that you, who, in consideration of the favors and privileges conceded to your University of Oxford by the apostolic see, and on account of your familiarity with the Scriptures, in whose sea you navigate, by the gift of God, with auspicious oar, you, who ought to be, as it were, warriors and champions of the orthodox faith, without which there is no salvation of souls—that you through a certain sloth and neglect allow tares to spring up amidst the pure wheat in the fields of your glorious University aforesaid; and what is still more pernicious, even continue to grow to maturity. And you are quite careless, as has been lately reported to us, as to the extirpation of these tares; with no little clouding of a bright name, danger to your souls, contempt of the Roman church, and injury to the faith above mentioned. And what pains us the more is that this increase of the tares aforesaid is known in Rome before the remedy of extirpation has been applied in England where they sprang up. By the insinuation of many, if they are indeed worthy of belief, deploring it deeply, it has come to our ears that John de Wycliffe, rector of the church of Lutterworth, in the diocese of Lincoln, Professor of the Sacred Scriptures (would that he were not also Master of Errors), has fallen into such a detestable madness that he does not hesitate to dogmatize and publicly preach, or rather vomit forth from the recesses of his breast, certain propositions and conclusions which are erroneous and false. He has cast himself also into the depravity of preaching heretical dogmas which strive to subvert and weaken the state of the whole church and even secular polity, some of which doctrines, in changed terms, it is true, seem to express the perverse opinions and unlearned learning of Marsilio of Padua of cursed memory, and of John of Jandun, whose book is extant, rejected, and cursed by our predecessor, Pope John XXII, of happy memory. This he has done in the kingdom of England, lately glorious in its power and in the abundance of its resources, but more glorious still in the glistening piety of its faith, and in the distinction of its sacred learning; producing also many men illustrious for their exact knowledge of the Holy Scriptures, mature in the gravity of their character, conspicuous in devotion, defenders of the Catholic church. He has polluted certain of the faithful of Christ by besprinkling them with these doctrines, and led them away from the right paths of the aforesaid faith to the brink of perdition.

Wherefore, since we are not willing, nay, indeed, ought not to be willing, that so deadly a pestilence should continue to exist with our connivance, a pestilence which, if it is not opposed in its beginnings, and torn out by the roots in its entirety, will be reached too late by medicines when it has infected very many with its contagion; we command your University with strict admonition, by the apostolic authority, in virtue of your sacred obedience, and under penalty of the deprivation of all the favors, indulgences, and privileges granted to you and your University by the said see, for the future not to permit to be asserted or proposed to any extent whatever, the opinions, conclusions, and propositions which are in variance with good morals and faith, even when those proposing strive to defend them under a certain fanciful wresting of words or of terms. Moreover, you are on our authority to arrest the said John, or cause him to be arrested and to send him under a trustworthy guard to our venerable brother, the Archbishop of Canterbury, and the Bishop of London, or to one of them.

Besides, if there should be, which God forbid, in your University, subject to your jurisdiction, opponents stained with these errors, and if they should obstinately perist in them, proceed vigorously and earnestly to a similar arrest and removal of them, and otherwise as shall seem good to you. Be vigilant to repair your negligence which you have hitherto shown in the premises, and so obtain our gratitude and favor, and that of the said see, besides the honor and reward of the divine recompense.

Given at Rome, at Santa Maria Maggiore, on the 31st of May, the sixth year of our pontificate.

❧ C. Wycliffe's Reply to the Pope's Summons to Come to Rome, 1384

Text in Thomas Arnold, Select English Works of Wyclif, *(London, 1861),* 3:504–6.

I have joyfully to tell to all true men that believe what

I hold, and algates to the Pope; for I suppose that if my faith be rightful and given of God, the Pope will gladly confirm it; and if my faith be error, the Pope will wisely amend it.

I suppose over this that the gospel of Christ be heart of the corps of God's law; for I believe that Jesus Christ, that gave in his own person this gospel, is very God and very man, and by this heart passes all other laws.

I suppose over this that the Pope be most obliged to the keeping of the gospel among all men that live here; for the Pope is highest vicar that Christ has here in earth. For moreness of Christ's vicar is not measured by worldly moreness, but by this, that this vicar sues more Christ by virtuous living; for thus teacheth the gospel, that this is the sentence of Christ.

And of this gospel I take as believe, that Christ for time that he walked here, was most poor man of all, both in spirit and in having; for Christ says that he had nought for to rest his head on. And Paul says that he was made needy for our love. And more poor might no man be, neither bodily nor in spirit. And thus Christ put from him all manner of worldly lordship. For the gospel of John telleth that when they would have made Christ king, he fled and hid him from them, for he would none such worldly highness.

And over this I take it as believe, that no man should sue the Pope, nor no saint that now is in heaven, but inasmuch as he sues Christ. For John and James erred when they coveted worldly highness; and Peter and Paul sinned also when they denied and blasphemed in Christ; but men should not sue them in this, for then they went from Jesus Christ. And this I take as wholesome counsel, that the Pope leave his wordly lordship to worldly lords, as Christ gave them—and move speedily all his clerks to do so. For thus did Christ, and taught thus his disciples, till the fiend had blinded this world. And it seems to some men that clerks that dwell lastingly in this error against God's law, and flee to sue Christ in this, been open heretics, and their fautors been partners.

And if I err in this sentence, I will meekly be amended, yea, by the death, if it be skilful, for that I hope were good to me. And if I might travel in mine own person, I would with good will go to the Pope. But God has needed me to the contrary, and taught me more obedience to God than to men. And I suppose of our Pope that he will not be Antichrist, and reverse Christ in this working, to the contrary of Christ's will; for if he summon against reason, by him or by any of his, and pursue this unskilful summoning, he is an open Antichrist. And merciful intent excused not Peter, that Christ should not clepe him Satan; so blind intent and wicked counsel excuses not the Pope here; but if he ask of true priests that they travel more than they may, he is not excused by reason of God, that he should not be Antichrist. For our belief teaches us that our blessed God suffers us not to be tempted more than we may; how should a man ask such service? And therefore pray we to God for our Pope Urban the Sixth, that his old holy intent be not quenched by his enemies. And Christ, that may not lie, says that the enemies of a man been especially his home family; and this is sooth of men and fiends.

✤ D. The Statute *De haeretico comburendo*

Text in Statutes of the Realm, *2:125–28: 2 Henry IV, c. 15.*

Whereas, it is shown to our sovereign lord the king on the advice of the prelates and clergy of his realm of England in this present Parliament, that although the Catholic faith builded upon Christ, and by his apostles and the Holy Church, sufficiently determined, declared, and approved, hath been hitherto by good and holy and most noble progenitors and predecessors of our sovereign lord the king in the said realm amongst all the realms of the world most devoutly observed, and the Church of England by his said most noble progenitors and ancestors, to the honor of God and the whole realm aforesaid, laudably endowed and in her rights and liberties sustained, without that the same faith or the said church was hurt or grievously oppressed, or else perturbed by any perverse doctrine or wicked, heretical, or erroneous opinions. Yet, nevertheless, divers false and perverse people of a certain new sect, of the faith of the sacraments of the church, and the authority of the same damnably thinking, and against the law of God and of the Church usurping the office of preaching, do perversely and maliciously in divers places within the said realm, under the color of dissembled holiness, preach and teach these days openly and privily divers new doctrines, and wicked heretical and erroneous opinions contrary to the same faith and blessed determinations of the Holy Church, and of such sect and wicked doctrine and opinions they make unlawful conventicles and confederacies, they hold and exercise schools, they make and write books, they do wickedly instruct and inform people, and as much as they may excite and stir them to sedition and insurrection, and make great strife and division among the people, and other enormities horrible to be heard daily do perpetrate and commit, in subversion of the said catholic faith and doctrine of the Holy Church, in diminution of divine worship, and also in destruction of the estate, rights, and liberties of the said Church of England; by which sect and wicked and false preachings, doctrines, and opinions of the said false and perverse people, not only most greatest peril of the souls, but also many more other hurts, slanders, and perils, which God prohibit, might come to this realm, unless it be the more plentifully and speedily holpen by the King's majesty in this behalf; especially since the diocesans of the said realm cannot by their jurisdiction spiritual, without aid of the said royal majesty, sufficiently correct the said false and perverse people, nor refrain their malice, because the said false and perverse people do go from diocese to diocese and will not appear before the said diocesans, but the same diocesans and their jurisdiction spiritual, and the keys of the church with the censures of the same, do utterly condemn and despise; and so their wicked preachings and doctrines do from day to day continue and exercise to the utter destruction of all order and rule of right and reason. Upon which novelties and excesses above rehearsed, the prelates and clergy aforesaid, and also the Commons of the said realm being in the same Parliament, have prayed our sovereign lord the king that his royal highness would vouchsafe in the said Parliament to provide a convenient remedy. The same our sovereign lord the king, graciously considering the premises, and also the laudable steps of his said most noble progenitors and ancestors, for the conservation of the said catholic faith and sustentation of the said divine worship, and also the safeguard of the estate, rights and liberties of the said Church of England, to the laud of God and merit of our said sovereign lord the king, and prosperity and honor of all his said realm, and for the eschewing of such dissensions, divisions, hurts, slanders, and perils, in time to come, and that this wicked sect, preachings, doctrines, and opinions, should from henceforth cease and be utterly destroyed; by the assent of the great lords and other noble persons of the said realm, being in the said Parliament, hath granted, established, and ordained, from henceforth firmly to be observed, that none within the said realm or any other dominions subject to his Royal Majesty, presume to preach openly or privily, without the license of the diocesan of the same place first required and obtained, curates in their own churches and persons hitherto privileged, and other of the Canon Law granted, only except; nor that none from henceforth anything preach, hold, teach, or instruct openly or privily, or make or write any book contrary to the catholic faith or determination of the Holy Church, nor of such sect and wicked doctrines and opinions shall make any conventicles, or in any wise hold or exercise schools; and also that none from henceforth in any wise favor such preacher or maker of any such and like conventicles, or persons holding or exercising schools, or making or writing such books, or so teaching, informing, or exciting the people, nor any of them maintain or in any wise sustain, and that all and singular having such books or any writings of such wicked doctrine and opinions, shall really with effect deliver or cause to be delivered all such books and writings to the diocesan of the same place within forty days from the time of the proclamation of this ordinance and statute.

And if any person or persons of whatsoever sex, estate, or condition that he or they be, from henceforth do or attempt against the said royal ordinance and statute aforesaid in the premises or any of them, or such books in the form aforesaid do not deliver, then the diocesan of the same place in his diocese such person or persons in this behalf defamed or evidently suspected and every of them may by the authority of the said ordinance and statute cause to be arrested and under safe custody in his prison to be detained till he or they of the articles laid to him or them in this behalf do canonically purge him or themselves, or else such wicked sect, preachings, doctrines and heretical and erroneous opinions do abjure, according as the laws of the Church do demand and require.

*   *   *

And if any person within the said realm and dominions, upon the said wicked preachings, doctrines, opinions, schools, and heretical and erroneous informations, or any of them be before the diocesan of the same place or his commissaries convict by sentence, and the same wicked sect, preachings, doctrines and opinions, schools and informations, do refuse duly to abjure, or by the diocesan of the same place or his commissaries, after the abjuration made by the same person be pronounced relapsed, so that according to the holy canons he ought to be left to the secular court (upon which credence shall be given to the diocesan of the same place or to his commissaries in this behalf), then the sheriff of the county of the same place, and mayor and sheriffs, or sheriff, or mayor and bailiffs of the city, town, and borough of the same county next to the same diocesan or the said commissaries, shall be personally present in preferring of such sentences, when they by the same diocesan or his commissaries shall be required; and they the same persons and every of them, after such sentence promulgate shall receive, and them before the people in an high place cause to be burnt, that such punishment may strike fear into the minds of others, whereby no such wicked doctrine and heretical and erroneous opinions, nor their authors and fautors, in the said realm and dominions, against the Catholic faith, Christian law, and determination of the holy church, which God prohibit, be sustained or in any way suffered; in which all and singular the premises concerning the said ordinance and statute, the sheriffs, mayors, and bailiffs of the said counties, cities, boroughs and towns shall be attending, aiding, and supporting to the said diocesans and their commissaries.

PART IV:

Moral and Miracle:
The Saint's Life
and the *Exemplum*

The thirteenth century witnessed the remarkable process of bringing together vast universal compendia summing up human knowledge, the *summae* of theology, law, history, and every other conceivable subject that is associated with the names of Thomas Aquinas, Vincent of Beauvais, and many other writers. The century also witnessed the production of two *summae* of moral stories collected for the edification of the faithful. At the beginning of the century Caesarius of Heisterbach, a Cistercian abbot, compiled the *Dialogus Miraculorum*, a vast compendium of miracle stories. At the end of the century Jacobus da Varazze compiled the *Legenda Aurea*, an immense collection of saints' lives retold in popular form. These two works and the many others compiled during the thirteenth and fourteenth centuries constituted a mine of moral tales that could be used by preachers, writers of tracts, and poets. The first selection below, from the *Legenda Aurea*, tells the stories of Longinus and Veronica, two figures who appear in *Piers Plowman*, in *Passus* V and XVIII, and were probably known to Langland in one variation or other of their story as told by Jacobus da Varazze. The remaining *exempla* come from the great thirteenth-century collections of Jacques de Vitry, Caesarius of Heisterbach, and Étienne de Bourbon, three of the most indefatigable compilers of anecdotes the world has ever known. On the genre itself, see J.-Th. Welter, *L'Exemplum dans la littérature religieuse et didactique du moyen age* (Paris-Toulouse, 1927; reprint ed., New York, 1973) and the works of Owst cited above.

The first selection is from Helmut Ripperger and Granger Ryan, trans., *The Golden Legend of Jacobus de Voragine* (London, 1941; reprint ed., New York, 1969). The remaining selections comprise the pamphlet *Monastic Tales of the XIIIth Century*, trans. Dana C. Munro, Translations and Reprints from the Original Sources of European History, vol. 2, no. 4 (Philadelphia, 1895). Each selection is cited by the author's name and the location in his own work. The works of Jacques de Vitry are from T. F. Crane, ed., *The Exempla . . . of Jacques de Vitry*, Publications of the Folk-Lore Society, vol. 26 (London, 1890; rpt. London, 1967); *Caesarii Heisterbacensis monaci ordinis Cisterciencis Dialogus Miraculorum*, ed. J. Strange, 2 volumes (Cologne, 1851); A. Lecoy de la Marche, *Anecdotes historiques . . . d'Étienne de Bourbon* (Paris, 1877). The substance of such collections as these touches, of course, upon other areas besides literary allusions and the history of belief; much folklore and learned antiquarianism are jumbled together in these collections, and brief extracts do not adequately give the flavor of the whole. A recent study dealing with a similar collection and its place in the history of popular belief is Juliane Matuszak, *Das Speculum Exemplorum als Quelle volkstümlicher Glaubensvorstellung des Spätmittelalters* (Siegburg, 1967). A more familiar collection of similar stories is the inexhaustible *Life in the Middle Ages*, by G. G. Coulton, 4 vols. (rpt. Cambridge, 1967), esp. vol. 1.

The final text in this section is the fable of the rat parliament, taken from Lucy Toulmin Smith and Paul Meyer, eds., *Les Contes Moralisées de Nicole Bozon, Frère Mineur*, S.A.T.F. (Paris, 1889). The fables of Bozon constitute yet another source in addition to saints' lives, *exempla,* and miracle stories for popular and learned views on society, including its vices and virtues, in the thirteenth and fourteenth centuries. See the use of Bozon's fable mentioned above, p. 87.

15

Longinus and Veronica: The *Legenda Aurea*

Introductory Note: Jacobus da Varazze's *Legenda Aurea,* written in the last decade of the thirteenth century, was one of the largest systematic collections of saints' lives before the sixteenth century and the beginnings of the *Acta Sanctorum* in the seventeenth. The following selection is from Granger Ryan and Helmut Ripperger, trans., *The Golden Legend of Jacobus de Voragine* (London, 1941; rpt. New York, 1969), pp. 191 and 214–15.

❧ A. Longinus

Longinus was the centurion who was assigned by Pilate to stand guard with his soldiers at the crucifixion of the Lord, and who pierced His side with a lance. He was converted to the Christian faith when he saw the signs which followed upon the death of Jesus, namely the darkening of the sun and the quaking of the earth. But it is said that what led to his conversion chiefly was that he was afflicted with a malady of the eyes; and by chance he touched his eyes with a drop of the blood of Christ which ran down the shaft of his lance, and immediately his eyes were healed. He then quit the military life, received instruction from the apostles, and for twenty-eight years led the life of a monk at Caesarea of Cappadocia, working many conversions by his word and his example.

He was brought before the governor of the province, and when he refused to sacrifice to the idols, his teeth were torn out and his tongue cut off. But this did not deprive Longinus of the power of speech. Laying hold of an axe, he set about smashing the idols, saying: "If these be gods, let them show themselves!" And demons issued forth from all the idols, and entered into the bodies of the governor and his aides. Longinus said to these demons: "Why do you dwell in the idols?" They ansered: "We dwell wherever the name of Christ is not invoked, and the sign of the cross does not appear!" Meanwhile the governor had lost his sight. And Longinus said to him: "Poor man, know that thou canst be cured only after thou hast put me to death! But as soon as I am dead I shall pray for thee, and shall obtain the salvation of thy body and of thy soul!" The governor therefore had him beheaded, and then, falling down before his corpse, wept and did penance: and at once he regained his sight and his health, and passed the rest of his life in doing good works.

✤ B. Veronica

When Pilate had handed Jesus over to the Jews to be crucified, he feared that this condemnation of innocent blood would give offense to Tiberius; and to justify himself he sent one of his courtiers to the emperor. At that time Tiberius was suffering from a grave malady, and heard that there was in Jerusalem a physician who cured all sicknesses by His word alone. Therefore the emperor, not knowing that this physician had just been put to death by Pilate, said to one of his followers, whose name was Volusian: "Cross the sea with all haste, and order Pilate to send this physician to me!" Volusian set out on his journey; but Pilate, terrified by his demands, asked for a fortnight's grace. During this delay Volusian made the acquaintance of a woman named Veronica, who had known Jesus, and asked her where he might find Him. And Veronica answered: "Alas, Jesus was my Master and my God, but Pilate, through envy, condemned Him to die on the Cross!" Volusian was aggrieved at this, and said: "Sad am I that I cannot carry our the commands of my master!" And Veronica rejoined: "As Jesus was always travelling about to preach, and I could not always enjoy His presence, I once was on my way to a painter to have the Master's portrait drawn on a cloth which I bore with me. And the Lord met me in the way, and learning what I was about, pressed the cloth against His face, and left His image upon it. And if thy master but looks upon this image, he shall straightway be cured!" And Volusian asked: "Can this image be bought for gold or silver?" "No," said Veronica, "but sincere piety will obtain its blessings. I shall go to Rome with thee and show the image to Cæsar, and then I shall return to my own land." Thus they did, and Volusian said to Tiberius: "This Jesus whom you wished to see was unjustly condemned and crucified by Pilate and the Jews. But I have brought back with me a woman who possesses an image of Jesus, and who says that if thou wilt look upon it with devotion, thou shalt soon regain thy well-being." Then Tiberius caused the road to be spread with silken stuffs, and had the image carried to him: and no sooner had he set his eyes upon it than he was made whole.

Thereupon Pontius Pilate was brought to Rome, and Tiberius, aroused to anger, sent for him. But Pilate had put on the seamless tunic of Our Lord, as a safeguard; and the result was that Tiberius, when he saw him, forgot his anger, and could not help treating him with deference. But hardly had he dismissed him, when all his wrath returned: yet each time that he saw Pilate, his ire subsided, to the wonderment of all. At last, at the order of God, or perhaps upon the advice of a Christian, Tiberius had Pilate stripped of his tunic; and then, being able to unleash his fury, he commanded him to be thrown into prison, to await the shameful death which was appointed for him. Learning of this, Pilate took his knife and killed himself. His corpse was weighted with a huge stone and thrown into the Tiber. But the foul and evil spirits laid hold of this foul and evil body;

and sometimes by plunging it into the waters, and other times by snatching it up into the air, they brought about countless floods, storms, and other ills, to the terror of the whole world. Therefore the Romans pulled the corpse out of the Tiber and sent it to Vienne as a mark of derision, because the name Vienne comes from the words *via gehennae*, the road of Hell: or it may have been called *Bienna*, because it was built in two years. But there again the wicked spirits began their foul play, until the people of Vienne, in haste to be rid of this vessel of abomination, buried it in the territory of Lausanne. But the inhabitants of this city also were anxious to rid themselves of the body, and cast it into a chasm surrounded by high mountains; and it is said that even now that place is turbulent with the evil doings of the devils.

16

Tales of Saints, Demons, and Relics

 A. Jacques de Vitry, CCLXXXII

In The Exempla . . . of Jacques de Vitry, *p. 117 f.*

A certain very religious man told me that this happened in a place where he had been staying. A virtuous and pious matron came frequently to the church and served God most devoutly, day and night. Also a certain monk, the guardian and treasurer of the monastery, had a great reputation for piety, and truly he was devout. When, however, the two frequently conversed together in the church concerning religious matters, the devil, envying their virtue and reputation, tempted them very sorely, so that the spiritual love was changed to carnal. Accordingly they made an agreement and fixed upon a night in which the monk was to leave his monastery, taking the treasures of the church, and the matron was to leave her home, with a sum of money which she should secretly steal from her husband.

After they had fled, the monks on rising in the morning, saw that the receptacles were broken and the treasures of the church stolen; and not finding the monk, they quickly pursued him. Likewise the husband of the said woman, seeing his chest open and the money gone, pursued his wife. Overtaking the monk and the woman with the treasure and money, they brought them back and threw them into prison. Moreover so great was the scandal throughout the whole country and so much were all religious persons reviled that the damage from the infamy and scandal was far greater than from the sin itself.

Then the monk restored to his senses, began with many tears to pray to the blessed Virgin, whom from infancy he had always served, and never before had any such misfortune happened to him. Likewise the said matron began urgently to implore the aid of the blessed Virgin whom, constantly, day and night, she was accustomed to salute and to kneel in prayer before her image. At length, the blessed Virgin very irate, appeared and after she had upbraided them severely, she said, "I am able to obtain the remission of your sins from my son, but what can I do about such an awful scandal? For you have so befouled the name of religious persons before all the people, that in the future no one will trust them. This is an almost irremediable damage."

Nevertheless the pious Virgin, overcome by their prayers, summoned the demons, who had caused the deed, and enjoined upon them that, as they had caused the scandal to religion, they must bring the infamy to an end. Since, indeed, they were not able to resist her commands, after much anxiety and various conferences they found a way to remove the infamy. In the night they placed the monk in his church and repairing the broken receptacle as it was before, they placed the treasure in it. Also they closed and locked the chest which the matron had opened and replaced the money in it. And they set the woman in her room and in the place where she was accustomed to pray by night.

When, moreover, the monks found the treasure of their house and the monk, who was praying to God just as he had been accustomed to do; and the husband saw his wife and the treasure; and they found the money just as it had been before, they became stupefied and wondered. Rushing to the prison they saw the monk and the woman in fetters just as they had left them. For one of the demons was seen by them transformed into the likeness of a monk and another into the likeness of a woman. When all in the whole city had come together to see the miracle, the demons said in the hearing of all, "Let us go, for sufficiently have we deluded these people and caused them to think evil of religious persons." And, saying this, they suddenly disappeared. Moreover all threw themselves at the feet of the monk and of the woman and demanded pardon.

Behold how great infamy and scandal and how inestimable damage the devil would have wrought against religious persons, if the blessed Virgin had not aided them.

✤ B. Caesarius of Heisterbach, Distinctio VII, Cap. xxxiv

In Caesarii Heisterbacensis . . . Miraculorum, *2:42–43*.

Not many years ago, in a certain monastery of nuns, of which I do not know the name, there lived a virgin, named Beatrix. She was beautiful in form, devout in mind, and most fervent in the service of the mother of God. As often as she could offer to the Virgin special prayers and supplications, she held them for her dearest delight. In truth, being made custodian, she did this more devoutly and more freely.

A certain clerk, seeing and desiring her, began to tempt her. When she spurned the words of lust, and he insisted so much the more strenuously, the old serpent enkindled her breast so vehemently, that she was not able to bear the flames of love. Finally, approaching the altar of the blessed Virgin, the patroness of the oratory, she spoke thus: "My lady, I have served thee as devoutly as I could. Behold, I resign thy keys to thee. I am not able any longer to withstand the temptations of the flesh." And, placing the keys on the altar, she followed the clerk secretly.

When that wretched man had corrupted her, he abandoned

her after a few days. Since she had no means of living and blushed to return to the convent, she led a life of shame. After she had publicly continued in that vice for fifteen years, she came, one day, in a lay habit, to the door of the monastery. She said to the doorkeeper, "Did you know Beatrix, formerly custodian of this oratory?" He replied, "Certainly, I knew her. For she is an honest and holy woman, and from infancy even to the present day she has remained in this monastery without complaint." When she hearing the man's words, but not understanding them, wished to go away, the mother of mercy appeared to her in her well-known image and said, "During the fifteen years of your absence, I have filled your office. Now return to your place and do penance; for no man knows of your departure." In fact, in the form and dress of that woman, the mother of God had performed the duties of custodian. Beatrix entered at once and returned thanks as long as she lived, revealing through confession what had been done for her.

✤ C. Caesarius of Heisterbach, Distinctio VII, Cap. xliv

Ibid., 2:262–63.

In the chapel of the castle of Veldenz there is a certain ancient statue of the blessed Virgin, holding her son in her bosom. This statue is, indeed, not very well made, but is endowed with great virtue. A certain matron of this castle—which is situated in the diocese of Trier—standing in the chapel, one day, looked at the image and despising the workmanship, said, "Why does this old rubbish stand here?"

The blessed Virgin, the mother of mercy, not, as I think, complaining to her son of the woman who spoke so foolishly, but predicting the future penalty for the crime to a certain other matron, said, "Because that lady"—designating her by name—"called me old rubbish, she shall always be wretched as long as she lives."

After a few days that lady was driven out by her own son from all her possessions, and up to the present day, she begs wretchedly enough, suffering the punishment for her foolish speech. Behold, how the blessed Virgin loves and honors those who love her, and punishes and humbles those who despise her.

✤ D. Etienne de Bourbon, No. 133

In Anecdotes historiques . . . d'Etienne de Bourbon, *p. 113.*

Also near Cluny it happened recently—namely, in the year of our Lord 1246, when I was there—that I heard from several how a certain tavern keeper on the Saturday before Advent, in selling wine and taking his pay, blasphemed Christ during the whole day. But when about the ninth hour, in the presence of a multitude of men, he had sworn by the tongue of the blessed Virgin, by blaspheming her he lost the use of his tongue; and by speaking basely of her, suddenly stricken he fell dead, in the presence of the multitude.

✤ E. Etienne de Bourbon, No. 119

Ibid., *p. 103.*

Also it is read that a certain robber had this much of good in him, that he always fasted on bread and water on the vigils of the blessed Mary. And when he went forth to steal, he always said, "*Ave Maria*," asking her not to permit him to die in that sin. When, however, he was captured and hung, he remained there three days and could not die. Then he called out to the passers by, that they should summon a priest to him. When the priest came and the prefect and others, the robber was removed from the gallows, and said that a most beautiful virgin had held him up by his feet during the three days. Promising reform, he was let go free.

✤ F. Etienne de Bourbon, No. 129

Ibid., *p. 110.*

Also it is said that there was a certain knight, lord of a castle in Auvergne, whom the devil served in human form for twelve years. He wanted to carry the knight off, if he should find him at any time unfortified, on account of crime. When this was revealed to a certain holy man, he approached the castle, saying that he wished to speak with the servants. When, moreover, the devil seeing the holy man, wanted to run and hide, the latter had him summoned, and adjured him to say what he wanted and who he was. He replied that he was the devil and that he had been waiting twelve years for a chance to carry off that lord. But he was not able to do so, because seven times each day the lord with bent knees saluted the Virgin, and said the *"Pater noster"* seven times. Adjured in the name of the blessed Virgin, he left the foul corpse in which he was and. fled.

✤ G. Caesarius of Heisterbach, Distinctio V, Cap. xi

In Caesarii Heisterbacensis . . . Miraculorum, *1:291.*

When our abbot was celebrating mass last year on the Mount of the Holy Saviour near Aachen, a possessed woman was brought to him after the mass. When he read the gospel lesson concerning the ascension over her head and at these words, "They shall lay hands on the sick and they shall recover," he placed his hands upon her head, the devil gave such a horrible roar that we were all terrified. Adjured to depart, he replied, "The Most High does not wish it yet." When asked in what manner he entered, he would not reply, nor would he permit the woman to reply. Afterward she confessed that when her husband in anger said, "Go to the devil!" she felt the latter enter through her ear. Moreover that woman was from the province of Aachen and very well known.

✤ H. Caesarius of Heisterbach, Distinctio VIII, Cap. lix

Ibid., *2:131 ff.*

In a village which is called Holenbach, there lived a certain knight named Gerard. His grandsons are still living and hardly a man can be found in that village who does not know the miracle which I am going to tell about him. He loved St. Thomas the apostle so ardently and honored him so especially, above the other saints, that he never refused any pauper seeking alms in the name of that apostle. Moreover he was accustomed to offer to the saint many private services, such as prayers, fasts and the celebration of masses.

One day, by the permission of God, the devil, the enemy of all good men, knocking at the knight's gate in the form and dress of a pilgrim, sought hospitality in the name of St. Thomas. He was admitted with all haste, and since it was chilly and he pretended to be catching cold, Gerard gave to him his own fur cape, which was not badly worn, to cover himself with when he went to bed. When the next morning he who had seemed a pilgrim did not appear, and the cape was sought and not found, his wife in anger said to the knight, "You have often been deceived by wanderers of this kind and yet you persist in your superstition." But he replied calmly, "Do not be disturbed, St. Thomas will certainly make good this loss to us."

The devil did this in order to provoke the knight to impatience on account of the loss of his cape, and to extinguish in his heart his love for the apostle. But what the devil had prepared for his destruction redounded to the glory of the knight. By it the latter was incited the more strongly; the former was confused and punished. For after a little time Gerard wanted to go to the abode of St. Thomas, and when he was all ready to start, he broke a gold ring into two pieces before the eyes of his wife, and joining them together in her presence, gave one piece to her and kept the other himself, saying, "You ought to trust this token. Moreover, I ask you to wait five years for my return, and after that you can marry anyone you please." And she promised.

He went on a very long journey and at length with great expense and very great labor, reached the city of St. Thomas the apostle. There he was saluted most courteously by the citizens, and received with as great kindness as if he had been one of them and well known to them. Ascribing that favor to the blessed apostle, he entered the oratory, and in prayer he commended himself, his wife, and all his possessions to the saint. After this, remembering the limit fixed, and thinking that the five years ended on that very day, he groaned and said, "Alas! my wife will now marry some other man." God had delayed his journey on account of what is to follow.

When the knight looked around in sorrow, he saw the above-mentioned demon walking about in his cape, and the devil said, "Do you know me, Gerard?" He said, "No, I do not know you, but I know my cape." The devil replied, "I am the one who sought hospitality from you in the name of the apostle; and I carried off your cape, for which I have been severely punished." And he added, "I am the devil, and I am commanded to carry you back to your own house before nightfall, because your wife has married another man and is now sitting with him at the wedding banquet." Taking him up, the devil crossed in part of a day from India to Germany, from the east to the west, and about twilight placed him in his own house without injury.

He, entering his own house like a stranger, saw his own wife eating with her husband. Drawing near, in her sight he drew out the half of the ring and sent it to her in a cup. When she saw it, she immediately took out her half and joining it to the part given to her, she recognized him as her husband. Immediately jumping up, she rushed to embrace him, proclaiming that he was her husband, Gerard, and saying goodbye to her new husband. Nevertheless, out of courtesy Gerard kept the latter with him that night.

In this as in the preceding miracle, it is sufficiently evident how much the blessed apostles love and glorify those who love them.

✣ I. Caesarius of Heisterbach, Distinctio V, Cap. xviii

Ibid., *1:296 ff.*

Two men simply clad, but not without guile, not birds but ravening wolves, came to Besançon, feigning the greatest piety. They were pale and thin. They went about bare-footed and fasted daily. They did not miss a single night the early service in the cathedral, nor did they accept any alms from anyone except necessary food. When by such hypocrisy they had attracted the attention of everyone, they began to vomit forth their hidden poison and to preach to the ignorant new and unheard of heresies. In order, moreover, that the people might believe their teachings, they ordered meal to be sifted on the sidewalk and walked on it without leaving a trace of a footprint. Likewise walking upon the water, they could not be immersed. Also, they had little huts burnt over their heads, and after those had been burnt to ashes, they came out uninjured. After this they said to the people, "If you do not believe our words, believe our miracles."

The bishop and clergy hearing of this were greatly disturbed. And when they wished to resist those men, affirming that those were heretics and deceivers and ministers of the devil, they escaped with difficulty from being stoned by the people. Now that bishop was a good and learned man and a native of our province. Our aged monk, Conrad, who told me these facts and who was in that city at the time, knew him well.

The bishop seeing that his words were of no avail and that the people entrusted to his charge were being subverted by the devil's agents, summoned a certain clerk that he knew, who was very well versed in necromancy, and said, "Certain men in my city are doing so and so. I ask you to find out from the devil by your skill, who they are, whence they come, and by what means so many and so wonderful miracles are wrought by them. For it is impossible that they should do wonders through divine inspiration when their teaching is so contrary to God's." The clerk replied, "My lord, I have long renounced that art." The bishop replied, "You see clearly in what straits I am. I must either acquiesce in their teachings or be stoned by the people. Therefore I enjoin upon you for the remission of your sins, that you obey me in this matter."

The clerk, obeying the bishop, summoned the devil, and when asked, told why he had called him. "I am sorry that I have deserted you. And because I intend to be more obedient to you in the future than in the past, I ask you to tell me who these men are, what they teach, and by what means they work so great miracles." The devil replied, "They are mine and sent by me, and they preach what I have placed in their mouths." The clerk asked, "How is it that they cannot be injured, or sunk in the water, or burned by fire?" The demon replied again, "They have under their arm-pits, sewed between the skin and the flesh my compacts in which the homage done by them to me is written; and by virtue of these they work such miracles and can not be injured by anyone." Then the clerk, "Suppose those should be taken away?" The devil replied, "Then they would be weak just like other men." The clerk having heard this, thanked the demon, saying, "Now go, and when you are summoned by me, return."

He went to the bishop and recited these things to him in order. The latter filled with great joy, summoned all the people of the city to a suitable place and said, "I am your shepherd, ye are my sheep. If those men, as you say, confirm their teaching by signs, I will follow them with you. If, however, they deserve punishment, you shall penitently return to the faith of your fathers with me." The people replied, "We have seen many signs from them." The bishop, "But I have not seen them."

Why protract my words? The plan pleased the people. The heretics were summoned. The bishop was present. A fire was kindled in the midst of the city. Nevertheless, before the heretics entered it, they were secretly summoned to the bishop. He said to them, "I want to see if you have any evil about you." Hearing this they immediately stripped and said with great confidence, "Search our bodies and our garments carefully." The soldiers, truly, following the instructions of the bishop, raised their arms, and noticing under the arm-pits some scars that were healed up, broke them open with their knives and extracted from them the little scrolls which had been sewed in.

Having received these, the bishop went forth to the people with the heretics, and having commanded silence, cried out in a loud voice, "Now shall your prophets enter the fire, and if they are not injured I will believe in them." Then the wretched men, trembling said, "We are not able to enter now." Then the bishop told the people of the evil which had been detected, and showed the compacts. Then all furious hurled the devil's ministers, to be tortured with the devil in eternal flames, into the fire which had been prepared.

And thus through the grace of God and the action of the bishop the rising heresy was extinguished and the people who had been seduced and corrupted were cleansed by penance.

✤ J. *Lucae Tudensis Episcopi De Altera Vita,* Lib. III, cap. 15

In Magna Bibliotheca Veterum Patrum (Cologne, 1618), 13:283. Translated in James Harvey Robinson, The Pre-Reformation Period, *pp. 6–7.*

From the lips of the same brother Elias, a venerable man, I learned that when certain heretics were scattering the virulent seeds of error in parts of Burgundy, both the Preaching Friars and the Minorities drew the two-edged sword of God's word against these same heretics, opposing them valiantly until they were finally taken by the magistrate of the district. He sent them to the fiery stake as they merited, in order that these workers of iniquity should perish with their wickedness as a wholesome lesson to others. Quantities of wood having been supplied in plenty to feed the flames, suddenly a toad of wonderful size which is sometimes called *crapaldus*, appeared, and without being driven betook itself of its own accord into the midst of the flames. One of the heretics, who was reported to be their bishop, had fallen on his back in the fire. The toad took his place on this man's face and in the sight of all, ate out the heretic's tongue. By the next day his whole body except his bones, had been turned into disgusting toads, which could not be counted for their great number. The inhabitants, seeing the miracle, glorified God and praised Him in His servants, the preaching monks, because the Lord had, in His mercy, delivered them from the horror of such pollution. God omnipotent surely wished to show through the most unseemly and filthiest of animals, how foul and infamous are the teachings of heretics, so that all might thereafter carefully shun the heretic, as they would the poisonous toad. Just as among four-footed creatures the toad is held the foulest, so the teachings of the heretic are more debased and filthy than those of any other religious sect. The blindness of heresy justifies the perfidy of the Jews. Its pollution makes the madness of the Mohammedans a pure thing in contrast. The licentiousness of the heretics would leave Sodom and Gomorrah stainless. What is held most enormous in crime, becomes most holy, when compared with the shame and ignominy of heresy. Thus, Dear Christian, flee this unspeakable evil, in comparison with which all other crimes are as trifles.

❖ K. Jacques de Vitry, CXII

In The Exempla . . . of Jacques de Vitry, *p. 52.*

Moreover, although poverty and other tribulations are advantageous, yet certain ones abuse them. Accordingly we read that when the body of St. Martin was borne in procession, it healed all the infirm who met it. Now there were near the church two wandering beggars, one blind, the other lame. They began to converse together and said, "See the body of St. Martin is now being borne about in procession, and if it catches us we shall be healed immediately, and no one in the future will give us any alms. But we shall have to work and labor with our own hands." Then the blind man said to the lame, "Get up on my shoulders because I am strong, and you who can see well can guide me." They did this, but when they tried to escape, the procession overtook them; and since, on account of the throng, they were not able to get away, they were healed against their will.

❖ L. Caesarius of Heisterbach, Distinctio VIII, Cap. liii

In Caesarii Heisterbacensis . . . Miraculorum, *2:125–26.*

Not long ago a certain merchant of our country, crossing the sea, saw the arm of St. John the Baptist in his hospital, and desired it. Learning that the custodian of the relics was following a certain woman, and knowing that there is nothing which women of that class cannot extort from men, he approached her and said, "If you will procure for me the relics of St. John the Baptist of which your lover has the charge, I will give you a hundred and forty pounds of silver." She, craving the money, refused to consent to the hospitaler until he obtained the sacred arm. This she immediately delivered to the merchant and received the promised weight of silver.

Do you perceive how great a mockery? Just as formerly the head of St. John was delivered by Herod to a lascivious girl as a reward for dancing, and by her was given to an adulterous mother, so at this time the hospitaler, no less wicked than Herod, gave the arm of the same saint to a base woman as the price of fornication, and by her it was sold to the merchant.

The latter, not consigning it to the ground like Herodias, but wrapping it in purple, fled almost to the extremities of the earth and arrived at the city of Gröningen, which is located at the entrance to Frisia. There he built a house and, hiding the arm in one of the columns, began to grow exceedingly wealthy.

One day when he was sitting in his shop, someone said to him, "The city is burning and the fire is now approaching your house." He replied, "I do not fear for my house. I have left a good guardian there." Nevertheless he arose and entered his house. When he saw the column unmoved he returned to his shop. All wondered what was the cause of so great confidence.

When questioned about the guardian of his house, the merchant replied ambiguously. But when he realized that his fellow-citizens noted it, fearing lest they might employ violence against him, he took out the arm and delivered it into the care of a certain hermitess. She, unable to keep the secret, told a man of her charge, and he told the citizens. They immediately took the relics and carried them to the church. When the merchant tearfully requested his relics, they replied harshly. When they asked him of what saint these were the relics, he not wishing to betray the facts said he did not know. Nevertheless in grief he deserted the city, and falling into poverty he became very ill not long after. When he feared death, he disclosed to his confessor what the relics were and how he had obtained them.

When the citizens learned this, they made a receptacle, in the form of an arm, of silver and gilt, adorned with precious stones, and placed the relics in it. I saw the same arm two years ago, and it is covered with skin and flesh. I also saw there among the relics a small gold cross of Frederick the Emperor, which had been given to the above-mentioned merchant at the same time as the arm.

NOVICE: "Since no one of the saints believed to be greater than St. John the Baptist, why is it that we do not read of any miracles in his life?"

MONK: "So that God may show that holiness does not consist in miracles, but in right living. For after death he was illustrious by innumerable great miracles. The aforesaid citizens, in truth, fearing for the relics of St. John, built of planks a very strong little house behind the altar, and by night they had a priest sleep in the top of it. The house was so shaken under him on the first night that he felt no slight horror. In the second night truly it struck him when asleep and hurled him onto the pavement. When one of the rulers of the city fell sick, at his request Theoderic, the priest of the church, carried the arm to his house and unwrapped it. He found the arm, as well as the purple in which it was wrapped, covered with fresh blood. He told me this with his own mouth. A priest cut off a small piece of flesh from the same arm, and when he carried it off secretly in his hand, he felt as much heat from it as if he had been carrying burning coal. Many miracles and healings indeed were wrought in that city by the same relics through the merits of St. John the Baptist."

✤ M. Caesarius of Heisterbach, Distinctio VIII, Cap. lxx

Ibid., *2:140.*

A certain knight loved most ardently the above mentioned martyr, St. Thomas of Canterbury, and sought everywhere to obtain some relic of him. A certain wily priest, in whose house he was staying, heard of this and said to him, "I have by me the bridle which St. Thomas long used, and I have often experienced its virtue." When the knight heard this, thinking it true, he joyfully paid the priest the money which he demanded, and received the bridle with great devotion.

God truly, to whom nothing is impossible, wishing to reward the faith of the knight, and for the honor of his martyr, deigned to work many miracles through the same bridle. The knight seeing this founded a church in honor of the martyr and in it he placed as a relic the bridle of that most wicked priest.

✣ N. Caesarius of Heisterbach, Distinctio III, Cap. ii

Ibid., *1:112–13.*

A certain soldier dwelt in a certain village, with whose wife the priest of the same village committed adultery. The soldier was told that the priest was carrying on an intrigue with his wife. He, since he was a prudent man and did not readily believe the story, wished to say nothing about it to his wife or the priest, but to learn the truth more fully. But he was not without some suspicion. There happened to be in another village, not far distant from the one in which the soldier lived, a possessed person, in whom the demon was so vile that in the presence of bystanders he revealed sins which were not cloaked by a true confession. The soldier learned this from the common report and asked the priest, whom he suspected, to go to a certain meeting with him. And the priest promised.

When they had reached the village where the possessed one was, the priest conscious of his guilt, began to suspect the soldier, because he was not ignorant that one possessed by so vile a demon dwelt there. And, fearing for his life if he was betrayed by the demon, feigning some necessity, he entered a stable and throwing himself at the feet of a servant of the soldier, said, "I ask you in the name of the Lord to hear my confession." The servant greatly terrified raised him up and heard what he had to say. After the confession had been made, the priest asked that a penance should be inflicted upon him; and the servant replied very prudently, saying, "Whatever you would enjoin upon another for such a crime, shall be your atonement."

And so going on now in greater security, the priest went with the soldier to the church. There meeting the possessed one, the soldier asked, "Do you know anything about me?" For he did this on purpose to take away any suspicion that the priest might have. When the demon made some reply to him which I do not know, he added, "What do you know about that master?" The demon replied, "I know nothing about this man." And after he had said this in German, he immediately added in Latin, "He was justified in the stable." No clerk was present at the time.

NOVICE: "I am sure that the devil did not speak Latin of his own free will at that time."

MONK: "He was not allowed to speak German, lest the knight should understand what he said and learn the truth. And he was not permitted to be silent, in order that he might show to the priest the virtue of confession."

NOVICE: "Great is the virtue of confession which blots out the crime of adultery from the devil's memory and liberates a man from imminent peril."

MONK: "I heard also the result of this confession. The priest, not unmindful of the benefit conferred upon him, deserted the world and became a monk in a certain monastery of our order. He is believed to be still living as I have learned from a certain abbot of the Cistercian order."

NOVICE: "The prophecy of that impudent demon was the cause of great salvation for him."

❖ O. Etienne de Bourbon, No. 176

In Anecdotes historiques . . . d'Etienne de Bourbon, *pp. 155–56.*

The manifold inconveniences and losses which our enemies suffer from the confession of our sins ought to incite us to confession. It destroys the devil's records. And note how, when a certain clerk was leading a most holy life, so that the devil envied him, the devil by tempting the clerk caused him to fall into grievous sin. When moreover the devil wished to confound the clerk, assuming human form he accused him before his bishop.

The day was fixed on which the devil was to prove his charges, by bringing to the judge his accounts, in which were recorded the place, the time, and the persons to whose knowledge the clerk had sinned. The said clerk, seeing that he was in hard straits, confessed all, grieving and purposing not to return to sin. When moreover they were in the presence of the judge and the devil said he had much against the clerk which he could prove by writing and witnesses, he unrolled his records and found all that had been in them erased. He said, "All that I had against this man was certainly written here this very day and I do not know who has destroyed it all." Having thus spoken, he vanished. The clerk, however, narrated all of these things to the bishop, in the secrecy of confession.

✤ P. Etienne de Bourbon, No. 177

Ibid., p. 156.

Also it is related that when a certain holy father was at one time engaged with the brethren in some work, he forgot to say the none at the right time, on account of his occupation. Afterwards he saw the devil passing before him, bearing on his shoulders a very large book in the shape of a roll which looked as large as a tower. And he adjured the devil in the name of the Lord to drop that book. When he unrolled the book, he found written on one page that he himself had not said the none on the day and at the hour when he ought to have said it. Moreover, prostrating himself at once at the feet of his companions, he confessed his negligence, and immediately looking again in the devil's roll, he found that what had been written there was erased, and thereby he knew the efficacy of confession.

✤ Q. Caesarius of Heisterbach, Distinctio III, Cap. xvii

In Caesarii Heisterbacensis . . . Miraculorum, *1:133–34.*

In the same city, namely Argentina which is Strassburg, ten heretics were seized. When they denied their guilt, they

were convicted by the ordeal of glowing iron and were condemned to be burnt. When on the appointed day they were
being led to the fire, one of the attendants said to one of them,
"Wretched one, you are condemned. Now do penance and confess your sins, lest after the burning of the body, which is only
momentary, hell-fire burns your soul eternally." When the man
replied, "I certainly think that I have been mistaken, but I fear
repentance in so great straits will be by no means acceptable
to God." The former replied, "Only confess from your heart.
God is merciful and will receive the penitent."

Wonderful fact! For as soon as the man confessed his
perfidy, his hand was fully healed. While he delayed in confession, the judge summoned him to the punishment. His confessor
replied to the judge, "It is not just that an innocent man should
be condemned unjustly." Since no trace of a burn was found
in his hand, he was dismissed.

The man had a wife living not far from the city and absolutely ignorant of these things which have been related. When
he came to her rejoicing and said, "Blessed be God who has
liberated me to-day from the loss of body and soul!" and explained to her the cause; she replied, "What have you done,
most wretched man, what have you done? Why have you withdrawn from your holy and sacred faith from fear of momentary
pain? You ought rather, if it were possible, to expose your body
a hundred times to the flames than once to withdraw from a
faith so well proven?"

Whom does not the voice of the serpent seduce? That man,
unmindful of the favor divinely conferred upon him, unmindful
of the so manifest miracle, followed his wife's advice and returned
to his former error. God, not unmindful truly of the crime, in
return for so great ingratitude, tortured the hand of each one.
The burn was renewed in the hand of the heretic and, because
his wife was the cause of his returning to his error, she was
made his companion in the renewed pain. So vehement was the
burn that it penetrated to the bones. And since they did not
dare in the village to utter the cries which the violence of the
pain extorted, they fled into the nearest woods, howling there
like wolves. Why protract my words? They were betrayed,

led back to the city, and together cast into the fire which was
not yet fully extinguished and they were burnt to ashes.
NOVICE: "They were very justly punished."

✤ R. Caesarius of Heisterbach, Distinctio IX, Cap. xxviii

Ibid., *2:186.*

In Hemmenrode a certain aged priest, Henry by name, died
a few years ago. He was a holy and just man, and had been
for many years sacristan in that monastery. When he was celebrating one day at the altar of St. John the Baptist, in the choir
of the lay-brethren, a certain one of the lay-brethren standing
near, saw, in the hands of the priest, the Saviour in the form
of a man. Nevertheless the priest himself did not see it. One of
the elders of that convent related this to me.

✤ S. Caesarius of Heisterbach, Distinctio IX, Cap. ix

Ibid., *2:173–74.*

On a certain island there was a certain possessed girl, not
a nun, whom I myself saw there. When the devil was asked
by a priest why he had so long and so cruelly tortured Hartdyfa
de Cogheme, he replied through the mouth of the girl. "Why?
She has most certainly deserved it. She scattered the Most High
upon her vegetables."

Since he did not at all understand the saying, and the devil
was unwilling to explain, the priest went to the woman and
told her what the devil had said about her, advising her not
to deny it, if she understood the saying. She immediately confessed her guilt, saying, "I well understand the saying, although
I have never told any man of it. When I was a young girl and
had a garden to cultivate, I received a wandering woman as
a guest one night. When I told her of my losses in my garden,
saying that all the vegetables were being devoured by caterpillars,
she replied, 'I will tell you a good remedy. Receive the body

of the Lord, break it in pieces, and scatter it upon your vegetables. And the caterpillars will disappear at once.' I, wretched one! who cared more for my garden than for the sacrament, when I received the body of our Lord at Easter, took it out of my mouth and did with it as I had been taught. What I had intended as a remedy for my vegetables, became a source of torment to me, as the devil is my witness."

NOVICE: "That woman was more cruel than the attendants of Pilate, who spared Jesus after His death, and did break up His bones."

MONK: "Therefore, up to the present day she atones for that heinous sin and suffers unheard of tortures. Let those who employ the divine sacrament for temporal gain, or—what is more execrable—for evildoing, give heed to this punishment. Also if vermin neglect to do reverence to this sacrament, they sometimes suffer punishment."

❧ T. Etienne de Bourbon, No. 317

In Anecdotes historiques . . . d'Etienne de Bourbon, *pp.* 266–67.

For I have heard that a certain rustic, wishing to become wealthy and having many hives of bees, asked certain evil men how he could get rich and increase the number of his bees. He was told by someone that if he retained the sacred communion on Easter and placed it in some one of his hives, he would entice away all of his neighbor's bees, which leaving their own hives, would come to the place where the body of our Lord was and there would make honey. He did this.

Then all the bees came to the hive where the body of Christ was, and just as if they had felt compassion for the irreverence done to it, by their labor they began to construct a little church and to erect foundations, and bases, and columns, and an altar with like labor. And with the greatest reverence they placed the body of our Lord upon the altar. And within that little bee-hive they formed that little church with wonderful and the most beautiful workmanship. The bees of the vicinity leaving their hives came to that one; and over that work they sang in their own manner certain wonderful melodies like hymns.

The rustic hearing this, wondered. But waiting until the fitting time for collecting the honey, he found nothing in his hives in which the bees had been accustomed to make honey. And finding himself impoverished through the means by which he had expected to be enriched, he went to that one where he had placed the host, where he saw the bees had come together. But when he approached, just as if they had wanted to vindicate the insult to our Saviour, the bees rushed upon the rustic and stung him so severely that he escaped with difficulty, and in great agony. Going to the priest he related all that he had done and what the bees had done.

The priest, by the advice of his bishop, collected his parishioners and made a procession to the place. Then the bees leaving the hive, rose in the air, making sweet melody. Raising the hive they found inside the noble structure of that little church, and the body of our Lord placed upon the altar. Then returning thanks they bore to their own church that little church of the bees constructed with such skill and elegance, and placed it on the altar.

By this deed those, who do not reverence, but offer insult instead to the sacred body of Christ or the sacred place where it is, ought to be put to great confusion.

17

Nicolas Bozon,
from *Les contes moralisées*

Introductory Note: Les contes moralisées of Nicholas Bozon is a collection of fables recounted under various headings, each with a moral attached—rather a Christianized version of Aesop. Bozon himself was a Franciscan, and he wrote his collection of fables around 1320. These fables, like the excerpts above, are in fact moral *exempla*, whose application is universal. The fable printed below, that concerning the rat parliament later used by Langland in *Piers Plowman*, was originally recounted about prelates and their parishioners. The moral, however, being universal, could and did apply to kings and their subjects as well, as it surely did in *Piers Plowman*. The French text is found in Lucy Toulmin Smith and Paul Meyer, eds. *Les Contes Moralisées de Nicole Bozon, Frère Mineur*, S.A.T.F. (Paris, 1889), pp. 143–45. This translation is by Jeanne Krochalis; Professor R. J. Dean has helped considerably with Bozon's Anglo-Norman.

❧ *Against Cowardly Parishoners and Prelates*

The nature of the snail is such that when they are quiet among their companions, they stick out their horns and consider themselves very great lords, but as soon as they feel hail or rain or wind, or meet any resistance, they immediately draw in their horns and shut themselves up in their shells. So do some prelates, and so do people generally. The prelates are joyful when making merry, and they hide themselves when threatened. Wherefore the prophet Osee says, in Chapter VIII [Hosea 13], "When Ephraim spake trembling he exalted himself in Israel, but when he offended in Bael he died." Great lords threatened and prelates are frightened, but as for the poor, they are merry enough and bold. So spake Daniel to the prelates of the old law: "You have done thus, and thus, to the simple ones of your people who, for fear, do not dare to speak," *Sic et sic faciebatis filiabus Israel, et ille timentes vobis loquebantur* [Daniel 13:57]. Wherefore the sheep said to the raven who sat on his back and pulled out his wool, "You did not do that to the mastiff who is called Griffin." And not only the prelates, but people generally are afraid to say the truth; but when they sit around in company and speak of the wrongs that are done in the country, or in religion, by the masters who are in charge of others, then they say and promise that they will bring about improvements if ever they see the place and the time. When the occasion arises when these improvements could be made, no one is bold enough to speak; rather, they behave as the mice did once upon a time.

�֍ *Fabula ad idem*

Once upon a time the mice held their parliament, and each one complained to the others about Monsieur Badde, the white cat who had decimated their families, and was exerting himself to destroy them. "What can we do," said one "about Sir Badde, who comes upon us privily, when we are at play, and makes us cower in corners for fear of his coming?" One said, "Let's put a bell around his neck, so that he can warn us by its sound; and thereby we can do him honor, and in this fashion we will be warned of his arrival." "What a good idea!" said the mice to one another. "Let's carry it through. But let us decide right away who will perform this deed we have planned." But each one made excuses. All said that the advice was good, but none wished to put it to the test. And Badde went about as before, and destroyed both large and small.

Thus many in a group promise to amend the outrages of sovereigns, but when they see them present, they cry out "Clym, clam, cat lep over dam" [Hush! Hush! The cat jumps over the fence], that is, "Hush! Hush! if you want to live in peace."[1]

1. Bozon gives both a middle English and a French proverb, implying that the French translates the English, but in fact ME "clym, clam" means "climb, climbed" not "hush, hush"—unless this is a very early instance of "Clam up," meaning "shut up."

PART V:

Instruction
and Action

Although the invention of universities was one of the greatest achievements of medieval Europe, universities and their graduates and masters play a small part in this book, in part at least, because they play a relatively small part in *Piers Plowman*. Of much greater importance are the lower levels of instruction (both in and out of schools), the range of private libraries and individual reading, and the common knowledge that most people shared about all sorts of subjects, from astronomy/astrology to physiognomy to moral and social guidance. It may be redundant, but it is always useful to remind students of fourteenth-century English society that not everyone constantly read St. Augustine and few had the whole corpus of Thomas Aquinas at their fingertips. Much more important are the informal instructional materials, the commonest schoolbooks, the few manuscripts that individuals might possess.

To understand a literary work, one needs only a good edition, or at least a manuscript, of the text itself. To understand the work's audience, however, it is important to know what other works were read or bound up with the work in question, who owned the manuscripts, and how they were circulated. The figure of Piers Plowman, to take a single pertinent example, appears in this book in John Ball's Letter to the Commons of Essex and elsewhere in fourteenth- and fifteenth-century English literature with considerably frequency. A knight, or franklin, or wealthy (or not so wealthy) urban merchant might own a few manuscripts, painfully and expensively collected, and these could often be bound together into commonplace books, sometimes containing the most diverse collection of literature imaginable. Other compendia, however, contained works that were considered to be related thematically, and in a number of *Piers Plowman* manuscripts, as suggested above, there precede or follow the poem itself other devotional works, and these constitute useful indicators of audience and general attitudes toward the poem and its content.

The selections printed below offer a variety of informal and formal educational texts, and the rules of various guilds are included to remind the reader that neither religious nor secular life was wholly contained in the more familiar associations of parish, diocese, kingdom, and city or village. In the guilds too, instruction and criticism took place, devotional movements flowered, and the individual was associated with other individuals in a common enterprise that had both spiritual and temporal dimensions. The blend of instruction, organization, advice, and learning contained in the following selections is certainly not "typical" of any single manuscript in particular, but all the texts below reflect half-learning, popular ideas, and formal and informal organizations.

The first selection, the *Septenarium*, is a popular compendium of history, devotion, and astronomy that represents one of the many popular versions of what C. S. Lewis has called the "mental Model of the Universe" that had been constructed by cosmologists and philosophers in the twelfth century out of the surviving late antique scientific cosmologies and earlier works of Christian cosmology. The taste for the model endured until the seventeenth century. The second selection, from the *Distichs of Cato,* was an elementary schoolbook in which children learned Latin and morals (and, it may be added, a certain tedious sententiousness). The third selection is one example of the vast practical instructional literature governing the devotional life. The fourth group of selections consists of guild rules and regulations. The final selection, *The Book of Physiognomy,* is the concluding section of the *Wise Book of Philosophy and Astronomy* already excerpted above (chapter 1). Both of the final two selections were bound in manuscripts with *Piers Plowman.* Taken as a whole, these texts illustrate the literature of guides to practical action in a world in which works, with faith, still played a crucial role in establishing the social order and leading to salvation.

18

Septenarium

Introductory Note: C. S. Lewis once said that, of all the inventions of modern man, the one the middle ages would have prized most highly was the card index. Ways of schematizing knowledge were dear to the medieval mind, and diagrams of various sorts abounded. There were trees of knowledge, trees of virtues and vices, trees of the genealogy of Christ, or of kings. One of the more inventive and delightful diagrams was inspired by a sermon of Alain de Lille on the six wings of the cherubim, where each feather on each wing on the right bore the name of a virtue, and each feather on the left was inscribed with the corresponding vice. Towers of wisdom could be built up, stone by inscribed stone. Hugh of St. Victor, for example, wrote a treatise entitled *De Quinque Septenis,* (On the Five Sevens) which drew parallels between the seven deadly sins, the petitions of the Lord's prayer, the gifts of the Holy Spirit, virtues, and Beatitudes. The text was often accompanied by some sort of diagram; in University College Oxford Ms. 45, where a shortened version of it follows *Piers Plowman,* the five sevens are laid out in columns across fol. 47v. But it was perhaps most commonly illustrated in five concentric circles.

The text and illustration given here are not Hugh's; they are a sort of expansion, and universalization, of Hugh's basic idea, in which the circles are framed in a double square, the outer line of which gives the four ages of the world, from Adam to eternity, and the inner line the corresponding parts of the church year. Septenarium texts are usually arranged within the frame, some around the wheel and some below it, and our text notes where this comes in a typical diagram.

These texts, of which at least half a dozen survive as single sheets or on rolls, seem to have been teaching devices. They often accompany the *Compendium Historiale* of Peter of Poitiers, a twelfth-century schoolmaster and later university lecturer. As a kind of enlarged geneaology of Christ, almost always illustrated, the *Compendium* served also as a school text, to provide a picture Bible History; the text is quite simple Latin.

The text given here comes from British Museum Ms. Royal 14. B. ix, a roll, of which this is the last sheet. It is a fourteenth-century English manuscript, and is unusual in the tradition of Septenarium Wheels only in the floral center medallion; usually there is a picture of God enthroned, illustrating *Pater noster*.

For discussions of schemes and diagrams, see F. Saxl, "A Spiritual Encyclopedia of the Later Middle Ages," *Journal of the Warburg and Courtauld Institutes* 5 (1942): 83–129, and R. W. Southern, *Medieval Humanism and other Studies* (Oxford, 1970), esp. Plates III-VIII, and charts 1 and 2. Peter of Poitiers is discussed in *The Works of Peter of Poitiers*, ed. Philip S. Moore, (Notre Dame, Ind., 1936), and *Septenarium* manuscripts in the description of Ms. Lyell 84 in A. C. Delamare, *Cataloque of the Collection of Medieval Manuscripts bequeathed to the Bodleian Library Oxford by James R. R. Lyell*, (Oxford, 1971).

Langland's method of personifying the seven deadly sins in *Passus* V is somewhat different from the treatment in the *Septenarium*, and on the surface somewhat less abstract. But, as here, each sin is opposed by pious practices and the gates of Heaven are guarded by virtues which one must cultivate in order to achieve salvation.

SEPTENARIUM WHEEL

A. GOD IN THE BEGINNING   C. CHRIST RISING
B. THE NATIVITY   D. CHRIST JUDGING
           E. OUR FATHER

a. Time of deviation, from Adam to Moses
b. First age, Second, Third, Fourth, Fifth, Sixth, Seventh to Second Passion Sunday
c. Time of revocation, from Moses to Christ
d. Advent
e. Nativity to Sunday before Septuagesima
f. Time of peregrination, as to Christ
g. Time of reconciliation, as to members
h. Time of revocation
i. Time of the perigrination of the Church, Antichrist, conversion of the rest of the world
j. Resurrection to Trinity Sunday
k. 33 Sundays, 45 days of penance

I. PRIDE (SINS)   1. PETITIONS
II. LUST   1. Hallowed be Thy name
III. GLUTTONY   1. Thy kingdom come
IV. AVARICE   1. Thy will be done
V. SLOTH   1. Give us this day our daily bread
VI. ENVY   1. Forgive us our trespasses as we forgive those...
VII. WRATH   1. Lead us not into temptation
VIII. VAIN GLORY   1. Deliver us from evil

I. 2. GIFTS   3. VIRTUES   4. REWARDS
II. 2. Wisdom   3. Peace   4. Children of God
III. 2. Understanding   3. Purity of heart   4. Sight of God
IV. 2. Counsel   3. Mercy   4. Granting of mercy
V. 2. Fortitude   3. Hunger for justice 4. Satisfaction
VI. 2. Knowledge   3. Mourning   4. Comfort
VII. 2. Piety   3. Meekness   4. Possession of the earth
VIII. 2. Fear of the Lord 3. Poverty of spirit 4. Kingdom of heaven

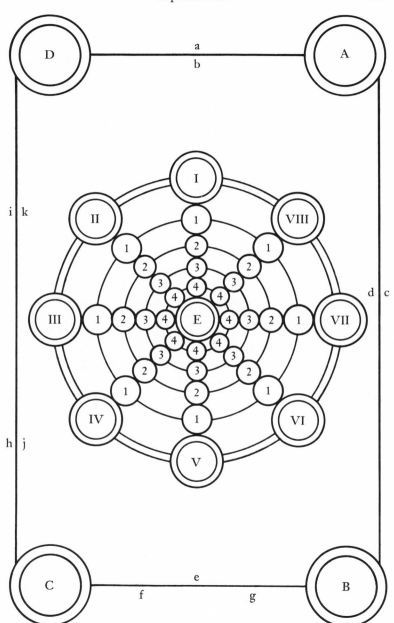

✤ Septenarium

There are four exterior lines which make a square, and they represent to us the four ages, which flow from the beginning of the world to the end. Inside these lines vices fill us, and must be expunged by the benefits, virtues, and gifts we need against them.

The first age lasted from Adam's going out [from Paradise] until Moses. In this age, Adam sinned, and was thrown out of Paradise, and Cain committed homicide, and Lamech committed bigamy, and men were drowned in the flood. Concerning this time, the Apostle said, "Death reigned from Adam to Moses, because sin then was scarcely known."

The second age was the time of revocation, from Moses until Christ. For through the law and the prophets, sins were made known more widely, and men began to be drawn back to truth by fear rather than by love.

The third was the age of reconciliation, from the birth of the saviour to the sending of the Holy Ghost. For Christ reconciled the world through all these things which He did: through his birth, circumcision, baptism, fasting, preaching, working of miracles, passion, death, resurrection, ascension, and the sending of the Holy Ghost. For God was reconciling the world to Himself through Christ. Concerning this age the Apostle says: *Behold now is the acceptable time, the time of grace.*

The fourth age is that of the peregrination, [which lasts] from the sending of the Holy Spirit to the day of judgment; in this time the Church wanders here in filth and battle, because, even if its fault should be forgiven, the punishment remains. This is signified in Absalom who, after he was reconciled to his father David, remained in Jerusalem for two years before he could see the face of his father.

Thus these four ages follow each other in order, as they are enumerated here and noted in the figures.

But in the scheme of the church year this is not the case. From the first Sunday of Advent until the Nativity, the Church cultivates the time of revocation; from the Nativity until Septuagesima the time of reconciliation, especially for the members, who are reconciled during this time, for this is the time of peregrination, particularly for Christ, who journeyed among us when He was born, circumsized, and baptized. From Septuagesima until the Passion the time of deviation is represented for the seven Sundays which illustrate the seven ages of the world. For indeed, the office of each of these Sundays pertains to the works of one of those seven ages, because some deviations are found in all ages. For this reason the seventh Sunday from the beginning is called the Sunday full of joy, when "Letare Jerusalem" is sung. Two Sundays belong to the term from the Passion to the time of reconciliation, and the peregrination of Christ, and the increase of sins in all men. During this time the office is mixed; it contains the memory of the perfidious Jewish people, and of the sins of the human race for which Christ suffered. And this office is said to pertain to the time of deviation, of resurrection, ascension, sending of the Holy Spirit, as much as it pertains to our reconciliation; but not to the wandering of Christ, for indeed He was already with God His father.

The Sundays which come from the octave of Pentecost to Advent, twenty-three of them, designate the time of the peregrination of the Church from now until the day of judgment. And this peregrination is twofold: first in the head, when we look toward our reconciliation, and second in the body, when we look at the peregrination at the end of which Antichrist will come. And after His reign, forty-five days will be granted for penitence, in which the rest of Israel will be converted. And afterwards Christ will come to give judgment.

[The following scheme of the seven ages of the world, which is added in the manuscript, comes from Peter of Poitiers, *Compendium Historiale*] The first age lasts from Adam to Noah, the second from Noah to Abraham, the third from Abraham to David, the fourth from David to the transmigration, the fifth from the transmigration to Babylon until Christ, the sixth from Christ to the end of the world. These six are of the living; the seventh will be of the dead, and it begins at the Passion of the Lord. The eighth will be the age of the risen, which will begin on the day of judgment, and will endure for all eternity.

[These are the verses which run down the center column of the wheel:]

Man is sick, God is the doctor, vices are the illnesses,
the petitions of the sick man are the laments and demands,
the gifts are the antidotes, the virtues are the remedies,
the beatitudes are the joys of felicity.

This prayer is worthier than others by reason of its authority because it came forth from the mouth of the Saviour; and by reason of its shortness in words, because no one can possibly be excused from getting it by heart; and by reason if its sufficiency, because it contains all things necessary for us; and by reason of its fecundity in mysteries of faith.

There are seven petitions of the Lord's prayer besides the salutation for capturing of good will. They begin: "Hallowed be thy name." Of these, the first three, which pertain to heaven, are worthier than the other four, which pertain to the earthly way. And therefore the first are put before the others, according to the order of their worthiness. This is the artificial order. But the holy ones that are shown forth, follow the natural order, which demands that we begin with the lesser, that is, temporal things, and proceed to the greater and eternal, according to the order of reason or of time. And the adaptation of petitions comes about, by which gifts are sought; and the adaptation of virtues, which are obtained by the gifts, and of beatitudes, which are acquired by the virtues. And all these fight against the seven vices. And in all these petitions, and gifts and virtues and beatitudes, a progression is followed. Nevertheless, the petitions proceed in retrograde order, unlike the gifts and virtues, which preserve the right order. And likewise the promises, which are nevertheless all one promise—the promise of the kingdom of God—although they have diverse names, which are varied for the sake of elegance. This can be done appropriately. For the poor, indeed, the kingdom is fitting; for the meek, the possession of the earth, which is greater; for those lamenting, consolation, which is greater still. And the following beatitudes progress in similar fashion.

✤ Exposition of the Lord's Prayer

It is said that "Our Father who art in heaven" is a brief capturing of good will. Through this utterance, "Our Father," we are urged away from two things: from pride, lest we say "My father," taking as our own personal thing something which is communal; and from unworthiness, lest we give ourselves back unworthily to such a father. It urges us to three things: to preserving the grace of adoption; the union of fraternity; and the promise of accomplishment, from whence He is not called a lord who is served as a father, but a father who is served in love.

Note that one says "Who art in heaven," that is, among the saints, through grace, so that thus it may make you holy; or in heaven, that is in the secret of divine majesty, through which is given the pledge of having the hidden things which the eye has not seen nor the ear heard, nor has it risen in the heart of man. [Here the text goes into the retrograde order discussed above.] "And deliver us from evil." That is, Give the spirit of piety of the Lord, by which habit we should have poverty of spirit, humility of heart, and should assent to good things within, not presuming concerning them, and we should reject exterior things, either by casting them away entirely, or by not placing the heart in them; and thus we are freed from the triple evil, innate, original, and additional, that is, actual sin, and from the concupiscence of the world, so that we are not seduced thereby. And thus, despising earthly things, we may have the eternal things of the kingdom, namely, whatever of the heavens Lucifer and the first parent lost through vainglory, through which fear and poverty of spirit dragged us back.

"And lead us not into temptation." Since a man may be freed from evil here, he is tempted while he is on the way. Therefore he petitions: "Lead us not into temptation," that is, give the spirit of piety, through which we have mildness, so that we might not succumb to temptation rendering back evil for evil, and so that we may possess the earth of the living, because we possess ourselves. By this we rule our wrath, which we repel by piety and mildness.

"Forgive us our trespasses &c." Since a man may be freed from evil when he conquers temptation, here nonetheless he is in some kind of sin as long as he is on the way. Therefore he petitions: "Forgive us our trespasses," that is, give us the spirit of knowledge, by which we may discern our own sins and those of others, and we may lament for them, so that we may know how to dismiss alien things; so you might dismiss our own sins. And thus we shall have consolation against envy, which makes a man dwindle away from an alien good; against which knowledge, accompanied by grief, prevails. This makes a man realize that all things are transitory. Our sins are called "debts" because they make us debtors, in particular to him against whom we sin.

"Give us this day our daily bread." When a man shall have been liberated from evil, when he shall have conquered temptations, when his sins shall have been dismissed, then it is even more necessary for him to have the spirit of fortitude, lest he fall short by expecting the reward while he is on the way. Therefore He says: "Give us this day our daily bread," that is, give the spirit of fortitude which strengthens the soul as bread strengthens the body, by which we habitually hunger after justice. For the hunger for justice is compared to [the hunger for] the fatherland, heaven. For justice does not exist in life, except where in the future we shall be sated, full of justice. This goes against sloth which expels the spirit of fortitude and lacks the hunger for justice.

"Thy will be done." The pleading of this petition is formulated on the way and is fulfilled in heaven, where we can wish nothing except what we know God to wish. Therefore one says: "Thy will be done," that is, give the spirit of counsel so that we may do thy will, give the greatest mercy, rather than merely what is necessary. God trains us up in the scriptures, so that we may pursue mercy, which is manifestly opposed to avarice, which expels the spirit of counsel, which advises that all things be distributed to the poor, and nothing be greedily retained.

"Thy kingdom come." That is, give the spirit of understanding, by which, with a heart already cleansed, we understand You to reign at present by faith, so that in the future we may see You reign in our sight. The seeking of this is manifestly opposed to gluttony. For it is fornication, wine, and drunkenness, as the prophet says: "They take away cleanliness of heart, which appeared in the three boys, who were made wiser in understanding by abstinence from food."

"Hallowed by thy name &c." That is, give us the spirit of wisdom, as it is said; that is, pleasure coming from understanding of the law; that is, peace in our generation; that is, interior quiet of movement. And thus shall Your name be hallowed, that is, Father, in this life we cannot be separated from You easily; in the future we cannot be separated at all, for we are undoubtedly Your sons. This obviously opposes lust, by which he who labors in the Lord is not delighted, nor does he have peace of mind when he drags himself about with bestial movements, nor is he the son of God, but is assimilated to the lowest sort of beast.

[On the left side of the wheel, within the frame:]
Three things placed here seem to be the same, namely humility, mildness, and peace. But they are really different things, because humility is called for in injuries of deeds, mildness in slander of words, while meekness might refer to either. For one has the following things in mind, in the prior order, and not on the contrary, for they occur in ascending order according to use, and none should occur habitually without the others. Peace is demonstrated in the quieting of movements, and if sensuality fights against reason, it does not prevail.

[On the right side of the wheel, within the frame:]
Wisdom and intelligence and knowledge are different in this way:

Wisdom is the pleasure arising from the intelligence of God, or the intelligence concerning God arising out of pleasure. Intelligence concerns invisible things under God. Learning concerns human or earthly things, which can be known from human sense and, through the power of the natural intellect, can be led to the effect. There are other gifts of the Holy Spirit, from natural powers, which are nevertheless strengthened through these gifts.

19

The *Disticha Catonis*: Petyt Caton and Book I

Introductory Note: No work was more generally familiar to students between the fourth and the sixteenth centuries than the moral *sententia* that passed under the authorship of "Cato." A detailed study with a modern English translation may be found in W. J. Chase, *The Distichs of Cato* (Madison, Wisc., 1922). The following text includes the Middle English and Latin texts of the preface, the "petyt Caton," and Book I (of Four) of the *Liber Catonis*. The juxtaposition of the Latin and Middle English texts is characteristic of the learned and half-learned jumble of Latin and vernacular languages, half-remembered and often misquoted biblical or secular *sententia*, and the veneer of formal learning superimposed over confused and confusing ideas that characterize much of fourteenth- and fifteenth-century social and cultural literature. The excerpts below are from *The Minor Poems of The Vernon Manuscript*, vol. 2 ed. F. J. Furnivall, Early English Text Society, original series, vol. 117 (London, 1901) 2:553–74. Langland frequently quotes Cato's *sententia*, and even uses Cato as Reason's servant in *Passus IV*.

✤ "petyt Caton"

How þe wyse mon tauhte his sone,
Þat was of tendere age.

Catun was an heþene[1] mon,
Cristned was he nouht:
In word ne in werk aȝeynes vr fey[2]
No techyng he non tauht.

To holy writ[3] al in his bok[4]
A-cordyng was he euere;
Of[5] god of heuene com his wit,[6]
Of oþer com hit neuere.

Þe lore[7] þat he tauȝte his sone,
Is neodful[8] to vs alle;
Vnderstond hose[9] wole,
ffor caas þat may be-falle.
  Whon[10] þat he sauȝ eny mon
Out of rihtful weye,
Hem to teche as hit was best
He letted[11] for non eiȝe,
  Þat þei mihte lerne and here
Siker[12] heore lyf to lede
And gedre[13] wit in heore ȝouþe
And God to loue and drede.—

Cum animaduerterem quam-plurimos homines grauiter errare in via morum, succurrendum opinioni eorum & consulendum forte existimaui, maxime ut gloriose uiuerent et honorem contingerent.

Nunc te, fili carissime, docebo quo pacto animi tui morem componas.

Deore sone, I schal þe teche
Þe maners of my wille,

1. *heþene:* heathen   2. *fey:* faith   3. *writ:* Holy scripture
4. *bok:* Bible   5. *Of:* From   6. *wit:* knowledge   7. *lore:* learning
8. *neodful:* needful, necessary   9. *hose:* whoso   10. *Whon:*When
11. *letted:* ceased, stopped   12. *Siker:* Surely   13. *gedre:* gather

Hou þou schat hem[14] ordeyne
And godes lawe to folfille.[15]

*Igitur mea precepta [ita] legito, vt intelligas: legere non intelligere est
negligere.*

Mi biddyng and my teching
In herte hem vnderstonde;
Ofte to here[16] & nouȝt lerne
Hit is boþe schame & schonde.[17]

Ideoque deo supplica. parentes ama. cognatos cole.

Worschupe god, & him biseche[18]
Of þing þou hast mestere.[19]
ffader & Moder loue þou wel
And hold hem leoue[20] and dere.

Datum serua. foro te para.

Keep þat þing þat þe is ȝiuen
Þorw[21] God or þorw mon.
Whon þou schalt to market,
A-tyre[22] þe as þou con.

Mutuum da. cum bonis ambula.
Cui des videto. ad consilium ne accesseris antequam voceris.

Lene[23] þi good to trewe men,
Þat þer-of falle[24] no wrake.[25]
Loke þat þou go wiþ þe goode,
And wikked men forsake.
To hem also þou ȝiue þi þing
Þerof þe wole bi-seke.
Neuer to counseyl þat þou come,
But ȝif þou cleped[26] be eke.[27]

---

14. *hem:* them   15. *folfille:* fulfill   16. *here:* hear   17. *schonde:* disgrace
18. *biseche:* beseech
19. *Of þing þou hast mestere:* About what you have mastery of
20. *leoue:* beloved   21. *Þorw:* By
22. *A-tyre:* attire   23. *Lene:* Give   24. *falle:* befall, happen
25. *wrake:* wreak, disaster   26. *cleped:* be called   27. *eke:* also

Conuiua raro. mundus esto.
Quod satis est dormi. saluta libenter.

Mak þi gestnyng[28] seldene,[29]
And be chast and clene.
Ȝif i-nouh with-outen more.
Grete men feire by-dene.

Coniugem ama. cede maiori.

Loue þi wyf, and ȝif stude[30] to þe grete.
Whon þi pouwer is lesse;
And whon þou metest hem in þe wey,
þou drede of heore[31] distresse.

Magistrum metue. vino te tempora. verecundiam serua.

A-Mesure þe in drynkynge;
To fleo folye be snelle.[32]
Gedere wit[33] of wyse men,
And let hit wiþ þe dwelle.

Libros lege; quod legeris memento. rem tuam custodi.

Bokes lere;[34] þat þou hast herd,
And hold hem in þi þouht.
Keep þi þing, & sone[35] hit not spende
In long tyme deore[36] was bouht.

Lib[e]ros erudi. diligenciam adhibe.
Blandus esto. iusiurandum serua.

Wit & wisdam, bleþeliche[37]
þi children þat þou teche!
Swere þou not but hit be soþ,[38]
ffor drede[39] of godes wreche.

28. *gestnyng:* conviviality, feasting   29. *seldene:* seldom
30. *ȝif stude:* give stead (place)   31. *drede of heore:* fear of their
32. *To fleo folye be snelle:* Be quick to flee folly
33. *Gedere wit:* Gather knowledge   34. *lere:* read   35. *sone:* immediately
36. *deore:* dearly, expensive   37. *bleþeliche:* gladly
38. *but hit be soþ:* unless it is the truth   39. *drede:* fear, pain

ffamiliam cura. irasci ab re noli.
Neminem irriseris. meretricem fuge.

C[h]astise feire þi seruauns.
ffor luitel beo not wroþ.[40]
Hordam[41] þou forsake,
And scornyng be þe loþ.

In iudicium adesto; ad pretorium stato.

Bleþeliche[42] þou hem helpe
Þat stonden in Iugement;
fflecche not for no bi-heste,
ffor ȝifte ne for rent.

Literas disce. consultus esto.

Let holy writ beo þi mirour
In word and eke[43] in dede.
Of wyse men tak þi counseyl,
Þat con þe wisse and rede.[44]

Bonis benefacito. virtute vtere.
Tutis consule. maledicus ne esto.

Bere þe wel to alle gode men;
And schrewes, forsake hem alle.
Haunte gode werkes & warie[45] not,
Þat[46] hit not on þe falle.

Troco lude; aleas fuge.

Tak a Toppe, ȝif þou wolt pleye,
And not at þe hasardrye.[47]
ffleo þou foles in alle wyse,
And vse no vileynye.

Patere legem quam ipse tuleris.
Equ[u]m iudica. nil mentire.

Such lawe as þou hast brouȝt
And haunted hast bi-fore,

40. *luitel beo . . . wroþ:* little be . . . angry   41. *Hordam:* Whoredom
42. *Blepliche:* Gladly   43. *eke:* also   44. *wisse and rede:* teach and advise
45. *warie:* weary   46. *Þat:* So that   47. *hasardrye:* gambling

þou most hit mekely suffre,
ffor winnyng or for lore.[48]

Beneficiȝ accepti memor esto.
Pauca in conuiuio loquere. minime iudica.

þe godnesse þat men do þe,
þou haue hit ofte in mynde;
Riȝt skile[49] hit wole eke,
Or elles þou art vn-kynde.

Illud stude agere quod iustum est. pugna pro patria.

þenk þou euere in þi lyue
þing þat falleþ to riht.
Ȝif þat Batayle[50] come in to londe,
Defende hit faste[51] wiþ fiht.

Aliena noli concupiscere. parem pacienter vince.

Oþer mennes þing with wronge
Coueyte hit nouȝt in herte.
Haue mesure al of þi-self,
þat wrong þe not smerte.[52]

Minorem ne contemseris.
Noli confidere in tua fortitudine.

Ȝif þou beo a strong mon
And riche of worldes good,
Dispyse þou no luytel mon,
Ne hate hym in þy mod.[53]

end
here endet petyt Caton

✿ Magnus Caton: Book I

Incipit liber catonis
Si deus est animus, nobis ut carmina dicunt,
Hic tibi precipue sit pura mente colendus.

48. *lore:* learning   49. *Riȝt skile:* Right reason   50. *Batayle:* Battle
51. *faste:* firmly   52. *smerte:* smart, sting   53. *mod:* mind, thought

ffor god is lord of alle þing,
As prophetes tellen i-mene,[1]
Þou schalt him in werk[2] honoure,
And wiþ þi þouȝtes clene.

Plus uigila semper: ne sompno deditus esto:
Nam diuturna quies uicijs alimenta ministrat.

Loke þou wake more þen sleple,[3]
And god in alle þing drede;
Long rest and luitel swynk[4]
To vices hit wol þe lede.[5]

Virtutem primam esse puta compescere linguam:
Proximus ille deo est qui scit racione tacere.

Kep þi tonge skilfulliche:
Þe furste vertu forsoþe hit is;[6]
He is next vnto god
Þat kepeþ hit wel i-wis.[7]

Sperne repungnando tibi tu contrarius esse:
Conueniet nulli qui secum desidet ipse.

Be not frouward to þi-self
In word ne in werk:
Wiþ such a mon may non acord—
So telleþ þe wyse clerk.

Si uitam inspicias hominum, si denique mores,
Cum culpas alios nemo sine crimine uiuit.

Whon þou blamest oþer men,
Þyn oune Iuge þou ne be![8]
Þer nis no[9] mon with-outen lak,
As men may wel ofte i-se.

---

1. *i-mene:* I think   2. *werk:* work   3. *sleple:* sleep
4. *swynk:* work   5. *lede:* lead
6. *Þe furste vertu forsoþe hit is:* It is truly the first virtue   7. *i-wis:* I know
8. *Þyn oune Iuge þou ne be:* Be not thine own judge   9. *nis no:* is no

Que nocturna tenes, quamuis sint cara, relinque:
Vtilitas opibus preponi tempore debet.

> þing þat wole apeire þi stat,[10]
> Beo hit þe neuer so lef,[11]
> Hastiliche do hit þe fro,[12]
> Or þou þole þe gref.[13]

Constans & lenis ut res expostulat esto:
Temporibus mores sapiens sine crimine mutat.

> Studefast[14] & stille þou be,
> As þi catel wol aske:[15]
> Þe wyse mon liueþ withouten blame,
> ffor he con wel hym taske.[16]

Nil temere uxori de seruis crede querenti:
Sepe etenim mulier quem coniux diligit odit.

> Leeue[17] not þi wyf fulliche
> Of þi seruans pleynande:[18]
> Ofte falleþ,[19] þe wyf hit hateþ
> Þat loueþ þe goode hosebande.

Cumque mones aliquem nec se uelit ipse moneri,
Si tibi sit carus, noli desistere ceptis.

> ȝif þou wolt chastise eny mon,
> Þouh he loue not þi lore;
> ȝif he be dere, leue him nouȝt,[20]
> But vndertake hym more.

Contra verbosos noli contendere verbis:
Sermo datur multis, animi sapiencia paucis.

> Aȝeynes men ful of wordes
> Stryue[21] þow riht nouht:

---

10. *stat:* harm   11. *lef:* dear   12. *do hit þe fro:* put it aside
13. *þole þe gref:* suffer grief yourself   14. *Studefast:* Steadfast
15. *catel . . . aske:* property . . . demand
16. *con wel hym taske:* knows well what to do   17. *Leeue:* Believe
18. *pleynande:* complaining   19. *Ofte felleþ:* It often happens
20. *leue him nouȝt:* don't let him off   21. *Stryue:* Strive, contend

Wordes is ȝiuen[22] to alle men,
And wisdom selden[23] brouht.

Dilige sic alios ut sis tibi carus amicus;
Sit bonus esto bonis ne te mala dampna sequantur.

Loue so wel oþure men,
Þin oune frend þat þou be;[24]
Beo so good to alle men,
Þat harm from þe fle.

Rumores fuge, ne incipias nouus auctor haberi:
Nam nulli tacuisse nocet, nocet esse locutum.

Of newe tales[25] þou ne be
ffurst makere I-founde:
Wikked tales a-mong men
Bringeþ loue to grounde.

Rem tibi promissam certam promittere noli:
Rara fides ideo quia multi multa locuntur.

Þing þat þe by-hoten[26] is,
Loke on none wyse[27]
Þat þou bi-hote hit to no oþer,
ffor þer mihte strif aryse.

Cum te aliquis laudat iudex tuus esse memento:
Plus alijs de te quam tu tibi credere noli.

Ȝif men preise þe for godnesse,
Þin oune herte þou tast;[28]
Leeue[29] non bettre þen þi self,
Wheþer þou þat vertu hast.

Officium alterius multis narrare memento,
Atque alijs cum tu benefeceris ipse sileto:

Þou maiȝt oþur mennes goodnesse
Preisen wiþ-outen blame,

22. *Wordes is ȝiuen:* Words are given   23. *selden:* seldom
24. *Þin oune frend þat þou be:* That thou be thine own friend
25. *newe tales:* rumors   26. *by-hoten:* promised
27. *on none wyse:* in no way   28. *tast:* taste   29. *Leeue:* Believe

But not þin owne be-fore men,
ffor hit were but a schame.

Multorum cum facta senex & dicta recenses,
ffac tibi succurrant iuuenisque feceris ipse.

> Sun, do her[30] in þi ȝouþe
> Þing þat þe mouwe[31] helpe;
> Whon þou art an old mon aftur,
> Þerof þenne maiȝt þou ȝelpe.[32]

Ne cures siquis tacito sermone loquatur:
Conscius ipse sibi de se putat omnia dici.

> Ȝif þou seo men speke stille,[33]
> A-Meoued beo þou nouȝt:[34]
> Þe wikked mon weneþ[35] þat alle men
> Haue him in heore þouht.

Cum fueris felixque sunt aduersa caueto:
Non eodem cursu respondent (vltima) primis.

> Ȝif þou, mon, be meke and mylde,
> ffleo al frouward[36] þing;
> Þe laste tale to þe furste
> Ȝif non onsweryng.

Cum dubia & fragilis sit nobis uita tributa,
In mortem alterius spem tu tibi ponere noli.

> Siþen þat vre lyf is frele[37]
> Þat to vs alle is ȝiuen,
> In non oþur monnes deþ
> Hope þou nouȝt to liuen.

Exiguum munus cum det tibi pauper amicus,
Accipito placide, plene laudare memento.

> Ȝif eny of þi pore frendes
> Ȝiue þe a ȝift smal,

30. *her:* here   31. *mouwe:* must   32. *ȝelpe:* boast
33. *seo . . . stille:* see . . . secretely
34. *A-Meoued beo þou nouȝt:* Be not upset   35. *weneþ:* thinks
36. *frouward:* adverse   37. *frele:* frail

Receyue þou hit bleþeliche,[38]
And þonk him feire[39] þou schal.

Infantem nudum cum te natura creauit,
Paupertatis onus pacienter ferre memento.

Siþen þat kynde haþ þe formed
A luytel naked chylde,
Þe charge of pouert loke þou bere,
And beo boþe meke & mylde.

Ne timeas illam que uite est ultima finis:
Qui mortem metuit amittit gaudia uite.

Whon þou schalt nedelich ones dye
And heþene[40] awey to wende,
Doute hit not, for þou3t þer-of
Mihte þe fulliche schende.[41]

Si tibi pro meritis nemo respondet amicus,
Incusare deum noli, set te ipse coerce.

3if no mon onswere to þe
ffor þi goddede[42] bi nome,
Wraþþe þe[43] not þerfore wiþ god,
Bote þi-seluen blame.

Ne tibi quid desit quesitis, vtere parce;
Vt-que quod est serues, semper tibi deesse putato.

Spene þi good mesurabliche,[44]
Purchased þau3 þei be;
And hope alle þinges þat þou hast
Awey mihte falle from þe.

Quod prestare potes, ne bis promiseris vlli,
Ne sis uentosus dum vis bonus esse videri.

Þing also þat þou may 3rue,
Twyes bi-hote[45] hit nou3t;

38. *bleþeliche:* gladly   39. *þonk him feire:* thank him fairly
40. *heþene:* have to   41. *schende:* make afraid
42. *goddede:* good deeds   43. *Wraþþe þe:* Be not angry
44. *Spene . . . mesurabliche:* Spend . . . moderately   45. *bi-hote:* promise

Beo not ful of wikked wynt[46]
And leose not þi fore þou3t.[47]

Qui simulat verbis, nec corde est fidus amicus;
Tu quoque fac simile: sic ars deluditur arte.

Hose feyneþ[48] him frend with word
And not wiþ herte stable,
With such a seruyse serue þou him,
And telle him tale of fable.

Noli homines blando nimium sermone probare:
ffistula dulce canit volucrem dum decipit auceps.

Preyse no mon but in his riht
With no losengerye;[49]
Þe foulere chaccheþ briddes feole[50]
Wiþ swete melodye.

Cum tibi sint nati nec opes, tunc artibus illos
Instrue, quo possint inopem defendere vitam.

3if þou haue children monye
And goodes none bute smale,
Sone þou hem to craft sette,[51]
Þer-wiþ to beeten heore bale.[52]

Quod vile est, carum; quod carum, vile putato:
Sic tibi nec cupidus, nec auarus nosceris vlli.

Þat is good chep may beo dere,
And deore good chep[53] also;
Loke þou beo not coueytous
Ne gredi ek þer-to.

Que culpare soles, ea tu ne feceris ipse:
Turpe est doctori, cum culpa redarguit ipsum.

Þing þat þou art wont to blame,
Loke þou do hit nouht!

46. *wynt:* wind   47. *leose . . . fore pou3t:* lose . . . fore thought
48. *Hose feyneþ:* Whoso deceives   49. *losengerye:* flattery
50. *Þe foulere chaccheþ briddes feole:* The fowler chases many birds
51. *Sone þou hem to craft sette:* Immediately set them to a trade
52. *beeten heore bale:* lessen their suffering   53. *good chep:* a good bargain

Schome hit is a mon to blame
þing þat he haþ wrouht.

Quod iustum est, petito, vel quod videatur honestum:
Nam stultum est petere, quod possit iure negari.

Aske þing þat rihtful is
Or honest in þi siht:
ffolye hit is to aske þe good
þat is to werne[54] wiþ riht.

Ignotum tibi tu noli preponere notis:
Cognita iudicio constant[i], incognita casu.

Loue bettre a knowen frend
þen mon of fer cuntre:
þorw de-faute of knoweleching
þou mai3t[55] i-greued be.

Cum dubia in certis uersetur vita periculis,
Pro lucro tibi pone diem, quocumque laboras.

Siþen dredful is deþ, diliueret[56]
In eorþe to al monkunne,[57]
Do þi labour eueri day
Sum good forte winne.

Vincere cum possis, interdum vince ferendo;
Obsequio quoniam dulces retinentur amici.

Sum tyme spare þi felawe
þou3 þou ouercome him miht;[58]
Parfyt[59] loue is þer non
Whon[60] 3e striue in riht.

Ne dubites, cum magna petas, impendere parua:
Hiis etenim rebus coniungit gracia caros.

To 3eue[61] luitel, dred þe nou3t,
þer[62] þou askest grete

54. *werne:* refuse   55. *mai3t:* might
56. *Siþen . . . diliueret:* Since . . . delivered   57. *monkunne:* mankind
58. *þou3 þou ouercome him miht:* Though you might (could) overcome him
59. *Parfyt:* Perfect   60. *Whon:* When   61. *3eue:* give   62. *þer:* When

Of þi frendes and neihebors—
Þat costum wol not lete.[63]

Litem inferre caue, cum quo tibi gracia iuncta est:
Ira odium generat, concordia nutrit amorem.

To þi felawe wel willynge
Sture[64] þou no chidynge;
Wraþþe gedereþ[65] gret hate,
Loue norisscheþ sauȝtynge.[66]

Seruorum ob culpam cum te dolor vrget in Iram,
Ipse tibi moderare, tuis ut parcere possis.

Ȝif serwe of gult of seruauns[67]
Wol þe bringe in care,
I rede[68] þou tempre þe so wel
Þat tyme þat þou hem spare.

Quem superare potes, interdum uince ferendo;
Maxima etenim morum est semper paciencia virtus.

Þe mon þat þou maiȝt ouergo,
Wiþ suffrance him ouercome;
Meknes[69] is vertu gret
Wiþ pure riht of dome.[70]

Conserua pocius, que sunt iam parta labore:
Cum labor in dampno est, crescit mortalis egestas.

Þinges þat þou hast gederet
Wiþ gret bisynesse,
Wysliche þou hem spene,[71]
ffor pereles more and lesse.[72]

Dapsilis interdum notis & carus amicis;
Cum fueris felix, semper tibi proximus esto.

---

63. *lete:* die out, abate   64. *Sture:* Stir up
65. *Wraþþe gedereþ:* Wrath gathers   66. *sauȝtynge:* reconciling
67. *gult of seruauns:* guilt of servants   68. *rede:* advise
69. *Meknes:* Meekness   70. *riht of dome:* judgment   71. *spene:* spend
72. *pereles more and lesse:* pearls great and small

20

"How men that ben in hele sholde visite sike folk..."

Introductory Note: "How men that ben in hele sholde visite sike folk" belongs to the large class of instructional literature directed at what came to be called the *ars moriendi*, the skill of holy dying. Although the rules insisted that it was always at least possible, right living might not always be achieved, for the world was a place full of temptations and dangers to the soul. The penitent Christian, however, could always achieve a good death. And so the layman, but even more the priest, should know what to say to a sick man or woman in order to prepare the dying for death and to assure the salvation of the soul. Part of this treatise takes the form of general instructions, and part a treatise of specific questions to ask the dying penitent. This tract follows *Piers Plowman* in Cambridge University Library Ms. Dd. 1. 17, fols. 550ʳ–551ʳ. It was edited for this volume by M. Vescott Driver and Jeanne Krochalis. The text can also be found in Gonville and Caius College, Cambridge, Ms. 209, fols. 149ᵛff and in Cambridge University Library Ms. Nn. 4. 12, vols. 29ᵛff.

In *Passus* XX, Will the Dreamer is attacked by Elde (Old Age), who makes him bald, deafens him, knocks out his teeth, and inflicts the gout upon him. Will's wife, seeing his misery, prays that he might be taken up to heaven, and the little scene echoes those texts on the proper preparation for dying that abounded in the fourteenth and fifteenth centuries. "How men that ben in hele sholde visite sike folk" is one such text, a manual for conduct at the death-bed that will save the soul of the decedent.

✣ *How men that ben in hele sholde visite sike folk*

My dere sone or doughter in God, it semees þat thow hiest[1] the fast in the way fra this lif to Godward. Thare shalt thow se al thi forine[2] faders, apostels, martirs, confessours, virgynes, and alle men and wymmen that ben saved. And for gladnesse of swich felawschip, be than of good conforth in God, and thenk how thow moost aftir this lif ligge[3] a stoon in the walle of the Citee of hevene, slighlich,[4] withouten any noys or strif. And tharfore, or[5] thow wende out of this world, thow moost polisshe thy stoon and make it redy, if thow wolt nat ther be letted.[6] This stoon is thi saule, wiche thou moost make stronge thurgh right bileve and faire. Thow moost it clense thourgh hope of Goddes mercy; and perfit charite the while helees the multitude of synnes. The noys þat thow moost make here in worthyng[7] of this stoon is ofte forthynkyng of thy synne, wich thow moost knowlich[8] to God, knowyng the gilty. And therafter it is profitabile to the to have conseil of trewe preestes, the whiche owen[9] to blisse the pepile, tellyng hem that ben sorwful for hir synnes that thay shalle, thurgh Goddes mercy, be assoiled[10] of hem.

The strook wharewith thow slikkest[11] this stoon is verreye repentaunce that thow shalt have in thyn herte, sorwyng of thy synne, smytyng thy self in the brest with grete sikyns[12] of sorwe, and stedfast wille to torne no more ayein to synne. And whan thow hast made redy thus thy stoon, that is thi saule, thanne myghte thow go the redy[13] way to God, and lay thy staan sikyliche[14] withouten noyful[15] noyse in the Citee of Hevene; and therfore I conseille the in this lif, that thow shryve[16] the clene to God, and make the redy

---

1. *hiest:* go   2. *forine:* ancestral   3. *ligge:* lie   4. *slighlich:* skillfully
5. *or:* before   6. *letted:* hindered   7. *worthyng:* making worthy
8. *knowlich:* acknowledge   9. *owen:* ought   10. *assoiled:* cleansed
11. *slikkest:* polish   12. *sikyns:* sighing   13. *redy:* quick
14. *silkliche:* quietly   15. *noyful:* harmful, annoying   16. *shryve:* confess

for grisly devels, the which han tempted men to synne in this lif wollen[17] in the last houre be ful bisy to bigile hem, and namely with despayr of Goddes mercy. And this is nat onlyche[18] to telle to sike men, but ek[19] to hale men, for every day a man neighed[20] his deth nere[21] and nere. For the more a man in this lif wexeth in dayes and yeres, the more he unwexes. For as sayntes sayen, the first day in the which a man is borne, is the first day of his deth, for every day he is dying while he is in this lif. And therfore, sayes the Gospel, awake, for thow wost[22] nevere whilc[23] houre God is to come, in thy youthe or in thy mydel age, or in thy laste dayes, or privelich[24] or openlich. And therfore loke that thow be alway redy, for it is semeliche[25] that the servant abide[26] the Lord, and nat the Lord the servant. And namelich, whan grete hast is, he is worthy blame that is unredy. But gretter hast no man redees[27] of, than shal be in the comyng of Crist; and therfore wakees in vertues, for whan the yate is schet,[28] it is nevere after opened. And therfore, brother or suster in God, wite[29] thow that God visites men for hir synnes diversliche. Som ben visited with scharp prisonyng, som with sclaunder and bakbityng, som with untrouthe of false men, and som with diverse siknesse. And if that synne were clene away, thane siknesse sholde slake;[30] hyreof berees the Gospel witnesse, where Crist saied to ten nicles[31] whan they were heled of hire lepere: "Goth," he sayes, "and nyl ye synne more, lest ye falle worse." Als who seith for youre synne ye hadde this sikenesse, and tharefor the lawe wolde by right justice that no leche[32] sholde yeve bodilich medycyne to a sike man, but he were in wille to take gostliche[33] medycyne, and for to leve synne that wondes[34] his saule, schryvynge hym trewlich with goode wille to do no more yvel. For so he receyvees God, dwellynge in perfit charite. And who that his thus trewlich schryvyng and dwellees in verray repentance, ydred nowht that ne thyne sikenesse shal salke which he had for his synne. Or elles hise peynes suffred with mekenesse shal torne hym to synne mykille[35] merite in bliss after this lif. Therfore if thy paynes slake nat, confort the in God on this manere.

17. *wollen:* will　　18. *onlyche:* only　　19. *ek:* also　　20. *neighed:* nears
21. *nere:* nearer　　22. *wost:* know　　23. *whilc:* what
24. *privelich:* privately　　25. *semeliche:* fitting　　26. *abide:* await
27. *redees:* imagines　　28. *yate is schet:* gate is shut　　29. *wite:* know
30. *slake:* let up　　31. *nicles:* lepers　　32. *leche:* doctor
33. *wille . . . gostliche:* willing . . . spiritual　　34. *wondes:* wounds
35. *mykille:* much, great

�֍ How a man scholde confort another that he
grucche nowth whan he hise sike.

Brother or syster, lovestow God thy lord? He or sche, if thay may
speke, wyle say "Ya." Or peraventure,[36] if thay mowe[37] nat speke,
thay wyle thynke she than thus: if thow lovest God, thow lovest al
that he does. And he scorgees[38] the for thy profet, and not for his;
and tharfore thow sholdest gladly suffre hym and love hym, for he
wyle nowht punyse hym twyes that mekelyche[39] suffres hym. And
that his chastisyng in this lif is al for love schewees[40] Salomon, where
he sayes "Sone, grucche nat ayeins[41] the chastisyng of thy fader, for
it is no sone who the fader chastise nowht." And this acordees with
reson, and als[42] with comune manere of speche. For if a man se
another mannes childe do yvele in his faderes presence, and his fader
chastise hym nouht, than wyle that other man say that it is nowht
hise childe, or elles that he lovees hym nowht. For if he were his
childe, or elles loved hym, he walde[43] chastise hym. And tharefore
be nat yvel payed of thy faderes chastisyng of hevene, fore he sayes
hym self: "Wham I love I chastise." Also siknese of body mekeliche
suffred makees hele of saule, and saule helthe[44] is nat bot oonlische[45]
of God. Therfore, dispise nat Goddes scourgyng, bot whan God
chastise the, thanke hym and love hym that he amendees the and
undirnymees[46] the, and blamees the. For al this is tokne of love that
God wyle not punysse the[47] in his wrathe ne in his wodnesse;[48] bot
of his grete godnesse, he wile have mercy on the if thow wolt leve
thy synne. And therfore thanke thi God and specialiche that he
hath larged[49] to synful men his mercy aboven his wrathe. Drede this
lord as sone[50] and nat as servaunt, for he his thi jugge[51] that wile
nat dampne the. But if thow wolt nat for lust and coveitise[52] leve thy
synne but he wole have mercy on the, and therfore mercyfulliche he
chastise the. And ther thow hast deserved everelastyng his wrathe,
and be dampned for evere, he puttes over[53] his vengeaunce; of his

36. peraventure: possibly, by chance   37. mowe: may
38. scorgees: scourges   39. mekelyche: meekly   40. schewees: shows
41. ayeins: complain   42. als: also   43. walde: would   44. helthe: heath
45. oonlische: only   46. undirnymees: undertakes
47. punysse the: punish thee   48. wodnesse: madness, rage
49. larged: increased   50. sonne: a son   51. jugge: judge
52. coveitise: covetousness, avarice   53. puttes over: puts by

grete mercy, he suffres us to amende oure defautes, and punysse us bot a while. And therfore, dispise nat his yerd[54] of mercy, ne grucche[55] nat ther ayeins,[56] bot suffre it gladliche for alle the domes[57] of God ben rightful.

Now sith sikenesse of body is hele of saule, and wil or nyl[58] thow, thow shalt have it or thow dye, and if þow grucche ayein God, with thy grucching thow makest thy self more fiebile,[59] and so thow harmest thy self with thy grucchyng, for no thyng is wors to a sik man than to be malencolyus.[60] And als thow grevest thy fadir, the whilc[61] coveites to be thy lecche;[62] and thus as a fool thow harmest thy self on double manere. Oon is that thow grevest thy God, and another is that thow lessest thy mede[63] that thow scholdest have if thow suffred eft alle manere of disese pacienliche[64] to þe deth. And though a man som tyme may nat kepe in siknesse pacience for grete accesse of diverse passiones, nertheles he shold, bifore thay come and after the passyng of hem, purpose[65] in his saule to suffre alle noyes paciencliche. And whan is hors[66] grucches, that is his flesshe, knowyng that alle bodily anoyes[67] suffred in this lif mekelich makes the soule faire and stronge and rightliche to passe fra[68] purgatorie to hevene; wherfore we shold with good wille hery God, and with good herte take diseises. Thenk that if thow haddest ben traitour to þe kyng, wherfore thow haddest disserved[69] hangyng and drawyng, and he had foryeve the thy deth, and punysshe the bot a litile while in a esy prisoun, how mykile were thow holde[70] to hym! Muche more thow sholdest bithynke the how thow hast ben traitour to God, and therfore deserved everelastyng payne, and yit this mercyful lord foryeves us here endeles deth, the which we han disserved, and punysshe us here but a little with bodiliche[71] sikenesse, if we wollen[72] mekeliche take his chastysyng.

✥ If Deth Go Faste on a Man, Speke to Hym Thus

Brother or syster in God, if thow sawe or bithoughtest the in thyn herte the meschiefs of this wrecched world, and the joies of

54. *yerd:* yard   55. *grucche:* complain   56. *ayeins:* against
57. *domes:* judgments   58. *nyl:* not wish   59. *fiebile:* feeble
60. *malencolyus:* melancholy   61. *whilc:* which   62. *lecche:* doctor
63. *lessest thy mede:* lose thy reward   64. *pacienliche:* patiently
65. *purpose:* intend   66. *is hors:* his horse   67. *anoyes:* annoyances
68. *fra:* from   69. *disserved:* deserved
70. *mykile . . . holde:* much beholden   71. *bodiliche:* bodily
72. *wollen:* will

hevene, thow sholdest desire to be with God. And thow were lord
of al this world and thow stode in grace, thow sholdest forsake it
to come to hevene, for Holy Writ sayes: "Blessed be thay that dyen
in God." Loke, the bigynnung of this lif is care, and sorwe; lyvynge
therinne, what is it but muche travaille withouten fruyt—tene and
disese whereþur3[73] many men ben overcomen with diverse temptacions, and forgeten hir God, and so thay come to an yvel ende.
Loke now wether it is better to dye wele or to lyve yvel? If thow
stande in verray repentaunce and last therinne stedfastlich, bilevyng
in the mercy of God, thow maist dye wele. Bot hard it is to lyve
wele fulliche in this wrecchid world, for the haly prophete sayes
that every man is a lier. That is to say, for his first forfeture everych
man synnees[74] whiles he lyvees in this wrecched lif, outher for
levyng of servyng of God after hise comandementes, or elles for
that he servees hym nough[75] after his worthynese. For Haly Writ
sayes that sevene sithes[76] in the day falles the rightful man, and
Saynt Poule[77] sayes that no man lyveth in this lif withouten defaute.
Therfore we shulden pray to God with grette disire, if it were his
wille that we weren dede and leveden[78] with hym, for the wrecchednesse of this world may no man telle. For here his[79] honger of
Goddes lawe, and few thad [sic] desires[80] therafter, and thay that
thristen[81] therafter ben oft tymes slaked with bitter venym;[82] and
therfore the charite of many waxes cold thurgh the hete of wikked
coveitise. For longe travaille and grete that men han after bodiliche
bisynesse and lustes maken many men so wery that thay suffisen
nat[83] to come to a good ende. For this lif is ful of envye, wrathe, and
glotonye, and lecherie, pride and sleuthe, coveitise, and falshed,
manslaughter and thefte, and of many other wikkednesse that
spryngen of thise. And ther nys no man that he ne hasse som of
thise, for no man in this lif lyvees withouten synne. And many men
ben combred[84] with alle thise, and yit thay kan not ne wollen nat
discharge hem. And therfore thise philosophres the which knowen
the wricchednesse of this lif made grete sorwe whan hir childerne
weren bore,[85] and grete joie whan thay dyeden, and passeden fro the
wo of this fals world. And as man fynden writen, Seynt Aystyn,[86]

73. *whereþur3:* through which   74. *synnees:* sins   75. *nough:* not
76. *sithes:* times   77. *Saynt Poule:* St. Paul   78. *leveden:* lived
79. *here his:* here is   80. *few thad desires:* few who desire
81. *thristen:* thirst   82. *venym:* venom   83. *suffisen nat:* do not suffice
84. *combred:* encumbered   85. *bore:* born   86. *Seynt Aystyn:* St. Augustine

whan he sholde be dede, spake to the deth on this manere: "Welcom, deth, ende of al wikkednesse! For thow are ende of travaille[87] to hem that hir[88] wele travailled, for than and nou rather bygynneth profitliche goode mennes eise[89] and endelees blisse! What man nay bithynke the profit, and the blisse, that thow bryngest with the? Therfore thow are desireful to me; for a trewe cristen man may nat yvel dyen, for after this lif he shal lyve with Crist."

 Whan thow Hast Tolde Hym Al This, or Ells If Thow Myght Nat For Hast of Deth, Bigyn Here or Hise Mynde Go Fro Hym.

Brother or Syster, artow[90] glad that thow shalt dyen in Cristen faith? Responsio: "Ye."

Knowlechest thow to[91] God that thow hast nat lyved after hise comandement? Responsio: "Ye."

Artow sory that thow levedest nat as thow shuldeste? Responsio: "Ye."

Artow in good wille to amende alle trespasses done ayeins[92] God and thyn evene Cristen, if thow haddest space to lyve? Responsio: "Ye."

Tristestowe[93] stedfastlich that God may forgeve the and alle men here[94] synnes, though thow ne noon other make here fullich asseeþ for hem? Responsio: "Ye."

Levestow[95] in God, Fader almyghty, maker of hevene and of herthe,[96] and of alle that ben in hem? Responsio: "Ye."

Levestow that Oure Lord Jhesu Crist, Goddes Sone of hene,[97] was conceyved oonliche of the Holy Goost, and took flessh and blood of Oure Lady Seinte Mary, and sho mayden and moder after his byrthe? Responsio: "Ye."

Levestow that Jhesy Crist suffred hard payne and deth for oure trespas, and nat for his gilt? Responsio: "Ye."

87. *travaille:* labor   88. *hir:* here   89. *eise:* ease
90. *artow:* are you   91. *Knowlechest thow to:* Do you acknowledge
92. *ayeins:* against   93. *Tristestowe:* Do you trust
94. *here:* their   95. *Levestow:* Do you believe   96. *herthe:* earth
97. *hene:* heaven

Levestow that he was after his deth byried, and roos in the thridde
day in flessh, and fleighe[98] to hevene, and sent the Holy Goost, and
shal come to deme[99] bothe wikked and good, yeldyng[100] hem after
hir travaille? Responsio. [Ye.]

Thankestow hym of alle thyne herte for this grete goodnesse that he
hase don wilfulliche to mannes kynde? Responsio: "Ye."

Levestow that thow ne no man may be saved bot thurgh his passion
and his[101] mercy? Responsio: "Ye."

While thy saule is in thi bodi, put al thi trist[102] in his mercy,
praying hym for his moder love that he wol of his goodnesse to do
the bettre that thow kanst desire; and have therfore stedfastlich to
thyn ende his passion and his grete mercy in thy mynde, for ther
thorugh onliche ben alle enemys overcomen. Therfore medele[103] thy
thought with his passion, and wrappe the as in a cloth in his mercy,
and trist stedfastliche on the passion of our Lord Jhesu Crist suffred
on the cros lastynglich in thy mynde. And if thow biholde any cros
or ymage made with mannes hondes, witow wele that it is nat God,
and therfore say or thynke in thyn herte and woot wele that thow
art not God, bot ymaged[104] after hym, to make men have more
mynde of hym after whom thow art ymaged. Therfor, Lord Fader
that art in heven, mercy I aske the, of al that I have trespassed; and
the wilful passion of Oure Lord Jhesu Crist, the which he suffred
for mankynde, mercyful fader, of thy goodnesse be it bytwine me
and myn evel dedes. And the gret merite of Oure Lord Jhesu Crist
queme[105] it to the, for al that ich shold have disserved and don and
did nat. Also mercy, ful god Fader of Heven, if it be thy wile, I
biseche the that alle the bienfates[106] of Oure Lord Jhesu Crist after
thy biddyng dide here in herthe[107] for savacioun of man stonde
bitwixe me and thy wrathe, and lady modder of mercy, Seint Marie,
quene of hevene and lady of this world, and Emperise of helle, as
thow deservest bifor alle wymmen thurgh thy goodnesse, of God to
beren withouten wein[108] of thy maidenhode, Jhesu Crist, saveour of
mankynde, thow bisech thy sone for me that my synnes alle forgyven

---

98. *fleighe:* flew, fled   99. *deme:* judge   100. *yeldyng:* giving, rewarding
101. *his:* his, i.e., Christ's   102. *trist:* trust   103. *medele:* mingle
104. *ymaged:* made in the image, fashioned   105. *queme:* comfort, soothe
106. *bienfates:* good deeds   107. *herthe:* earth   108. *wein:* lamenting

me, lord Jhesu Crist, sith[109] thy Haly Gospel witnesseth that thow wolt nat deth of a synful man, bot that he be torned fram synne and lyve. Have mercy of me, synful, after thy word, and as thow blamedest Symond,[110] for he had indignacion that Marye for hir synnes shold neighe[111] the, have mercy on me, moost synful. And as thow clepedest[112] Zachee and Poule and other diverse fram hir synnes, dispise nat me that cometh to the wilfulliche, withoute swich clepyng,[113] and though I have leye[114] longe in my synne, thenke on the grete mercy that thow haddest, and sholdest to mankynde that he sholde nat shame ne dispise of thy mercy, though al he hadde longe leye in synne. Whan thow haddest no desdeyn to rere Lazer[115] though al he hadde leye in his grave four dayes stynkyng, and herefore I trist to the, for thow are fader almyghty, in whos mercy I triste, to whose refute[116] I flee with grete desire. I come to the, heigh Jugge; Lord, dispise nat me though I be wrycched and synful, for I triste to thyn help in al my grete nede. For I knowlich[117] I may nat helpe my self, ne ayein bygge[118] me with my dedes, bot stedfastlich I trist in thi passion, that it suffises to make ful asseeth to þe fader of hevene for my synnes. Therfore, Lord, bryng me out of care, and have mercy of me. I triste nat to my dedes, bot I dispise to trist in hem, fullich tristyng in the grette mercy, dispysing my wikked dedes, for thow art my God, in whom, I trowe stedfastliche, is al myght and mercy and good wille, what thurth[119] I hope to be saved. And therfore to the that art ful of mercy, I knowlich my synne, the whiche I have don thurgh myn owene defaute. I knowliche my gilt; have mercy of me, for I trow trewliche that thow denyest thy mercy to non that trewlich tristen therto. And in Crist therfore I forsake with al myn herte this lif, to lyve with the, and in thyn hondes, Lord almyghti and merciful, I bitake my soule, for fra the bigynnyng of this world hath thy mercy be redy to synful men, and so I triste it shal be to me in my ende. Therfore, God my Lord, ful of trouthe, take my saule, for it is thyn. Do therto as the likes, for I woot of thy goodnesse it shal fare better than it hase disserved. Receyve it, and help it, for in thy merciful handes I put it. Amen. Amen.

---

109. *sith:* since   110. *Symond:* Simon Peter
111. *neighe:* come near, approach   112. *clepedest:* called
113. *clepying:* calling   114. *leye:* lain   115. *rere Lazer:* raise up Lazarus
116. *refute:* refuge   117. *knowlich:* acknowledge
118. *bygge:* buy   119. *what thurth:* through which

21

Guild and Fraternity

Introductory Note: The extraordinary variety of forms of association in the Middle Ages and in traditional Europe generally has often been obscured by the more familiar hierarchical arrangement of society. In spite of the theoretical and real power of superiors, however, what Marc Bloch has called "horizontal associations" played an important role in all aspects of social life. Religious guilds and fraternities constituted another way of organizing the village or parish, a way which often gave their lay members considerably more scope and authority than they normally possessed in devotional affairs. Commercial guilds, including the guilds merchant, organized the practitioners of a trade or profession and had considerable impact on legal and economic institutions. Sometimes, as in Dante's Florence, for example, guild membership became a prerequisite for holding political office, and in general guilds played many roles, few of which were exclusive. Thus, to consider the guilds and fraternities of traditional Europe as close equivalents of modern labor unions, marketing associations, or trade institutes is to miss the multiplicity of functions that all guilds performed for their members.

Few guilds, no matter how economically oriented, were wholly without their religious and social dimensions. In a world where the sacramental and legal supports of the family were slight and the larger organizations were supervised by lay or spiritual lords, the guilds formed an important association in the life of each of their members. Like the religious orders, in a sense, they constituted a legitimate and protected area for lay association, and they too expressed individual and collective concern for the problems that other selections in this book also tried to deal with. Their variety, the wide scope of their activities, and their role in developing lay devotion and bonds of association make the guilds an important and powerful element in the life of later medieval society.

The following selections are taken from E. P. Cheney, *English Towns and Gilds*, Translations and Reprints from the Original Sources of European History, vol. 2, no. 1 (Philadelphia, 1900). A larger collection of documents is that of Lucy Toulmin Smith and Lujo Brentano, *English Gilds*, Early English Text Society, Original Series, vol. 40 (London, 1870; rpt. London, 1963), and a fine study of a particular group of guilds is that of Pierre Duparc, "Confraternities of the Holy Spirit and Village Communities in the Middle Ages," in Fredric L. Cheyette, ed., *Lordship and Community in Medieval Europe* (New York, 1968), pp. 341–56.

Passus VI in *Piers Plowman* shows Piers setting the world to work, allocating jobs and functions and generally organizing society along the lines of separate crafts and arts that the documents below reveal. The little communities that these guilds constituted absorbed much of their members' lives and energies. At the end of *Passus* VI, when Piers' little world has collapsed, the poet denounces the circumstances of a world in which such organization is not permitted to succeed:

> And that he was werkman wrou3t waille the tyme,
> A3eines Catones conseille comseth he to Iangle—
> *Paupertatis onus pacienter ferre memento.*
> He greuth him a3eines god, and gruccheth a3eines resoun,
> And thanne curseth he the kynge and al his conseille after,
> Suche lawes to loke, laboreres to greue.

❧ A. Articles of the Spurriers of London, 1345

In English Towns and Gilds, *pp. 21–23. Original text in*
H. T. Riley, Memorials of London (*London, 1868*), *pp. 226–28.*

Be it remembered, that on Tuesday, the morrow of St.
Peter's Chains, in the nineteenth year of the reign of King Edward III, the articles underwritten were read before John Ham-
mond, mayor, Roger de Depham, recorder, and the alderman;
and seeing that the same were deemed befitting, they were accepted and enrolled in these words.

In the first place—that no one of the trade of spurriers shall
work longer than from the beginning of the day until curfew
rung out at the Church of St. Sepulchre, without Newgate; by
reason that no man can work so neatly by night as by day.
And many persons of the said trade, who compass how to practice
deception in their work, desire to work by night rather by day;
and then they introduce false iron, and iron that has been
cracked, for tin, and also they put gilt on false copper, and
cracked. And further—many of the said trade are wandering
about all day, without working at all at their trade; and then,
when they have become drunk and frantic, they take to their
work, to the annoyance of the sick, and all their neighborhood,
as well by reason of the broils that arise between them and the
strange folks who are dwelling among them. And then they blow
up their fires so vigorously, that their forges begin all at once
to blaze to the great peril of themselves and of all the neighborhood around. And then, too, all the neighbors are much in dread
of the sparks, which so vigorously issue forth in all directions
from the mouths of the chimneys in their forges. By reason
thereof it seems unto them that working by night should be
put an end to, in order such false work and such perils to avoid:
and therefore the mayor and the aldermen do will, by the assent
of the good folks of the said trade, and for the common profit,
that from henceforth such time for working, and such false work
made in the trade, shall be forbidden. And if any person shall
be found in the said trade to do the contrary hereof, let him
be amerced, the first time in 40d., one-half thereof to go to the

use of the Chamber of the Guildhall of London, and the other half to the use of the said trade; the second time, in half a mark, and the third time in 10s., to the use of the same Chamber and trade; and the fourth time, let him forswear the trade forever.

Also that no one of the said trade shall hang his spurs out on Sundays, or any other days that are double feasts; but only a sign indicating his business. And such spurs as they shall so sell, they are to show and sell within their shops, without exposing them without, or opening the doors or windows of their shops, on the pain aforesaid.

Also, that no one of the said trade shall keep a house or shop to carry on his business, unless he is free of the city; and that no one shall cause to be sold, or exposed for sale, any manner of old spurs for new ones, or shall garnish them or change them for new ones.

Also, that no one of the said trade shall take an apprentice for a less term than seven years, and such apprentice shall be enrolled according to the usages of the said city.

Also, that if any one of the said trade, who is not a freeman, shall take an apprentice for a term of years, he shall be amerced as aforesaid.

Also, that no one of the said trade shall receive the apprentice, serving-man or journeyman of another in the same trade, during the term agreed upon between his master and him; on the pain aforesaid.

Also, that no alien of another country, or foreigner of this country, shall follow or use the said trade, unless he is enfranchised before the mayor, alderman and chamberlain; and that by witness and surety of the good folks of the said trade, who will undertake for him as to his loyalty and his good behavior.

Also, that no one of the said trade shall work on Saturdays, after None has been rung out in the City; and not from that hour until the Monday morning following.

❖ B. Ordinances of the White-Tawyers

In English Towns and Gilds, *pp. 23–25, and Riley,* Memorials of London, *pp. 232–34.*

In honor of God, of Our Lady, and of All Saints, and for the nurture of tranquillity and peace among the good folks the megueers, called white-tawyers, the folks of the same trade have, by assent of Richard Lacer, mayor, and of the aldermen, ordained the points under-written.

In the first place, they have ordained that they will find a wax candle, to burn before our Lady in the church of Allhallows, near London wall.

Also, that each person of the said trade shall put in the box such sum as he shall think fit, in aid of maintaining the said candle.

Also, if by chance any one of the said trade shall fall into poverty, whether through old age or because he cannot labor or work, and have nothing with which to keep himself, he shall have every week from the said box 7d. for his support, if he be a man of good repute. And after his decease, if he have a wife, a woman of good repute, she shall have weekly for her support 7d. from the said box, so long as she shall behave herself well and keep single.

And that no stranger shall work in the said trade, or keep house for the same in the city, if he be not an apprentice, or a man admitted to the franchise of the said city.

And that no one shall take the serving-man of another to work with him, during his term, unless it be with the permission of his master.

And if any one of the said trade shall have work in his house that he cannot complete, or if for want of assistance such work shall be in danger of being lost, those of the said trade shall aid him, that so the said work be not lost.

And if any one of the said trade shall depart this life, and have not wherewithal to be buried, he shall be buried at the expense of their common box. And when any one of the said trade shall die, all those of the said trade shall go the vigil, and make offering on the morrow.

And if any serving-man shall conduct himself in any other manner than properly towards his master, and act rebelliously toward him, no one of the said trade shall set him to work, until he shall have made amends before the mayor and aldermen; and before them such misprison shall be redressed.

And that no one of the said trade shall behave himself the more thoughtlessly, in the way of speaking or acting amiss, by reason of the points aforesaid; and if any one shall do the contrary thereof, he shall not follow the said trade until he shall have reasonably made amends.

And if any one of the said trade shall do the contrary of any point of the ordinances aforesaid, and be convicted thereof by good men of the said trade, he shall pay to the Chamber of the Gildhall of London, the first time 2s., the second time 40d., the third time half a mark, and the fourth time 10s., and shall forswear the trade.

Also—that the good folks of the same trade shall once in the year be assembled in a certain place, convenient thereto, there to choose two men of the most loyal and benefitting of the said trade, to be overseers of work and all other things touching the trade for that year; which persons shall be presented to the mayor and aldermen for the time being, and sworn before them diligently to inquire and make search, and loyally to present to the said mayor and aldermen such defaults as they shall find touching the said trade without sparing anyone for friendship or for hatred, or in any other manner. And if any one of the said trade shall be found rebellious against the said overseers, so as not to let them properly make their search and assay, as they ought to do; or if he shall absent himself from the meeting aforesaid, without reasonable cause, after due warning by the said overseers, he shall pay to the Chamber, upon the first default, 40d., and on the second like default, half a mark; and on the third, one mark; and on the fourth, 20s., and shall forswear the trade forever.

Also, that if the overseers shall be found lax and negligent about their duty, or partial to any person for gift or for friendship, maintaining him or voluntarily permitting him to continue in his default, and shall not present him to the mayor and aldermen, as before stated, they are to incur the penalty aforesaid.

Also, that each year, at such assemblies of the good folks of the said trade, there shall be chosen overseers, as before stated. And if it be found that through laxity or negligence of the said governors such assemblies are not held, each of the said overseers is to incur the said penalty.

Also, that all skins falsely and deceitfully wrought in their trade which the said overseers shall find on sale in the hands of any person, citizen or foreigner, within the franchise shall be forfeited to the said chamber, and the worker thereof amerced in manner aforesaid.

Also, that no one who has not been an apprentice, and has not finished his term of apprenticeship in the said trade, shall be made free of the same trade; unless it be attested by the overseers for the time being, or by four persons of the said trade, that such person is able and sufficiently skilled to be made free of the same.

Also, that no one of the said trade shall induce the servant of another to work with him in the said trade, until he has made a proper fine with his first master at the discretion of the said overseers, or of four reputable men of the said trade. And if any one shall do to the contrary thereof, or receive the serving workman of another to work with him during his term, without leave of the trade, he is to incur the said penalty.

Also, that no one shall take for working in the said trade more than they were wont heretofore, on the pain aforesaid; that is to say, for the dyker of Scotch stags, half a mark; the dyker of Irish stags, half a mark; the dyker of Spanish stags, 10s.; for the hundred of goat skins, 20s.; the hundred of roe leather, 16s.; for the hundred skins of young deer, 8s.; and for the hundred of kid skins, 8s.

✛ C. Order of the Pageants of the Corpus Christi Play in the City of York, 1415

In English Towns and Gilds, *pp. 29–32, and L. T. Smith,* York Plays (Oxford, 1885), *p. xix. Among the many guild functions was sometimes that of participating in the religious plays that mark the cultural life of the late fourteenth and fifteenth centuries, particularly in England. Sometimes, as can be seen below, there is a distinct connection between the guild function and its responsibility in the play.*

Tanners—God the Father Omnipotent creating and forming the heavens, the angels and archangels, Lucifer and the angels who fell with him into the pit.

Plasterers—God the Father in his substance creating the earth and all things which are therein, in the space of five days.

Cardmakers—God the Father forming Adam from the mud of the earth, and making Eve from Adam's rib, and inspiring them with the breath of life.

Fullers—God forbidding Adam and Eve to eat of the tree of life.

Coopers—Adam and Eve and the tree between them, the serpent deceiving them with apples; God speaking to them and cursing the serpent, and an angel with a sword driving them out of Paradise.

Armorers—Adam and Eve, an angel with a spade and distaff appointing them their labor.

Glovers—Able and Cain sacrificing victims.

Shipwrights—God warning Noah to make an ark out of planed wood.

Fishmongers and Mariners—Noah in the ark with his wife, three sons of Noah with their wives, with various animals.

Parchment-makers and Book-binders—Abraham sacrificing his son Isaac on the altar.

Hosiers—Moses lifting up the serpent in the wilderness, King Pharaoh, eight Jews looking on and wondering.

Spicers—A doctor declaring the sayings of the prophets concerning the future birth of Christ. Mary, the angel saluting her; Mary saluting Elizabeth.

Pewterers and Founders—Mary, Joseph wishing to send her away, the angel telling them to go over to Bethlehem.

Tilers—Mary, Joseph, a nurse, the child born and lying in a manger between an ox and an ass, and an angel speaking to the shepherds, and to the players in the next pageant.

Chandlers—Shepherds speaking to one another, the star in the East an angel announcing to the shepherds their great joy in the child which has been born.

Goldsmiths, Goldbeaters, and Moneyers—Three kings coming from the East, Herod questioning them about the child Jesus, and the son of Herod and two counsellors and a herald. Mary with the child, and the star above and three kings offering gifts.

(*Formerly*) *The House of St. Leonard, (now) Masons*—Mary, with the boy, Joseph, Anna, the nurse, with the young doves. Simeon receiving the boy into his arms, and the two sons of Simeon.

Marshalls—Mary with the boy and Joseph fleeing into Egypt, at the bidding of the angel.

Girdlers, Nailers, and Sawyers—Herod ordering the male children to be slain, four soldiers with lances, two counsellors of the king, and four women weeping for the death of their sons.

Spurriers and Lorimers—Doctors, the boy Jesus sitting in the temple in the midst of them, asking them questions and replying to them, four Jews, Mary and Joseph seeking him, and finding him in the temple.

Barbers—Jesus, John the Baptist baptizing him, and two angels attending.

Vinters—Jesus, Mary, bridegroom with the bride, ruler of the feast with his slaves, with six vessels of water in which the water is turned into wine.

Smiths—Jesus on a pinnacle of the temple, and the devil tempting him with stones, and two angels attending, etc.

Curriers—Peter, James, and John; Jesus ascending into a mountain and transfiguring himself before them. Moses and Elias appearing, and the voice of one speaking in a cloud.

Ironmongers—Jesus, and Simon the leper asking Jesus to eat with him; two disciples, Mary Magdalene bathing Jesus' feet with her tears and drying them with her hair.

Plumbers and Patternmakers—Jesus, two apostles, the woman taken in adultery, four Jews accusing her.

Pouchmakers, Bottlers, and Capmakers—Lazarus in the sepulchre, Mary Magdalene and Martha, and two Jews wondering.

Spinners and Vestmakers—Jesus on an ass with its colt, twelve apostles following Jesus, six rich and six poor, eight boys with branches of palm, singing Blessed, etc., and Zaccheus climbing into a sycamore tree.

Cutlers, Bladesmiths, Sheathers, Scalers, Bucklermakers, and Horners—Pilate, Caiaphas, two soldiers, three Jews, Judas selling Jesus.

Bakers—The passover lamb the Supper of the Lord, twelve apostles, Jesus girded with a towel, washing their feet, institution of the sacrament of the body of Christ in the new law, communion of the apostles.

Cordwainers—Pilate, Caiaphas, Annas, fourteen armed soldiers, Malchus, Peter, James, John, Jesus, and Judas kissing and betraying him.

Bowyers and Fletchers—Jesus, Annas, Caiaphas, and four Jews beating and scourging Jesus. Peter, the woman accusing Peter, and Malchus.

Tapestrymakers and Couchers—Jesus, Pilate, Annas, Caiaphas, two counsellors and four Jews accusing Jesus.

Littesters—Herod, two counsellors, four soldiers, Jesus, and three Jews.

Cooks and Watercarriers—Pilate, Annas, Caiaphas, two Jews, and Judas bringing back to them the thirty pieces of silver.

Tilemakers, Millers, Furriers, Hayresters, Bowlers—Jesus, Pilate, Caiaphas, Annas, six soldiers holding spears with banners, and four others leading Jesus away from Herod, asking to have Barabbas released and Jesus crucified, and likewise binding and scourging him, and placing the crown of thorns upon his head; three soldiers casting lots for the clothing of Jesus.

Shearmen—Jesus, stained with blood, bearing the cross to Calvary. Simon of Cyrene, the Jews compelling him to carry the cross; Mary the mother of Jesus; John the apostle then announcing the condemnation and passage of her son to Calvary. Veronica wiping the blood and sweat from the face of Jesus with a veil on which is imprinted the face of Jesus, and other women mourning for Jesus.

Pinmakers, Latenmakers, and Painters—The cross, Jesus stretched upon it on the ground; four Jews scourging Him and binding Him with ropes, and afterwards lifting the cross, and the body of Jesus nailed to the cross on Mount Calvary.

Butchers and Poultry Dealers—The cross, two thieves crucified, Jesus hanging on the cross between them, Mary the mother of Jesus, John, Mary, James, and Salome. A soldier with a lance, a servant with a sponge, Pilate, Annas, Caiaphas, the centurion, Joseph of Arimathea and Nicodemus, placing Him in the sepulchre.

Saddlers, Glaziers, and Joiners—Jesus conquering hell; twelve spirits, six good, and six evil.

Carpenters—Jesus rising from the sepulchre, four armed soldiers, and the three Marys mourning. Pilate, Caiaphas, and Annas. A young man seated at the sepulchre clothed in white, speaking to the women.

Winedrawers—Jesus, Mary Magdalene with aromatic spices.

Brokers and Woolpackers—Jesus, Luke, and Cleophas in the guise of travelers.

Scriveners, Illuminators, Pardoners, and Dubbers—Jesus, Peter, John, James, Philip, and the other apostles with parts of a baked fish, and a honey-comb; and Thomas the apostle touching the wounds of Jesus.

Tailors—Mary, John the evangelist, the eleven apostles, two angels, Jesus ascending before them, and four angels carrying a cloud.

Potters—Mary, two angels, eleven apostles, and the Holy Spirit descending upon them, and four Jews wondering.

Drapers—Jesus, Mary, Gabriel with two angels, two virgins and three Jews of Mary's acquaintance, eight apostles, and two devils.

Linen-weavers—Four apostles carrying the bier of Mary, and Fergus hanging above the bier, with two other Jews and an angel.

Woolen-weavers—Mary ascending with a throng of angels, eight apostles, and the apostle Thomas preaching in the desert.

Innkeepers—Mary, Jesus crowning her, with a throng of angels singing.

Mercers—Jesus, Mary, the twelve apostles, four angels with trumpets, and four with a crown, a lance, and two whips, four good spirits, and four evil spirits, and six devils.

✤ D. Rules of a Guild at Exeter Before the 11th Century

The roots of later guilds sometimes extend back in time to the earliest periods in the history of traditional Europe. The following rules of what E. P. Cheney calls a "social or non-industrial" guild suggest the religious and communal character of the guilds from a very early date.

This assembly was collected in Exeter, for the love of God and for our soul's need, both in regard to our life here, and to the after days which we desire for ourselves by God's doom.

Now we have agreed that our meeting shall be thrice in the twelve months; once at St. Michael's Mass, secondly at St. Mary's Mass, after mid-winter, and thirdly at Allhallow's Mass after Easter; and let each gild-brother have two sesters of malt, and each young man one sester, and a sceat of honey; and let the mass-priest at each of our meetings sing two masses, one for our living friends, the other for the dead; and let each brother of common condition sing two psalters of psalms, one for the living and one for the dead; and at the death of a brother, each man six masses; or six psalters of psalms; and at a death each man five pence; and at a house-burning each man one penny. And if any one neglect the day, for the first time three masses, for the second five, and at the third time let him have no favor, unless his neglect arose from sickness or his lord's need. And if any one neglect his subscription at the proper day, let him pay double. And if any one of this brotherhood misgreet another, let him make boot with thirty pence. Now we pray for the love of God that every man hold this meeting rightly, as we rightly have agreed upon it. God help us thereunto.

✤ E. Report of Wardens of the Guild of St. Katharine at Norwich, 1389

In English Towns and Gilds, *pp. 34–35. Original in* Smith and Brentano, English Gilds, *pp. 19–21. Comparison with the*

preceding selection suggests the continuity of devotional and
social services among the guilds. In 1398, five hundred guilds
sent reports of their rules to the king, of which this selection
is one example.

To the most excellent prince and lord, our lord Richard, by
the grace of God, king of England and France, and to his council
in his chancery, his humble lieges, the guardians of a certain
fraternity of St. Katharine the virgin and martyr, in the church
of St. Simon and St. Jude in Norwich, all subjection and reverence
and honor. By virtue of a certain proclamation recently made
according to royal command by the sheriff of the county of
Norfolk at Norwich, we certify to your excellency according
to the form of the aforesaid proclamation, that our aforesaid
fraternity was founded in the year 1307, by certain parishioners
of the said church, and by others devoted to God, to the honor
of the Holy Trinity, and of the blessed Virgin Mary, and of
St. Katharine the virgin and martyr, and of all saints and for
keeping up an increase of light in the said Church; under certain
ordinances made and issued with common consent of the brothers
and sisters of the aforesaid fraternity. The tenor of these ordinances follows in these words.

In the first place with one assent it is ordained that all the
brethren and sisters of this gild shall come together to the parish
church of St. Simon and St. Jude, in Norwich, on the day of
St. Katharine, to go in the procession with their candle, which
is borne before them, and to hear the mass of St. Katharine
in the aforesaid church; and at that mass every brother and sister
shall offer a half-penny.

And also it is ordained that what brother or sister shall be
absent at the procession aforesaid, or at mass, or at offering, he
shall pay to the chattels of the gild two pounds of wax, but
they may be excused reasonably.

And also it is ordained, that where a brother or a sister
is dead, and every brother and sister shall come to *dirige* and
to mass; and at the mass, each shall offer a half-penny, and give
a half-penny to alms; and for a mass to be sung for the soul
of the dead, a penny. And at the *dirige*, every brother and sister

that is lettered shall say, for the soul of the dead, *placebo and dirige*, in the place where they shall come together; and every brother and sister that is not lettered shall say for the soul of the dead, twenty times, the *Paternoster*, with *ave Maria;* and from the chattels of the gild shall there be two candles of wax, of sixteen pounds weight, about the body of the dead.

And also it is ordained, that if any brother or sister die out of the city of Norwich, within eight miles, six of the brethren that have the chattels of the gild in keeping, shall go to that brother or sister that is dead; and if it be lawful, they shall carry it to Norwich, or else it be buried there; and if the body be buried out of Norwich, all the brethren and sisters shall be warned to come to the foresaid church of St. Simon and St. Jude, and there shall be done for the soul of the dead all service, light and offering as if the body were there present. And what brother or sister be absent at *placebo* and *dirige*, or at mass, he shall pay two pounds of wax to the chattels of the gild, unless he be reasonably excused. And nevertheless he shall do for the dead as it is said before.

And also it is ordained that, on the morrow after the gild day all the brethren and sisters shall come to the aforesaid church, and there sing a mass of requiem for the souls of the brethren and sisters of this gild, and for all Christian souls, and each offer there a farthing. And whoso is absent he shall pay a pound of wax.

And also it is ordained that if any brother or sister fall into any discord between brothers and sisters, that discord shall be helped by every brother and sister of the gild, with a farthing in the week.

And also it is ordained by common assent that if there be any discord between brothers and sisters, that discord shall be first showed to other brothers and sisters of the gild, and by them shall accord be made, if it may be skillfully. And if they cannot be so brought to accord, it shall be lawful to them to go to the common law, without any maintenance. And whoso does against this ordinance, he shall pay two pounds of wax to the light.

Also it is ordained, by common assent, that if any brother

of this gild be chosen into office and refuse it, he shall pay two pounds of wax to the light of St. Katharine.

Also it is ordained, by common assent, that the brethren and sisters of this gild, in the worship of St. Katharine, shall have a livery of hoods in suit, and eat together in their gild day, at their common cost; and whoso fails, he shall pay two pounds of wax to the light.

Also it is ordained, by common assent, that no brother or sister shall be received into this gild but by the alderman and twelve brethren of the gild.

And as to the goods and chattels of the said fraternity, we make known to your excellency, likewise, that we the aforesaid guardians, have in our custody, for the use of the said fraternity, twenty shillings of silver.

22

The Book of Physiognomy

Introductory Note: The Book of Physiognomy which follows can be found as a concluding section of *The Wise Book of Philosophy and Astronomy*, in Cambridge University Library Ms. Ll. 4. 14, which also contains *Piers Plowman*. It tells the art of reading faces, from two different points of view. The planet under which a man is born influences his moral qualities, and his basic character. Parts of this read like a brief summary of *The Wise Book*. But this is only the introduction to the art of reading the faces themselves; certain shapes and sizes and colors of heads, mouths, ears, eyes, and noses have significance in reading a man's character, and these are all expounded here. The treatise is anonymous, and has not been printed before. It was edited for this volume by M. Wescott Driver and Jeanne Krochalis, with the assistance of Laurie Finke. There is a leaf missing in the manuscript, so the description stops at the ear.

The description of individuals, whether human characters or literary personifications, in *Piers Plowman* owes much to the kind of physiognomy discussed in this document. In a sense, The Book of Physiognomy completes the picture of the macrocosm and microcosm considered in the first section of this book by revealing the ways by which the stars and planets affect character differentiation among humans.

✤ Physiognomy

Here bygynneth þe tretis of þe booke of phisonomye. A nobile knowinge of nature ys þe whiche enserchiþ[1] qualities within a man by fformes withoute; and þat doþe þe tretis of þe science of phisonomye. And this word *phisonomea* ys saide of *phisis*, þat is nature, and *gnomos*, þat is dyvynynge. Fforsothe he is wonte to be made mevyngis, within fforth as by sy3th of inner colour3 of beynge, as þe urinis.[2] Ffor sothe knowinge of nature ys sotillere and openere, whiche schewith þe levynge withoute in þe superfficie;[3] þat is to seie, þe seyth of many eye, ffor þus in þe name of Crist here we dispersid ffriste. Now of þe complexicioun.

The fforge of manys body hath take his bygynnynge of elementis and of nurshingis, whereof þe substances of humour3 drawith nature of elementis: as colrere of ffyre, blode of eyre, fflemne of water, malancolie of erthe. Blode makith naturaliche donne,[4] mesurable, vikele,[5] and well fformed. Colre makith naturaliche ruffe or citrine, oþer blak withoute, within lyght and witti, lene, and soluble,[6] and companied in body. Fflemne hath no coloure propre, but of humoure regnynge next undir him; ffor sothe, he makiþ bodies ffatte, and wakynge, and thenkinge withinne hem self; comynge sone hore. Malancolie makith white oþer blake. If it be white withoute, withinne gylfull, coveitys, sory, mysbelevyd oþer wickid; slepy, or dredffull. And if it be blak, distrumbling, witti and lyght; lene, insoluble, not compouned of body. Be þis knowinges yt is lyghte, to wytte: þat whiche hature of planetis ys in a man, þat is to saye to have lordschipe in him, þat whiche makiþ þe disposynnge of lyvynnge. Fforþermore, in summe, humours regneth meddelid, in whiche þe lasse certeyne dome schewith in men. Alle þese with þe helpe of god we shulleth schewe.

---

1. *enserchiþ:* examines   2. *urinis:* urine   3. *superfficie:* outward appearance
4. *donne:* darkly colored   5. *vikele:* fickle   6. *soluble:* fluid

The disposiscion of þe planetis, and ffrist of Saturne

Hit is to knowe þat Saturne makiþ qualities withinne men after his lordschepe in all spisis[7] of malancolie. And he betoneth Chaunce[8] not to be ffolwid. Saturne makiþ gylffull, sore welspekinge; not mevable; hatynge not pleynge, but with disturbaunce; coveytous; desiringe; moche thenkenge withinne him self, and not lyghtly wille schewe. And as þey beth hard to be plesid, þey beth durable in elde,[9] more amyable inneþe[10] ffolwinge a good ende. Also fformes beth in men, be þe whiche qualities beth knowe. The semblaunge beth ofte tyme swelle, þe browes grette and honginge, þe eyne ʒelow; a thynne berde, a gret nose, eyne[11] unmevable; slowe in goynge, þe semblant bowynge towarde þe erthe. Moche he þenketh of erthely þingis, and blake clothis he loveth more þan white.

The planete of Jupiter

The qualities of Jovis beth regynynge in blode; ffor why Jupiter makith a man merie, menable, coveitous and glosinge,[12] amyable, moche desiringe, gracious, havynge lordschepe; naþeles, not moche duringe; unneþe he durith to þe age.

The signs of Jupiter beth a brode fforhed; browis bent; eyne citrine; meke syʒth; a riʒth nose; an even longe fface; a mene mouþe; teeþ even and white, and reed lyppis; a fface sanguyn; ryth lymes; meke goynge withoute noyse.

Now of þe planete Mars

Mars makyth a man lyght, wytty, bacbytynge, lene, ffytthynge, myssaynge,[13] coveytous of wurschepe, bostynge of here owen dedis, undernemynge[14] other ffolkis, ianglynge, moche wakynge, unnethe overe passynge þe age of 40 ʒere.

The signes of Mars and þe complesions beth þese: a brode ffronte; ryth browis and scharpe eyne; a long fface, and lene; a longe nose, and bocchy;[15] a moche mouþe, and ofte opeyd; longe teth. Also he puttiþ him self to þe companye of men. He shall love reed cloþis,[16] and unnethe he will here any manere of science.

---

7. *spisis:* species   8. *Chaunce:* chance   9. *elde:* old age
10. *inneþe:* in   11. *eyne:* eyes   12. *glosinge:* of fair appearance
13. *myssaynge:* evil speaking   14. *undernemynge:* reproving
15. *bocchy:* swollen   16. *cloþis:* clothing

Now of þe planete of Sol
Sol makyth a man glosynge, meke, lyght to teche, and tacffull of lore; and of wondyr witte, and moste duringe; ffayre spekynge, and without boste; gladeliche purchasinge, and curteysliche ȝevenge; amyable, and lovynge privyliche wyse men and women; and doynge all þingis with his owen disciscion; comynge lyghteliche to manys age perffightliche, and ffolwinge þe ende of men.

The sign of Sol, þat is þe sonne, beth þese: mene stature; a round fforhed; smale browis; rounde eyne, and diverse; a right nose, not moche longe, a litill bochy in þe myddill; a fface clere, long and reed; a mene mouth; al þe body ffull ffayre. He lovethe moste clothe of golde.

Now planete of Venus
Venus makith men burgenyng,[17] lovng, gladynge, desiringe diverse kyndes of instrumentis, good to speke with, not moche wrothe, lyȝteliche fforȝevynge; wrathe unneþe trowynge[18] oþer ffellis; lyvynge conceill,[19] ffaynynge large, and of lyght mynde.

The signes of Venus beth þese: a semblante chaungeable; a mene fforheed; smale browis; lawinge eyne; a white nose crekid and scharpe; and a large mouþe, and reed lyppis yswolle; white teeth and ychinge. And þey takyth hede to many þingis, and þey loveth moste cloþe þat is white.

Now of planete of Mercurie
Mercurie makyth men to speke well; bostinge; well schape; gladeliche purchasynge; and levynge more his owen conseyll þan oþers; lyinge; prout;[20] of good witte and of better mynde; lyth and menable;[21] walkynge dyverse kyngdomys and gladdeliche ffolowynge.
The signes of Mercurie ben þess: a streigh fforheed; longe browis; blake eyn; a rith nose; a clere fface, lyghtliche reed; grett lyppis; even teeþ; a longe chynne; he loveth wommen well, and he shall love well grene clothe.

Now of þe planete of þe mone
Luna makith men wakynge and thenkynge moche withinne hem self; unstable lynge;[22] unwitteliche spekynge; colde, and lyghteliche wexinge seke þerwith; drawynge into lyth wrath, and sone ffor-

yevynge; pa(r)tinge his goodis not lyghtelich, coveytinge oþer strange þingis; moche desiringe silvere; and never comynge perffightliche to þe age of 60 ʒere. *The signes of luna* ben þese: þe fface is pale and clere; brode ffronte; browis bente; þe eyne meke; a low nose; noseþrellis[23] openyd; a littil mouthe; a opyn chynn; and neygh þe chekis sone hore; a ffatt navell; moche thenkynge on erthely þingis.

Be þese signes þe certeyne knowinge of men ys proved: Saf disposinge of þingis ʒevyth knowinge of þe bone lyme be lyme. Oþer disposinge of þe bodie ʒevyth knowinge of þingis lyme bi lyme. We shull trete nobiliche of yche sygnes in a man, and of þe singnificaciouns of hem with Goddis helpe. It is to knowe þat divers singnificaciouns of lymys beth ofte cordinge[24] togedir, þe whiche beth ffailinge. And þerffore þe singnifaciouns of þe principall lymes above ffordemeþ[25] all þe oþer. Therffor þe heed in a manys body ys principalere þan oþer, and it hath a serteyne betokenynge; and oþer disposiciouns of lymys schewith a deseynable[26] image of signes. Neþeles, þe doctrine of pawmistre[27] is wonte to enserche þe knowinge of ffortunys, and fforsoþe þis is more opyn in þe quikker schewinge, þe whyche we have expoundid ellis where, dillgentliche.

The signes of þe heed

Now we shull speke of þe heed, and of þe signes of him by everyche parties of him. An heed round in þe moste schewynge place, havynge him to þe manere of a crowne, betokeneth without douute a wyse man and well avisid, and meke kepinnge wrath, and amyable. And if it be whiʒte, it betokeneth a man of ffull witte, and of holdinge ffaste mynde, saf[28] he is ffoliche[29] large. And if it be blake it betokenet a man ffull of witte, and of holdinge ffast mynde, of lygh wrath, of stedffaste ffrenshipe, and of sothe word. And if it be citrine, it betokeneth a man swythe meke, and large kepinge parffitnliche ffellawschepe and stedffaste. And if it be ruffe, it betokeneþ (a man) well spekinge another, helynge wrathis, inow[30] amyable and wyse; saf he is lesse to be levede in worde, he is of best mynde, and caccyinge[31] of witte; and if þe heed be ffulle, it betokeneth a meke man, and a

---

23. *nose prellis:* nostrils   24. *cordinge:* in accord
25. *ffordemeþ:* takes precedence   26. *deseynable:* discernable
27. *pawmistre:* palmistry   28. *saf:* except   29. *ffoliche:* foolishly
30. *inow:* enough   31. *caccyinge:* piercing

deboner in word, and moche gay, and holdinge of perffith ffellaw-schepe, and of blessid reson. An heed even longe in þe schewynge partie, betokeneth a man of scharp witte, doynge many þingis un-wysliche and lyght, menable, wrothi; not well kepinge prementees,[32] nother naturaliche gay; scharpe in speche; commendid in dedis; over-well avisid in þingis to be disposid; lovynge gretteliche his owen. And if it be white, it betokeneth a man lesinge[33] reson in wrath, and ffull large; boystusliche[34] and naturalliche coveitous. And if it be blake, it betokeneth a man of lyght witte, and al moste of non reson in wrath, and unnethe abowynge lordis; and a grette distroubelere of many þingis. And if it be ruffe, it betokeneth a man of beste witte, and proute and unworthy, and lyghtly myssaynge, and lufsom,[35] and large. And if it be doun,[36] it betokeneth a may ty3th, and gay, and ffre and unstedeffaste, and lyinge in heed in þe sythtier stede. Ffoure square betokeneth a man of good deth, and meke and mylde, softe and deboner, not moche wroth, well avisid, wyse—saff coveitous—in word envious, desiringe moche ioye, and ffavor of men. And if it be white, it betokeneth a man more coveytous, and lasse meke, and more amyable, and more boringe. And if it be blak, it betokeneth a man more stedeffaster in soule, purschasinge sone ffrenschepis, and kepinnge longe, proute in aray, and well helinge privytes. And if it be ruffe, it betokeneth a man disposynge well of þingis þat beth prophetable and chaungeable, well avisid, and no þing fflateringe, saf be wratthingis; gladeliche wull lye. And if þe heed be dun, it be-tokeneth a man better þan þe oþer, and meker, and larger, save lyghtloker, coveitous, gylffull, hither proute, ofte seke, travelinge in akynge of þe heed; wytty and lyvynge dredffull, and moche of oþer many dedis bacbitinge. And if it be blake, it betoneth more fforth brekynge into ffoly dedis. And if it be whi3te, it betoneth a man lesse malicious. And if it be ruffe, or citrine, it betokeneth a man more better and more liberall. These ben certeine domms[37] of qualitis in þe wyche no man may be disceyved: fforsoþe in þe disposicion of þe oþer lymes is iwonte to be lettinge[38] of discrecion. Neþerles, þese ffore demeth[39] hem not. Þerffor a wyse phisonomyer shuld be ware to deme, but if he can perseyve or likene þe knowinge of signes ffolowinge.

32. *prementees:* promises   33. *lesinge:* losing   34. *boystusliche:* violently
35. *lufsom:* lovable   36. *doun:* dun   37. *domms:* judgments
38. *lettinge:* hindering   39. *ffore demeth:* condemn

Now of þe nature of heere

Heere[40] þat is blak, grette and þicke, betokeneth a man ffull of noyse, oþer distroubelinge[41] of good witte, or parffight mynde; of good maners; of noble ffaconde,[42] and proute; and a gloton, desiringe good metis and drinkis; lyghteliche scabbid;[43] kepinge þe bondis of good ffelawschepe; not moche getynge, disposynge many þingis, and ffewe endid. Here þynne and blake, and rith, betokeneth a ffooll, proute; a gloton; lygthliche brekinge into chistis; not gladeliche bowinge to no man; levynge lyghtliche a purpose moche hatynge; unneþe endinge his purpos. He is lyveliche, and moche duringe. Here blake and crispe[44] betokeneth moche wrathe, proute, and a gloton; sone sokeringe[45] all þingis, gretteliche gay, save in gamys moche my3th.[46] Heere þat is ruffe, þicke and ri3th betokeneth a man gretteliche acursid, prout, lyght of wylle, envious and malicious, seynable; gylffull he ys. Heere ruffe, thynne and crispe betokeneth a man more brekynge into wrathe, and bethenkynge longe of wrathe; a fflaterer, and not kepinge perffi3thly love. Heere ruffe, þicke and crispe betokeneth a man prout, bostinge and lygh wakynge; þat ffaynith gretteliche; neþeles ffre in ffelawschipe, and grantinge many þingis; and disturbanthliche,[47] and noyuslicke.[48] Heere glauk[49] and þikke betokeneth a man meke in word, desiringe, prayingis, and ffavor of þe peple; envious and ffayned in ffrenschipe. Heere glauk and þinne betokeneth a man more meker, and overe meke lyvinge, and overe meke be hotynge[50] of all þingis; not grantinge gladliche withoute dissposiscion. Heere glauk and crispe betokeneth a man leccherous, not moche desiringe metis, ne to be no gloton; moche envious and ffayned, and glad lokere; grauntynge of his goodis. Heere donn, þicke and grette betokeneth gretteliche liberall and meke, and tame, bihotynge more þan he may perfforme; disposinge many þingis with him self; wakynge grettely myndynge of good dedis; desiringe gretteliche þe ffrenschepe of men; not ffaynynge ne lyinge. Heere dunn and crispe betokeneth a man gladeliche acusinge, not gladeliche fforberinge any man; behotinge and grauntinge many þingis; many þingis to him self.

---

40. *Heere:* Hair   41. *distroubelinge:* troubled   42. *ffuconde:* eloquence
43. *scabbid:* scabbed   44. *crispe:* curly   45. *sokeringe:* securing
46. *my3th:* might   47. *disturbanthliche:* in a disturbed manner
48. *noyuslicke:* noisily   49. *glauk:* grey   50. *þe hotynge:* promising

Of hoorenesse.[51] Pe man þat is hoore in his ȝouthe, betokeneth a gyloure,[52] and harde and undi(r)stondinge in wraþe. And þe heere be crispe and hore,[53] he is avisid in his dedis. And þe heere be blake hoore, and þicke, it betokenyth a man disposinge in all þingis, and disceyve.

Now of þe ffaçe

A round fface betokeneth a man well manered, symple and meke, not þinkynge moch on high þingis, and disposinge mekeliche all þingis, and kepinge ffrendis trewly. A fface square betokeneth a man wyse and curteys of speche, well sounnynge, stedeffaste, and ordaynynge of good concellis. A longe fface betokeneth a prout man, noble of witte and of wille, bostinge more of him self þan of oþer; moche fflaterrere he is. A fface trianglid betokeneþ a curteise spekinge man, gylfull and ffaynynge wrothy and unwurþi. A fface pale betokeneþ a coveitouse man, backebitinge; not gabbinge, gylfull and not misturnyd. A reed fface betokeneth a man lyght and movable, and lyghtlyche brekinge into wrathis; maliciouse, and sone fforthenkynge, and gadering lyghtly togedris malafficia, þat is to saye evyll doynges.

The singnificaciouns of þe fforehede

A fforheed brode and square betokeneth a liberall man, and gay, lygh, unstable, almest of no ffith[54] in wordis. A fforheed trianclid betokeneth a man worthy and stable in love, gladeliche chiding and fforberinge; ffewe in wrathe. A rounde fforheed betokeneth a meke man in wordis, large in wystis,[55] paciente in chidinge. A fforheede swythe streit in a blake man betokeneth a gay man, and a gloton, and gladeliche wrothe; neþeles gretteliche ffree, ffrenchippe gladeliche purschasinge, and not lyghly lesinge. In a white man it betokeneth a ffole, and unstedeffaste, not gladeliche spekinge to ony man. In crispe man it betokneth sone wrothe. In a dun man it betokeneth a ffull liberall man, and moche unworþeringe, and litill noynge.

Now of þe eyne þe significaciounis

Grette eyne and rounde and glauk[56] bitokeneth a man malancoliouse in ffaynynge, ryth prut, unworthy, coveytynge many thyngis,

51. *hoorenesse:* grayness   52. *gyloure:* deceiver   53. *hore:* grey
54. *ffith:* faith   55. *wystis:* wisdom   56. *glauk:* greenish-grey

and gay spekynge; sownynge liche, and lyghtliche with wrathe losyng reson. A moche eyne, rounde and blake, betokeneth a man resonable, not well riche, þinkinge many þingis by him self. A moche eye even, longe and white betokeneth a luthir man, þenkynge many thretingis, not trewe in ffelawschepe; in wrathe gladeliche backbitinge; chalangynge to him strange dedis; and bostinge. A meche eye, glauk and even longe, betokeneth a man sobre, chaste, righffull in dome, not gladeliche levinge, and to go be many kyngedomys. A moche eie, blak and even longe, betokeneth a lovynge man, and suffringe, ofte tyme akynge in his herte, and many traveylis, and þenkynge of nessessarius to him self. An eie white and purblinde[57] betokeneth a man to suffre many happis,[58] oþer beprecyngis, oþer bygile, and þenkinge moche on his owne good and ffayned in wordis. An eie moche, and blak, and purblynde betokeneth a man proute and liberall in ffellawschep, and meke to meke, and prout to prout. An eie moche, blake and purblynde betokeneth a gylleffull man, gretteliche gylinge, suffringe many sorwes and akyngis,[59] bisyinge him gretteliche to gette ffellawschepe, saf to ffewe curteys oþer kynde. A litill eye, rounde and white, betokeneth a sley man in worde and moche aviside, holdinge ffaste, not grauntynge, and kynde gladeliche to manye. An eie litill, round and glauke, betokeneþ a man gretteliche amyable, prut in his aray, and swithe liberall; unstedeffast grettelich affor 30 3ere, and after hem moche stabelers, and litill grauntinge affor his deth of ony þinge. A litill eye even, longe and white betokeneth a man styinge moche to hie dingnitys, saf litill profetinge; moche ffiateringe, and to ffewe kynde. A litill eye, even, longe and glauk, betokeneth a man moche enviouse, and he wull love prophiliche hem þat hath begunne to love onys. An eye litill, crokide and blake bytokeneth a man malicious, gylffull; þingz many luthir thou3tys, unneþe sewinge a good ende in his dedis, ne in non oþer þingz. A litill eye, white and purblynde betokeneth a wickyd man in his dedis, large in 3iftys, ffell in speche and enviouse to ham. A litill eye, purblynde and glauke betokeneth a man lyghtly discuringe of wrathe, traveylinge gretteliche and unstedeffaste also. A litill eye, purblynde and blake betokeneth moche thou3th and gylffull and wickyd, backebitinge be grette pride of herte. Eyen white and in a

---

57. *purblinde:* defective vision   58. *happis:* chance events
59. *akyngis:* achings

white man betokeneth a man unstedeffaste lyvinge and curteisliche
spekynge, ffollyliche, large with noyse, and naturaliche coveitous.
Eyen blake in a whiʒte man betokeneth a man disposinge many
þingis, and rechynnge⁶⁰ to many richessis, be many traveilis. Eyne
glauke boþe in a whiʒte man and in a blake man bytokenith a man
well maried beffoure and ffre granteliche þat is his. Eyn white in a
blake man betokeneth a man gretteliche wrethe, disciscuringe of lyght
causis, and not of hooll. The ruth eye in a man more þan þe lyʒft eye
betokeneþ a man resonable and sotill in worde, meke and mylde, and
well avisid, saf he is prout, and gladeliche graunting his þingis, and
sone fforþinkinge. The lyfte eye more þan þe ryth betokeneth a man
gay and ffayre of spekynge, in sownynge and travesinge moche.

The significacionis of þe nose
A nose moche bocchy bytokeneth a man moche dronke, lew,
gloton, proute, gay, and grauntinge gladeliche his þingis. A nose ryth
and crokide in þe myddis betokeneth a man grettely wrothy, almoste
no man fforberinge, and unworthy. A nose sumwhat bochy in þe
myddis, not havynge large nosþrellis betokeneth a man mysseggyng,
and a gloton and delicious. An scoʒte nose betokeneth a wrothy man
and iffayned and backbitinge ofte tyme or repentinge of his (good
wille) or repungynge. A longe nose betoneth a man þinkynge many
þingis, ʒevynge him to grete þingis, a'nd sone he wull be wrothe. A
nose grete in þe lownesse betokeneth a gloton and a ffooll, not
þinkinge moche of þingis to come. A nose scharpe beneþe betokeneth
a coveytous man, and a well avisid, grauntinge gladliche his, and
envious gretteliche. A nose naturaliche reed betokeneth a sotill man
and a witti, and of lyght mynde, purchasinge many ffrenschippis,
kynd to many and stedeffaste. A nose naturaliche pale betokeneth
an harde man of witte, and of unstable mynde, stedeffaste in ffrenschipe and pacient in word.

The Singnificaciouns of þe browys
Browis ryth and grette betokeneth a man swithe cruell in rith
gladeliche purschinge worschipe, backebitinge and enviouse, gladeliche grauntinge ffor wurscheppe. Browis yarchide⁶¹ and smalle bytokeneth a man swythe meke and debonere, saff lyghliche slydinge
ffrom purpos, gay and hidynge and most his gaynes and in all his

60. *rechynnge:* reaching   61. *yarchide:* arched

wyllys. Browis smale and rith betokeneith a man gretteliche coveitous
and wrothi in witte, oþer in soule, and rith venemouse.

The significaciouns of þe mouth
A moche mouthe, havynge smale lyppis betokeneth a man coveitouse in witt, and of unstable wrethe, not moche of durable lyff,
purschasinge many thingis, and kepinge well þinges purschasid. A
mouthe havynge grette lyppis betokeneth a gloton, gretteliche gay,
worþi, stedeffaste and swithe lefsom.[62] A mouthe havynge grette
lyppis and soteler in þe ende betokeneth a man unstable, liberall and
not duringe lyff. A mouthe havynge grette lyppys in þe myddill and
pale, betokeneth a man wrothy and a brawler, of unsteffaste mynde
and of duringe ffrenscheppe. A mouthe crokide betoneth untrewe,
evyll wyllyd to summe men, and to summe good willyd, gladeliche
descevynge his ffellawe, and ffull of malice, backebytinge and not
well stedeffaste. A lyppe gretter above þan benethe betokeneth a
man clenge and wickyd in thoughte.

Significaciouns of teeth
Teeth white in a man bitokeneth curteyse man, desiringe gretteliche preysinge. Teeth blake betoneth a man gladeliche backebytinge,
acusinge and also pretinge,[63] not lying. Teeth even betokeneth a man
well spekinge, wrothi, disposinge many þingis, and ȝevynge many
conceyulls. Teeth unevene betokeneth a man to þenke many þingis,
and veyne in thoughtys. Teeth þynne betokeneth a man mysseggynnge
and gay. Teeth þicke betokeneth a gloton and delyciouse in metis and
drinnkis. Teeth rounde betokeneth a man stedeffaste and unworthy.
Teeth longe betokeneth a lyght man in wordis, and in wille to be
bowide lyghteliche. Teeth dunne in þe myddill betokeneth a man
ffree and unsteffaste. Teeth grette and hele betokeneth a prute man,
and in wyll unworthy, and lyinge. An even chyn betokeneth a man
even, debonere and meke.

The significaciouns of þe eere
A grette eere betokeneth a man gylouse[64] yffayned and bostinge
many þingis. A litill eere betokeneth a man meke, debonere and lyghte.
An harde eere betokeneth a man of good disposicion of body.

[The manuscript stops here]

62. *lefsom:* pleasant   63. *pretinge:* prating   64. *gylouse:* jealous

PART VI:

Paysage Moralisée

Few elements in medieval literature are as readily misunderstood as allegory, the expression of multiple meanings on different planes of understanding in a single work. The bulk of allegorical literature, to be sure, encourages misunderstanding, for much of the commonest sort of allegory suffers from mechanical separations of levels of meaning and the dominance of one or two levels over the others. What suffers most often is the level of literal description, which usually becomes an improbable showcase crowded with elements whose literal significance veers toward the nonsensical or improbable, while their spiritual value is diminished by their wooden inconsistency with realistic description. When, as often in *Piers Plowman*, allegorical techniques are used in the grand harmonious manner, when commonplace literalness is lifted to higher and broader levels of perception, the literal level becomes charged with poignance and the experiences of daily life transformed into universal patterns of significance and illumination. The quality of few of the following selections is up to that of Langland at his best, but they do suggest the variety of allegorical approaches to certain themes that Langland uses. The first two selections are short poems newly edited for this volume. The third and fourth selections are from two of the best known allegorical poems of the thirteenth and fourteenth centuries, Robert Grosseteste's *Castle of Love* and Guillaume de Deguille-ville's *Pilgrimage of the Soul*.

23

"In place as man may se . . ."

Introductory Note: This poem is found in British Museum Ms. Harley 3954, fol. 87^r. It is a lengthy meditation on Christ's life and death, but it begins with an extended metaphor about a child's horn-book, the A B C from which children learned their first letters. The blood-red paraph marks indicate the wounds, and the blue fluorishes indicate the blows inflicted upon Christ's body. The complete poem has been printed by F. J. Furnival, *Political, Religious and Love Poems,* Early English Text Society, Original Series, vol. 15 (London, 1866), pp. 271–78. In *Passus* VII of the B-Text, a priest asks Piers who taught him the little learning he has, and Piers replies: "Abstinence the abbesse . . . myne a. b. c. me tauȝte, / And Conscience came afterward and kenned me moche more." Learning, for Langland and the author of this poem, was fundamentally an introduction to meditation on religion.

> In place as man may se,
> Quar a chyld to scole¹ xal² set be,

1. *scole:* school   2. *xal:* shall

A bok hym is browt
Naylyd on a brede[3] of tre
þat men callyt an abece[4]　　　　　　5
Pratylych Iwrout.[5]

Wrout[6] is on the bok withoute
A paraffys[7] grete and stoute
Bolyd[8] in rose red
that is set withoutyn doute[9]　　　　　10
In tokenyng of Crist ded.

Red letter in perchemyn[10]
Makyth a chyld good and fyn
lettrys to loke and se.
Be[11] þis boke men may dyvyne　　　　15
þat Cristis body was ful of pyne[12]
that deyid on rode tre.[13]

In tre he was don ful blythe,[14]
With grete paraffys þat ben wondis five,
As ye mon[15] understonde.　　　　　20
Loke in hys body, mayde and wyfe!
Won[16] hee gun[17] naylys drive
In fot and in honde.

Hond and fout þer was ful woo,
And þer were lettrys many moo　　　　25
Within and withoute.
With rede wondys and strokis blo[18]
He was dryve[19] fro top to þe too,
Hys fayre body aboute.

3. *brede:* plank　　4. *abece:* abecedary
5. *Pratylych Iwrout:* Prettily wrought　　6. *Wrout:* Wrought
7. *paraffys:* ornamental paragraph mark or initial　　8. *Bolyd:* colored
9. There is presumably a line missing here, which the rhyme scheme, though not
the sense, demands.
10. *perchemyn:* parchment　　11. *Be:* By　　12. *pyne:* pain
13. *rode tre:* tree of the cross　　14. *In . . . blythe:* On . . . willingly, gladly
15. *mon:* may　　16. *Won:* When　　17. *gun:* began to
18. *strokis blo:* strokes blue　　19. *dryve:* pierced

About this a pece I wyl spede,[20]   30
Þat I myth[21] þis lettrys rede,
Withoutyn ony dystaunce.
But God that let hys body sprede
Upon the rode for manys nede
In hevene us alle avaunce.[22]

20. *spede:* hasten   21. *myth:* might   22. *avaunce:* advance

24

Moralisacio sacerdotis

Introductory Note: This section of a longer poem is edited from British Museum Additional Manuscript 31042, fol. 104ʳ. It offers another version of the allegorical arming of Christ which Langland describes in Piers Plowman, *Passus* XVIII, letting the armor represent Human Nature in the battle with Death and the Devil. This poem has not been printed before.

 Moralisacio sacerdotis tocius apparatus
in missa &c.

> Uppon his hede an amyte[1] fyrste he laythe
> Wich is a syegne,[2] a tokenn, and a figure
> Owtewarde a schewynge growndide in faythe.
> The large albe by recorde of scripture
> A ryghtwysnesse[3] perpetually to endure.   5

---

1. *amyte:* amice   2. *syegne:* sign   3. *ryghtwysnesse:* justice

The longe girdille[4] Clennesse and chastytee
Rownde of the arme the ffanonn dothe assure
Alle sobirnesse knyttes with humylitee.
The stole also strechynge ferre in lengthe
Is of doctours the angelike doctryne   10
Mowgre[5] of heretikes to stande in his strengthe,
Fro[6] Cristes lawe never to declyne.
The shesepul[7] abouthe with charyte to schyne
Brighte as Phebus[8] in his myddedaye spere[9]
Holdes evere his course in the righte lyne,   15
To friend and foo strechyng owte his bemyse[10] clere,
A perfite preste made stronge with armoure
Afore the awtre[11] as Cristes champyoun
Schalle stounde up righte and make a discomfitoure;
Alle oure thre Enymys venquwesse[12] and bere
      downne—   20
The flesche, the worlde, Sathane the folle Dragownne.[13]
Fyrste to bygynne or he ferrare[14] passe,
With contrite herte and lufe, confessyoune;
And so procedes devoutely to masse,
To god aboufe settys holy[15] his desire   25
Soo that his charytee schyne clere and bryghte.
Afore the gospel he nedis muste have fyere—
Torche, tapure, or waxe kandle or lighte—
Tokenn that Criste[s] woo,[16] consider se[17] aryghte
Is verrey[18] bryghtenesse of lighte wiche is eterne   30
To chasse awaye alle dirknesse of the nyghte
In perfite lighte to gyde us and governe.

4. *girdille:* belt   5. *Mowgre:* In spite (French: *maugre*)
6. *Fro:* From   7. *shesepul:* chasuble   8. *Phebus:* Apollo, the sun
9. *spere:* sphere   10. *bemyse:* beams   11. *awtre:* altar
12. *venquwesse:* vanquish   13. *folle Dragownne:* foul serpent
14. *ferrare:* farther   15. *settys holly:* sets entirely (wholly)
16. *Criste[s]woo:* Christ's sorrow   17. *se:* so   18. *verrey:* true

25

The Castle of Love:
The Four Daughters of God
and the Harrowing of Hell

Introductory Note: The following selections are excerpts from the edition of the thirteenth-century Middle English text of Robert Grosseteste's poem by Carl Horstmann, *The Minor Poems of the Vernon Manuscript*, Early English Text Society, Original Series, vol. 117, part 1 (London, 1892), pp. 355–406. Grosseteste, first Chancellor of Oxford University and later Bishop of Lincoln (1235–1253) wrote this fifteen hundred-line allegorical description of the story of the fall of Adam and the redemption of mankind by Christ early in the thirteenth century. The translator explains the need for an English translation at the outset: "We are not all of one people / Nor born together in one land / No common speech do we understand / Nor do we all know Latin / Nor Hebrew nor Greek." The first 274 lines of the poem describe the creation, Adam's fall, and the necessity of the human regaining of Paradise by some man's alighting in a fair Castle, "that Mary's body was." Following a brief discourse on Doomsday, Heaven, and Hell, the first excerpt (lines 275–564) describes the arguments among the Four Daughters of God concerning Adam's punishment, a discourse closely echoed in

Passus XVIII of *Piers Plowman*. Lines 565–1330 begin with a summary of Old Testament prophecies concerning Christ, followed by a detailed allegorical description of the Castle, the Virgin Mary, Jesus' combat with the Devil and his death on the cross, and a reworking of Gospel stories to prove Christ's divinity. The second selection (lines 1331–54) describes the Harrowing of Hell, a favorite theme of medieval literature and drama. The end of the poem, lines 1355–1524, recount the fulfillment of Isaiah's prophecies in Jesus' acts after the resurrection, a summary of the materials in the *Acts of the Apostles*, and a description of the new status of mankind and the promise of salvation. Grosseteste's poem is remarkably economical, and its widespread influence in the later thirteenth and fourteenth centuries is well-attested. A discussion of this poem and related texts, with editions, may be found in Kari Sajavaara, *The Middle English Translations of Robert Grosseteste's Chateau d'Amour*, Mémoires de la Société Néophilologique de Helsinki, vol. 32 (Helsinki, 1967).

✤ (a) lines 275–564

Hit was a kyng of muche miht,
Of good wille and gret in-siht.
And þis kyng hedde a Sone,
Of such wit and of such wone,[1]
Of such strengþe and of such chere
As was his ffader in his manere;   280
Of on wille heo weoren bo,
And of on studefastschipe also,
Of on fulnesse[2] heo weoren out-riht
And boþe heo weoren of on miht.
Þorw þe Sone þe ffader al be-gon[3]   285
Þat bi-lay[4] to his kynedom;
Wiþ wit was his be-gynnynge,
Þe ffader wolde to ende bringe.
Foure douhtren hedde þe kyng,
And to vchone sunderlyng[5]   290
He ȝaf a dole of his fulnesse,

---

1. *wone:* habit   2. *fulnesse:* substance   3. *be-gon:* overcome
4. *bi-lay:* beseiged, beset   5. *sunderlyng:* sister

Of his miht and of his wysnesse,
As wolde bi-fallen to vch on;
And ȝit was al þe folnesse on,
Þat to him-self bi-lay;   295
Wiþ-oute whom he ne mai
His kindom wiþ pees wysen,[6]
Ne wiþ rihte hit Iustisen.[7]
Good is to nempnen hem forþi.
Þe furste douȝter hette Merci—   300
Þe kynges eldeste douȝter heo is;
Þat oþer hette Soþ, I-wis;
Þe þridde soster Is cleped Riȝt;
Pees hette þe feorþe a pliȝt.
Wiþ-outen þeos foure wiþ worschipe   305
Mai no kyng lede gret lordschipe.
Þis kyng, as þou herdest ar þis,
Hedde a þral þat dude amis,
Þat for his gult strong and gret
Wiþ his lord was so I-vet,[8]   310
Þat þorw be-siht of riht dom[9]
To strong prison was I-don
And bi-taken to alle his fon,[10]
Þat sore him pyneden euerichon;
Þat of no þing heo nedden onde[11]   315
Bote him to habben vnder honde;
Heo him duden in prisun of deþ,
And pyneden him sore wiþ-outen meþ.[12]

De misericordia.

Merci þat a-non I-seiȝ;
Hit code hire herte swiþe neih,   320
Ne mai hire no þing lengore holde,
By-foren þe kyng comen heo wolde
To schewen forþ hire Resoun
And to dilyuere þe prisoun.

6. *wysen:* rule   7. *Iustisen:* administer justice.   8. *I-vet:* odious
9. *dom:* judgment   10. *fon:* foes   11. *onde:* desire, envy   12. *meþ:* mercy

"Vnderstond," quaþ heo, "ffader myn!   325
Þow wost þat I am douȝter þyn,
And am ful of Boxumnes,
Of Milce and of Swetnes,
And al Ich habbe, ffader, of þe.
I beo-seche þat þou here me,   330
Þat þe [sorful] wrecche prisoun
Mote come to sum Raunsum
Þat a-Midden alle his fon
In strong prison [þou] hast I-don.
Heo him made agulte, þulke vnwreste,   335
And bi-swikede[13] him þorw heor feire beheste,
And seiden him ȝif he wolde þe Appel ete,
Þat whon he hedde al I-ete,
He scholde habbe al þe miht of gode
Of þe treo þat him was forbode;   340
And be-gylen him þerof, and heo luytel ronȝ
ffor falshede euerȝite heo souhten.
And falshede hem I-ȝolde be,
And þe wrecche prisun I-sold to me!
ffor þow art kyng of Boxumnes,   345
Of Milce and of Swetnes,
And I þi douhter alre[14] eldest,
Ouer alle þe oþere beldest;[15]
Neuere I þi douhter neore
Bote Milce toward him were.   350
Milce and Merci he schal haue,
Þorw Milce I-chulle þe prisun craue;[16]
ffor þin owne swete pite
I schal him bringe to sauete.
Þi Milce for him I crie euermore,   355
And haue of him Milce and ore!"[17]

De veritate.

Anon whon Soþ þis I-seiȝ
Hou Merci, hire soster, hir herte beiȝ[18]

13. *bi-swikede:* tricked   14. *alre:* first   15. *beldest:* boldest
16. *craue:* claim   17. *ore:* mercy, grace   18. *beiȝ:* bowed

And wolde þis þral of prisun bringe
Þat Riht hedde him I-demet wiþ-outen endinge: 360
Al heo chaunged hire mood,
And bi-foren þe kyng heo stood.
"ffader, I þe bi-seche, herkne to me!
I ne may for-bere to telle hit þe
Hou hit me þinkeþ a wonder þing   365
Of Merci, my suster, wilnyng,
Þat wolde wiþ hire Milsful sarmon
Diliuere þe þral out of prison
Þat swiþe agulte, þer ich hit seih
And tolde hit to Riht þat stood me neih.   370
ffader, ich sigge[19] þe for-þi:
Þou ouhtes nouȝt to heere Merci,
Of no boone þat heo bi-secheþ þe,
Bote Riht and Sooþ þer-mide be.
And þow louest soþ and hatest lees,   375
ffor of þi fulnesse I-comen Ich wes;
And eke þow art kyng Rihtwys,
And Merci herte so reuþful is
Þat, ȝif heo mai saue wiþ hire mylde speche
Al þat heo wole fore bi-seche,   380
Neuer schal be mis-dede abouht,
And þou, kyng, schalt be douted riȝt nouht.
Þou art also so trewe a kyng,
And stable of þouȝt in alle þyng.
ffor-þi me þinkeþ Merci wilneþ wouȝ,[20]   385
And spekeþ to-ȝeynes Riȝt I-nouȝ;
ffor Riht con hym in prison bynde
He ouȝte neuere Milce to fynde,
Milce and Merci he haþ for-loren—
He was warned þerof bi-foren;   390
Whi scholde me helpe þulke mon
Þat nedde of him-self pite non?
His dom he mot habbe as Sooþ con sugge,[21]
And al his mis-dede a-bugge."[22]

---

19. *sigge:* tell   20. *wouȝ:* evil   21. *sugge:* tell   22. *a-bugge:* pay for

De Iusticia.

Riht I-herde þis talkyng: 395
Anon heo stod bi-fore þe kyng,
"Þi douȝtur," heo seiþ, "I am, I wot bi þon,
ffor þou art, kyng, Riht domes-mon;[23]
Þe beþ rihte domes mitte,
Alle þine werkes beþ ful of witte.   400
Þis þral of whom my sustren deeþ mene,[24]
Haþ deseruet as at ene;[25]
ffor in tyme, while þat he freo wes,
He hedde wiþ him boþe Merci and pees,
And soþ and riht he hedde bo,   405
And wiþ his wille he wente hem fro
And tyed hym to wraþþe and wouȝ,
To wreccheddam and serwe I-nouȝ.
So þat, ȝif Riht geþ,
He schal euere þolyen deþ;   410
ffor þo þow him þe heste hiȝtest,
Þorw Soþ þou him þe deþ diȝtest,[26]
And I my-self him ȝaf þe dom,
As sone as he hedde þe gult I-don;
ffor Soþ bereþ witnesse þer-to,   415
And elles nedde I no dom I-do.
Ȝif he in Court bi-foren vs were,
Þe dom þou scholdest sone I-here.
ffor Riht ne spareþ for to Iugge
What-so-euere Soþ wol sugge;   420
Þorw wisdam heo demeþ alle,
As wole to his gult bi-falle."—
Soþ and Riht, lo þus heo suggeþ,
And þis þral to deþe Iuggeþ;
Neuer nouþer ne spekeþ him good,   425
Ne non þat Merci vnderstood.
Ac as a Mon mis-I-rad[27]
On vche half he is mis-bilad.[28]

---

23. *domes-mon*: judge   24. *mene*: pity   25. *at ene*: at once
26. *diȝtest*: gave   27. *mis-I-rad*: given bad advice   28. *mis-bilad*: led astray

Ne helpeþ him no þing wher-so he wende,
þat his fo fetteþ him In vche ende   430
And I-strupt him al start-naked,
Of miȝt and strengþe al bare I-maked;
Him and al þat of him sprong
He dude a þeuwedam²⁹ vyl and strong
And made agult[en] swiþe I-lome,³⁰   435
And Riht com after wiþ hire dome;
Wiþ-outen Merci and Pees heo con Iugge,
Euer aftur þat Soþ wol sugge.
Ne Pees mot not mid hem be,
Out of londe heo mot fle,   440
ffor pees bi-leueþ in no londe
Wher þer is werre,³¹ nuy³² and onde;
Ne Merci mot not a-Mong hem liue,
Ac boþe heo beþ of londe I-driue.
Nis þer nout in world bi-leued   445
þat nis destrued and to-dreued,
And dreynt,³³ for-loren and for-demed,
But Eiȝte soulen, þat weren I-ȝemed³⁴
In þe Schup,³⁵ and þar weoren heo:
Noe, and his sones þreo,   450
And heore wyues þat heo hedden bi-fore—
Of al þe world nas be-leued more.
Careful herte him ouȝte come
þat þencheþ vppon þe dredful dome!
And al hit is þorw Riht and Soþ,   455
þat wiþ-outen Pees and Merci doþ."

De pace

So þat Pees a last vp breek³⁶
And þus to hire ffader speek:
"I am þi douȝter sauȝt³⁷ and some,³⁸

---

29. *þeuwedam:* serf, slave   30. *I-lome:* frequently, often
31. *werre:* strife   32. *nuy:* annoyance, hurt
33. *dreynt:* flooded, engulfed   34. *I-ȝemed:* protected saved
35. *Schup:* Ship   36. *breek:* jumped   37. *sauȝt:* reconciled
38. *some:* accordant

And of þi fulnesse am I-come.   460
To-fore þe my playnt I make:
Mi two sustren me habbeþ forsake,
Wiþ-outen me heo doþ heore dom,
Ne Merci a-mong hem nouȝt ne com.
ffor no þing þat I miȝte do   465
Ne moste Merci hem come to,
Ne for none kunnes fey[39]
Ne moste ich hem come neyȝ,
Ak þat dom is al heore owen.
ffor-þi Ich am of londe I-flowen,   470
And wole wiþ þe lede my lyf,
Euer o þat Ilke stryf
Þat a-mong my sustren Is a-wake,
Þorw sauhtnesse[40] mowe sum ende take.
Ac what is hit euer þe bet   475
Þat Riht and Soþ ben I-set,
Bote heo wite wel pees?
Rihtes Mester hit is and wes
In vche dom pees to maken.
Schal I þenne beo forsaken   480
Whon eueriche good for me is wrouht
And to habben me bi-þouht?[41]
And he me louede neuere to fere[42]
Þat Merci, my suster, nul not here.
Off vs foure, ffader, I-chul telle þe   485
Hou me þinkeþ hit ouȝte to be.
Whon ffoure beþ to-gedere I-sent
To don an euene Iuggement,
And schul þorw skil alle and some
Ȝiuen and demen euene dome,   490
þer ne ouȝte no dom forþ gon
Er þen þe foure ben aton;
At on heo moten at-stonden alle
And loken seþþen hou dom wol falle.
Be vs ffoure þis I telle: 495

39. *fey:* faith   40. *sauhtnesse:* reconciliation   41. *bi-þouht:* forever
42. *fere:* mate, wife

We beoþ not alle of on spelle;
Boþe Ich and Merci.
We be-clepeþ þe dom forþi;
Hit is al as Riȝt and Soþ wol deme,
Merci ne me nis hit not qweme.[43]   500
Wiþ-outen vs þer is bale to breme:[44]
ffor-þi, ffader, þow nime ȝeme![45]
Of vche goodschipe Pees is ende,
Ne fayleþ no weole[46] þer heo wol lende,
Ne wisdam nis not worþ an hawe   505
Þer Pees fayleþ to felawe;[47]
And hose Pees loueþ, wiþ-outen gabbe,[48]
Pees wiþ-outen ende he schal habbe.
Mi word ouȝte ben of good reles,[49]
ffor þou art kyng and prince of pes.   510
ffor-þi þou ouȝtest to here me,
And Merci my suster, þat clepeþ to þe
Þat þe þral, þe prisoun,
Mote come to sum Raunsoun.
Vre wille, ffader, þou do sone   515
And here vre rihte bone!
ffor Merci euere clepeþ to þe
Til þat þe prison dilyuered be,
And I-chul fleon and neuere come
Bote my sustren ben sauȝt and some."   520
Þe kynges sone al þis con heren
Hou his sustren hem to-beeren,[50]
And seiȝ þis strif so strong awaken,
And Pees and Merci al forsaken;
Þat wiþ-outen help of his wisdome   525
Ne mihten heo neuere to-gedere come.
"Leoue ffader," quaþ he, "Ich am þi sone,
Of þi wit and of þi wone,
And þi wisdam [me] clepeþ me;
And so muche þou louedest me   530

43. *qweme:* pleasing   44. *breme:* cruel   45. *nime ȝeme:* take care
46. *weole:* wealthy, happiness   47. *felawe:* join   48. *gabbe:* deception
49. *reles:* taste, odor, relish   50. *to-beeren:* set at variance

Þat al þe world for me þou wrou3test,
And so þou me in werke bou3test;
ffor we beoþ on in one fulnesse,
In miht, in strengþe, and in hei3nesse;
I-chulle al don þat þi wille is,   535
ffor þou art kyng Rihtwis.
So muche, ffader, ich nyme 3eme
Of þis strif þat is so breme,
Þat for þe tale þat Merci tolde þe
fful sore þe prisun reweþ me;   540
ffor-þi he reweþ me wel þe more
ffor Merci euere clepeþ þin ore.
Þou art, ffader, so milsful kyng:
Hire we schul heren of alle þing.
Al i-chul hire wille done   545
And sauhten⁵¹ Soþ and hire ful sone.
Nimen I-chulle þe þralles weden,⁵²
As Soþ & Riht hit wolden and beoden,
And al one I-chul holde þe doom
As Iustise ouhte to don,   550
And maken I-chule Pees to londe come,
And Pees & Riht cussen & be sau3t & some,
And druyuen out Werre, Nuy and Onde,
And sauen al þe folk in londe."
Hose þis forbysene⁵³ con,   555
He may openliche i-seo bi þon
Þat al þis ilke tokenynge
Is Godes in-siht, Almihti kynge.
Wiþ-[out] God þe ffader nis maked nouht,
Þorw God þe Sone is al þing wrouht,   560
And alle þing is folfuld out-riht
Þorw God þe holigostes miht:
And alle þreo beþ on, þouh hit be so,
In one fulnesse and in no mo.

. . . .

51. *sauhten:* reconcile   52. *weden:* mad, angry, raging
53. *forbysene:* exemplum, allegory, lesson

❧ (b) lines 1331–1354

To þe croys he con come
And wolde habben his soule I-nome.
Ac he faylede, þe Traytour!
He was a-bated[1] of his tour![2]
ffor Godes Godhede hin haþ doun cast   1335
In to helle, and I-bounden fast.
ffor þorw his Godhede his soule eode
Þidere, for hise þat hedden neode,
Þat ȝore hedden him a-bide
And sore longeden to gon him mide.   1340
Helle-ȝates he al to-breek,
And to-daschte al þe fendes ek,
A gret bite he bot, of helle nom
And drouh alle hise out, vchen,
Þat leeueden his come & him knewe   1345
And serueden him wiþ herte trewe.
Such strengþe nas neuer I-herd ar þis,
Ne neuer schal, but of him, I-wis!
ffor þe meste strengþe he al bi-reuede,
Þat þe fend in þe world heuede.   1350
He was en-Armed ful stronge,
Þat his ȝat wuste ful longe:
Ac þo þe strengore him ouer com,
Gret preye he him bi-nom.

1. *a-bated:* deprived of   2. *tour:* turn

26

The Pilgrimage of the Soul:
The Green Tree
and the Dry Tree

Introductory Note: In the early decades of the fourteenth century, Guillaume de Deguilleville wrote three immensely long and detailed "Pilgrimage" allegories that became extremely popular for the next two centuries and were translated into several languages. The first of these may be found in *The Pilgrimage of the Life of Man*, Englished by John Lydgate, A.D. 1426, from the French of Guillaume de Deguileville, A.D. 1335, ed., F. J. Furnival (London, E.E.T.S., 1899). This work begins with the soul's vision of Jerusalem, the heavenly city, and traces the Pilgrim's life allegorically and at enormous length from birth, through the encounter with Grace-Dieu, Baptism, the meeting with Reason and Moses, the sacraments, the great debate between Grace-Dieu and Nature over their respective provinces in Creation, the meeting with Penance and the bread of Charity, the debate between Grace-Dieu and Aristotle, and on to the pilgrim's death. In *Passus* XII of *Piers Plowman* the character Imagination discusses the figure of Aristotle and secular learning in general somewhat less harshly than the Stagirite is treated here.

The second of Deguilleville's allegories was entitled *Le Pélérinage de l'Ame, The Pilgrimage of the Soul.* It begins where the *Life of Man* ended, and the Soul, freed by death, rises from the earth to become the subject of a dispute between Satan and the Angels, another common medieval literary motif. Justice pleads on the soul's behalf. At the beginning of Book IV the Soul has a vision of the Green Tree and the Dry Tree, the meaning of which is explained by his Angel. The beginning of this vision and the explanation are given here.

This text is taken from the early printed edition, in the translation sometimes attributed to Lydgate, but almost certainly not his work: *The Booke of the Pylgremage of the Sowle*, translated from the French of Guillaume de Guilevile, and printed by William Caxton, an. 1483. The copy from St. John's College Library, Oxford, was used for this text. The copy at the Beinecke Rare Book Library at Yale was also consulted, and the editors are indebted to Dr. Maureen Quilligan of the Department of English at Yale and to Christina Hanson of the Beinecke Library for assistance in tracking down editions and relevant passages.

A partial text, not including the passage printed here, can be found in *The Booke of the Pylgremage of the Sowle . . .* , ed. Katherine Isabella Cust (London, 1859; rpt. New York, 1973). Miss Cust systematically omitted those parts of the poem pertaining to Mariolatry and "quaint descriptions of purgatory and other abstruse metaphysical doctrines, which it was felt could neither be of advantage nor interest to the general reader," that is, most of the more complicated and intricate parts of the allegory. On the work itself, see the dissertation of James S. Flynn, "Pilgrimage of the Soul: An Edition of the Caxton Imprint," (Ph.D. diss., Auburn University). In *Passus* XVI of *Piers Plowman*, the discussion of the Tree of Charity echoes the images of the green tree and the dry tree in Deguilleville, who in this case may be the direct source of Langland's image.

❧ The Pilgrimage of the Sowle, Caxton, 1483

Liber Quartus

The fourthe book begynneth of the grene tree and the dry and other wonderful sygthes. Capitulo primo.

In this mene tyme[1] that we thus talked, me semyd that helle wente awey fro me, and that I also departid fer fro[2] it. Nevertheles, I sawe hit contynuelly, so ferre ne passed I nought,[3] that it ne was sene of me what tyme that I retourned my vysage[4] thyderward. Neverthelater longe ne was it nought er that we were retourned ayene abouven the erthe fro[5] thens that we departid. Thenne sawe I before me a thyng wherof I wondred, for such a maner syght hadde I not sene byfore. I sawe in a fayre playn a multytude of pylgryms pleyenge with an appel bytwene twoo greete trees, one of the whiche was fayr and grene, full fresshe and lusty to loke upon, and that other drye withoute only maner lustynesse[6] or vendure.[7] "Seest thou," quod myn Aungel "the yonder pylgrumes?" "Ye" quod I, "I see them wel, but it wold full gretely ease my herte yf that ye wold telle what that pleye meneth."

"There nys," quod he," no pylgrym so wyse ne soo holy that soo certeynly can holden his wey, that he ne shall fynde somtyme hevynesse and sorowe at his herte. Wherfore hym nedeth of[8] solace and disport, wherewith to appesen his herte as who soo wold styllen[9] a child with some maner of comfortable myrthe of recreacion. Wherfore wyte it well, that these that thus pleyen here to avoyden theyr hevynesse, they have founden under the yonder grene tre an appel, wherof they haven grete joye and comfort, with the whiche appel they playen as oftymes as they ben annoyed.[10] And wyte it wel that this appel is nought withouten grete comfort, for this is nought the Appel whereof Aristotiles wrote that merveylous book. Ne this is nought sothely[11] Adam's appel, by whiche so moche meschyef come to the world, but it is the appel that by cause of Adam and this lygnage[12] was hanged upon this drye tree, whiche that grewe before hand[13] upon this grene florisshynge tree. And fro one tree to another was he translated and borne fro the grene tree and put upon the drye tre for to restoren this drye tree to verdure and to fresshenes, that was by laste[14] hym of old tyme by the surfet[15] of your fyrst fadre."

1. *mene tyme:* meantime   2. *fer fro:* far from
3. *passed I nought:* I did not depart   4. *vysage:* gaze
5. *fro:* where   6. *lustynesse:* vigor   7. *verdure:* greenness
8. *hym nedeth of:* he has need of   9. *styllen:* quiet
10. *annoyed:* distressed   11. *sothely:* truly   12. *lygnage:* lineage
13. *before hand:* previously   14. *by laste:* left to   15. *surfet:* sin

Here foloweth of the Appel tree. Capitulo Secundo. "Now take hede and here, for first wyll I tell the of this appel tree er[16] than I telle ought of this fayr appel. And I shal telle the fro whens hit come and how hit ymped.[17] What tyme that Adam hadde eten of the Appel to grete harme of hym self and alle his yssue after hym, the pepyns[18] of that appel he plantid withynne his owne hert. Wherfore his trees or braunches spryngynge of the pepyns were bycomen wylde and unfructuous[19] into the tyme that upon his braunche was ymped[20] a graf,[21] that was taken fro a free appel tree and a fructuous.

Soothly the appel whiche that Adam ete was of a ful good tre and the fruyt it self full good fayre and swete, al be it that hit was of hym mystaken and eten oute of tyme.[22]

But for as moche as Adam was nought soo well disposyd to etyng of this appel, as it had ben nedeful for inconvenyence of the season in whiche he receyved it, these pepyns myghe nought kyndely as they shold renewen[23] into a good appel tree. Wherof hit befelle that in these pepyns was bredde[24] a worme, and closid withynne Adam's herte the unthryfty[25] vyce of dis-obedyence, whiche worme soo[26] had forfaren[27] these pepyns and corrumped[28] them withynne, that they myght nought kyndely[29] sprynge to a fayr appel tree, but to fowle buskes[30] and wylde that myght nought fructyfyen[31] no holsome ne lusty fruyte, but bytter and unsavoury. Whiche fruyt the Mayster gardyner ne wold nought putte amonge his other store among his other fruyte, but lete caste it to the swyne of helle in to the tyme that it lyked to[32] the hyghe lord to ympen a good graf as is byfore said. Whiche that was to hym ful dere and precious, and taken froo that ryal[33] and worshypful Root Jesse. Noughtwithstand-ynge that this Roote soo noble a braunche that was ordeyned and predestynate[34] by the blyssynge of the good Lord for to receyven exempcion of this forsayd wyldenesse after that hit

16. *er:* before   17. *ymped:* was implanted, engrafted
18. *pepyns:* pips, seeds   19. *unfructous:* unfruitful   20. *ymped:* grafted
21. *graf:* graft   22. *tyme:* season   23. *renewen:* sprout
24. *bredde:* bred   25. *unthryfty:* injurious   26. *soo:* thus
27. *forfaren:* destroyed   28. *corrumped:* corrupted
29. *kyndely:* by their nature   30. *buskes:* bushes   31. *fructyfyen:* produce
32. *lyked to:* pleased   33. *ryal:* royal   34. *predestynate:* predestined

were graffed[35] uppon the stokke uppon the whiche hit sholde be ympyd.[36]

"This stok[37] was that noble and trewe and vertuous wyf Seynt Anne uppon whiche full covenably[38] was ympyd that noble forsaid braunche oure blessid lady, whiche that we clepen[39] the soverayne solace and the welle of salvacion of the kynd of man,[40] whiche that God despoilled[41] and made very clene, and naked of al maner vyce[42] and corrupcion, whiche that come by nature of this roote fully halewed[43] and preserved fro all maner tatches of[44] synne, Orygenal[45] and other. So that, when that this graffe had taken kynde[46] and moysture of this forsaid stock on whiche hit was ympyd it bycome a ful swete and grafted convenable[47] appel tre for to beren good fre fruyte, agreable and holsome to the etyng of ony wel disposid[48] creature. An appel eyther fruyte of more noble valewe or more worthy prys ne was there never none than this gentyll[49] appel tree brought forth after a fewe yeres. Sothely[50] this was the very tree in understandynge, wherof wrote Danyell the prophete, whiche that Nabugodonosor sawe in his slepe, standyng in myddes of the erthe, soo that fro every parte of the world, every creature that nede hadde myght yf hum lyst[51] behold it to his hertes solace and comforte, soo forforth[52] that excusen hym self ne may none at al, that he ne maye ful lyghtely fynden this tree yf that hym lyst for to loken toward. Ful many trees ther ben that nowhere ben knowne but only in the countre where that they growne. But this tree the good Lord hath sette as seyth Ezechyel in myddes of his people al londes abouten hit, soo that who soo hath any need onythyng to done,[53] he maye ful well and easyly fynde it; he faileth not therof. Wherof seith Seynt Bernard, her owne subtil clerke: In hyt as in a myroure that standeth in the muddes[54] every creature may setten his syght in what place or what parte that he be ynne, in heven or in

35. *graffed:* grafted   36. *ympyd:* grafted   37. *stok:* stock
38. *covenably:* fittingly   39. *clepen:* call, name   40. *kynd of man:* mankind
41. *despoilled:* stripped   42. *vyce:* vice   43. *halewed:* purified
44. *tatches of:* spots of   45. *Orygenal:* original   46. *kynd:* nourishment
47. *convenable:* suitable   48. *ony wel disposid:* any well-disposed
49. *gentyll:* noble   50. *Sothely:* truly   51. *lyst:* pleased
52. *ferforth:* entirely   53. *onythyng to done:* anything to be done
54. *muddes:* midst

erthe, al thylke[55] that have be or shalle ben herafter, yf that them lyketh[56] to geten here grace and hyr benyvolence. This tree also is wondre stronge and myghty, aretchyng[57] in to heven, soo that she suffyseth to sustene and to bere al tho[58] that wyllen resten and lene[59] them selven to hyr. And fynally, she wylle and also she may senden grace fro heven ful redyly, as often as it nedeth. She that hyr reward and beholdynge aboute by all the erth soo that she knoweth and seeth every mans herte of tho that here Biseketh,[60] whether that it be of hole[61] entent or elles. She knoweth what they ben, and how they demenen[62] the dayes of theyr lyves and what weyes they wenden,[63] be it ryght or other. Here wordes ben leves[64] of ful huge beaute, and all that she seeth hit is full of amyable ful swete, and ful lusty[65] enlumyned all with soverayn charyte.

"And wondre wele she maye kepen and byshadowyn under hyr fayr braunches al tho that ben wery of theyr laboure. Under this tree dwelen al beestes. For why al that lyven bestyally[66] encombred with synnes under hyr shadowe, they ben favoured and spared, and longe tyme, for to that ende that they maye take better avysement[67] for to amenden theym selven withouten fowle rebukynge, or hastenesse of vengeaunce.

"In here lusty bowes and here fayre braunches, that is in hyr plentious benefetys,[68] the birdes of hevene ben alwey coversaunt,[69] that ben spyrituel men, that ben contemplatyf, and haven sette theyr hertes in heyghte[70] and drawen them oute of this moddy[71] erthe. This tree is so fructuous,[72] that al folk ben refresshed and fulfylled every day and every hour; noo tyme ne fayleth them therof, but yf it be long uppon[73] theyr owne slouthe. This fruyte is the Appel with whiche men must pleyen them[74] to avoyden theyr hevynesse.[75] This tree that bare this appel, she bare never no moo, ne never shalle herafter. And now is she discharged therof, and shalle no more beren it, but it must

55. *thylke:* such   56. *lyketh:* pleases   57. *aretchyng:* arching
58. *tho:* those   59. *lene:* lay   60. *Biseketh:* seek her   61. *hole:* proper
62. *demenen:* conduct   63. *wenden:* go   64. *leves:* leaves
65. *lusty:* vigorous   66. *bestyally:* bestially   67. *avysement:* counsel
68. *benefetys:* benefits   69. *coversaunt:* conversing   70. *in heyghte:* on high
71. *moddy:* muddy   72. *fructuous:* fruitful   73. *long uppon:* be the result
74. *pleyen them:* amuse themselves   75. *hevynesse:* trouble

be restored to the Tree that Adam despoylled instede of the appel that he ete. Wherof we have spoken and more note herafter.

"And ryght it is that thou knowe clerely how that this drye tree was restablysshed. And how the forsaid appel was restored, withoute whiche restitucion Adam ne none of his lygnage ne myght nought be quyte[76] of the surfet of thylk noyous[77] appel, whiche he thus hadde spoylled fro this tree and eten hit ageyne the wylle of the soverayne gardyner."

76. *quyte:* relieved   77. *thylk noyous:* that poisonous

PART VII:

This is the Way
the World Ends

So far, in the course of this book we have found *Piers Plowman* in manuscripts in company with treatises of general information and instruction, like *The Wise Book of Philosophy and Astronomy*, and *Physiognomy;* with instructions for dying penitents and descriptions of England. Here we find it with the kind of text one might have guessed would most logically accompany it—a sermon. *Wrecchednesses* can be found in Trinity College Cambridge Ms. B. 15. 17, following *Piers Plowman.* It is a sermon meant to call to mind the last things, man's eventual fate, and inevitable unpreparedness. About the first half of it appears here and was edited for this volume by M. Kathryn Taylor.

Medieval meditations on the end of the world took many forms. One of the most vivid and grisliest is the illustrated Dance of Death, in which kings and queens, bishops, knights, and ladies appear first in all their worldly glory, then as skeletons, suffering in Hell. Another theme sometimes illustrated—memorably in the large east window of All Saints Church in York—was the end of the world and the fifteen signs leading up to it. The fifteen signs were derived from the description of the end of the world in Revelation 8–9, and there are a number of late Middle English poems about them. Many of the sentiments expressed in these two selections may be compared with those expressed by the figure of Conscience in *Passus* XX of *Piers Plowman*, and with the general eschatological tone of the close of the poem.

Wrecchednesses is one of the few English prose works which can definitely be attributed to the best-known of fourteenth-century English devotional writers, Richard Rolle of Hampole. Many religious poems and prose works were assigned to him, both by his contemporaries and by later scholars; some, like the poem on the Fifteen Days of Doom with which we conclude the volume, are certainly not his, but *Wrecchednesses*, which enjoyed a wide circulation, is, according to its earlier twentieth-century editor, Hope Emily Allen, the best of his English prose works. A more northerly version of the complete text, taken from Cambridge University Library Ms. Dd. v. 64, can be found in H. E. Allen, *English Writings of Richard Rolle, Hermit of Hampole* (Oxford, 1931), pp. 85ff.

27

"Wrecchednesses"

In euery synful man or womann þat is bounden in dedly synne ben þre wrecchednesses, þe whiche bringeþ hem to þe deiþ of helle Þe firste is defaute[1] of goostly[2] strengþe: þat þei are so feble wiþ inne hire herte þat þei ne may noþer stonde ayeins temptacions of þe fend, ne þei ne may lifte up hir wille to desire þe love of God and folwen it.

Þat ooþer is use of flesshly desires. For þei have no wille ne myght to stonde, þei falle in lustes and likynges of þis world. And for þei þynken hem swete þei dwelle in hem stille, manye til hire lyves ende. And so þei come to þe þridde wrecchednesse.

Þe þridde wrecchednesse is chaungynge of lastynge good for a passinge delit, as who seye þei yeue[3] endelees joye for a litel joye of þis lif.

If þei wole turne and risen up to penaunce, God wole ordeyne hire wouyng[4] with aungeles and holi men. But for þei chese pe vile synne of þis world and have moore delit in filþe of hir flessh þan in

---

1. *defaute:* lack   2. *goostly:* spiritual   3. *yeue:* give   4. *wouyng:* wooing

þe fairhede[5] of hevene, þei lese boþe þe world and hevene. For he þat
haþ noȝt Iesu Crist, he leseþ al þat he haþ and al þat he is and al
þat he myghte gete. He nys noȝt worþi þe lif, ne to be fed wiþ
swynes mete. All creatures shulle be stired in his vengeaunce at þe
day of dome.[6]

Þise wrecchednesses þat I haue told of are noght oonly in
wordly men and wommen þat usen glotonye or leccherie and oþer
aperte[7] synnes, but þei aren also in some þat semeþ in penaunce and
in good lif. For þe devel þat is enemy to al mankynde, whan he seeþ
a man or a womman among a þowsand turne hym oonly to God and
forsaken alle þe vanytees and þe richesse þat men þat loven þis world
coveiten[8] moore þan seke þe joye euer lastynge, a þowsand wiles
he haþ on what manere he deceyven hem. And whan he may noȝt
bryngen hem into swiche synnes þe whiche myȝte maken alle men
wondren on hem þat knewe hem, he bigileþ so manye pryvely[9] þat
þei kan noȝt ofte siþe[10] felle þe trappe þat haþ taken hem.

Somme he takeþ wiþ errour þat he putteþ hem inne. Somme wiþ
singuler wit whanne he makeþ wene[11] þat þe þyng þat þei þenkeþ or
dooþ is best. And þer fore þei wol no conseil have of oþer þat are
bettre and wisere þan þei. And þis is a foul stynkyngge pride. For
he wolde noȝt setten his wit beforn alle oþer but if he wende þat
ouþer he knewe bettre or dide bettre þan oþer.

Somme þe devel deceyveþ þorugh vayne glorie. Þat is ydel joye
whan any haþ pride and delit in hem self of þe penaunce þat þei
suffre, of goode dedes þat þei do, of any vertue þat þei have; ben
glad whan men loveþ hem, sory whan men blamen hem, haveþ
envye to hem þat is spoken moore good of þan of hem. Þei holde hem
self so glorious and so fer passynge þe lif þat ooþer men leden, þat
hem þynkep þat no man sholde repreven[12] hem in any þyng þat þei
do or seyen, and despisen synful men and oþere, þe whiche wol noȝt
do as þei biddeþ hem.

Þow myȝtow fynde a synfuller wrecche þan swich oon. And
so muchel is he þe werse þat he woot[13] noȝt þat he is yvel, and is
holden good and is honoured of men as wys and holy.

Somme are deceyved wiþ ouer much lust and likynge in mete
and drinke when þei passe mesure and come in to outrage and haue

5. *fairhede:* beauty   6. *dome:* judgment   7. *aperte:* open, public
8. *coveiten:* covet   9. *pryvely:* secretly   10. *siþe:* time   11. *wene:* think
12. *repreven:* reprove   13. *woot:* knows

delit þer inne, and weneþ þat þei synneþ noȝt. And þer fore þey amenden hem noȝt, and so þei destruyen vertue of soule.

Somme are bigiled wiþ over muchel abstinence of mete and drynke and sleep. Þat is of temptacions of þe devel for to maken hem faylen amydde hire werkes so þat þei brynge it to noon ende, as þei sholde have doon if þei hadde knowe reson and holden discrecion. And so þei lesen hire merite for hire frowardnesse.[14]

Þis panter[15] leyeþ owre enemy to taken us wiþ whan we bigynne to haten wikkednesse and turne us to goodnesse.

Þanne manye bigynneþ þat þei may never mo brynge to an ende. Þanne þei wene þat þei may do what so hire herte is set up on. But ofte þei faile er þei come amydde þe weye, and þat þyng þat þei wende were for hem is lettyngge[16] to hem. For we have a long wey to hevene. And as manye goode dedes as we do, as manye prayeres as we make, and as manye goode þoȝtes as we þenkeþ in bileve and hope and charite, as manye paas[17] we gon to heveneward.

Þanne if we maken us so feble þat we ne maye neiþer werke ne praye as we sholde do, ne þenke, are we noȝt gretly to blame þat fayle whan we hadde moost nede to be strong? And wel I woot þat is noȝt Goddes wille þat we so do.

For þe prophete seiþ, "Lord, I shal kepe my strengþe to þee," þat he may susteyne Goddes servyce til his deeþ day, noȝt in a litel nor in a short tyme wasteþ it, and siþen lien[18] wendynge[19] and gronynge by þe wal. And it is muche moore peril þan men weneþ.

For Seint Ierome seiþ þat he makeþ of ravyne[20] offrynge þat outrageously tormenteþ his body in over litel mete or sleep.

And Seint Bernard seiþ, "Fastynge, wakynge letteþ[21] noȝt goostly goodes, but helpeþ, if þei be don wiþ discrecion. Wiþ outen þat, þei are vices." Þer fore it is noȝt goode to peyne us so muche and siþen have maugre[22] for our dede.

Þer have ben manye, and are, þat wene þat it is noȝt yvel þat þei do, but if þei be in so muchel abstinence and fastynge þat þei make men to speke of hem þat knowen hem. But ofte siþe it falleþ þat ever þe moore joye and wondrynge þat þei have wiþ outen of preisynge of men, ever þe lasse joye þei have wiþ inne of þe love of God.

---

14. *frowardnesse*: perversity   15. *panter*: trap, snare
16. *lettyngge*: a hindrance   17. *paas*: steps   18. *lien*: lie
19. *wendynge*: turning, winding   20. *ravyne*: raving   21. *letteþ*: hinders
22. *maugre*: displeasure, spite

To my doom, þei sholde paye Iesu Crist muche moore if þei toke for his love, and in þonkynge and preisynge of hym for to susteine þat body in his servyse, and to holde hem fro muche speche of men what so God sente, for þe tyme and þe stede,[23] and ȝeve hem siþþe holly and parfitly to þe love and the preisynge of hir lord Jesu Crist, þat wole stalworþely be loved and lastyngly be served, so þat hire holynesse were moore seene in Goddes sight þan in mannes sighte. For ever þe bettre þat þou art, and þe lasse speche þow hast of men, þe moore is þy joye bifore God.

And what it is muche to be worþi preisynge and be noȝt preised. And what wrecchednesse it is to have þe name and þe habite of holynesse, and be noȝt so but covereþ pride or wraþþe or envye under þe cloþes of Cristes childhood.

A foul leccherie it is to have likynge and delit in mannes wordes þat kan namoore deme what we ben in oure soule þan þei wite what we þenke. For ofte syþe þei seye þat he or she is in hyere degree þat is in þe lowere degree, and þat þei seye is in þe lower is in þe hyer. Þer fore I holde it but a woodnesse[24] to be gladder or sorier wheiþer þei seye good or yvel.

If we be aboute to hiden us fro speche and preisynge of þe world, God wole shewen us to his preisynge and our joye. For þat is his joye, whan we ben stronge to stonde ayeins þe pryve[25] and þe apperte[26] temptacions of þe devel, and seken no þyng but þe preisynge and þe worshipe of hym, and þat we myȝte entierly love hym. And þat ouȝte to ben oure desir, oure preiere, and oure entente nyght and day, þat þe fir of his love alighten our herte, and þe swetnesse of his grace be oure confort and oure solace in wele[27] and woo.

Þow hast now herd a party how þe fend deceyueþ wiþ his subtile craftes unwise men and wommen. And if þou wolt doon good conseil and folwe holy techynge, as I trow þat þow wolt, þu shalt destruyen hise trappes and brennen in þe fir of love alle þe bondes þat he wole bynde þee wiþ. And al his malice shal turne þee to joye and hym to moore sorwe.

God suffreþ hym for to tempten goode men for hire profit, þat þei may þe hyer be corouned[28] whan þei haue þoruȝ his help overcome so cruwel an enemy þat ofte siþe, boþe in body and in soule, confoundeþ many man.

---

23. *stede:* place   24. *woodnesse:* madness   25. *pryve:* secret
26. *apperte:* open   27. *wele:* prosperity   28. *corouned:* crowned

In þre maneres he haþ power to ben in a man. In oo manere, hurtynge þe goodes þat þei have of kynde,[29] as in doumbe men, and in oþere, blemysshynge hire þo3t.

In anoþer manere, birevynge[30] þe goodes þat þei have of grace. And so is he in synful men, þe whiche he haþ deceyved, þoru3 delit of world and of hire flessh, and ledeþ hem wiþ hym to helle.

In þe þridde manere, tormentynge a mannes body, as we rede þat he was in Job. But wite þow wel, if he bigile þee no3t wiþ inne, ne dar þow no3t drede what he may do wiþ outen. For he may do namoore þan God yeveþ hym leve for to do.

For þat, þow hast forsaken þe solace and þe joye of þis world and take þee to solitarie lif, for Goddes love, to suffren tribulacion and angwissh here, and after come to þe rest and joye in hevene. I trow stedefastly þat þe confort of Jesu Crist and swetnesse of his love wiþ þe fir of þe Holi Goost þat purgeþ all synne, shal be in þee and wiþ þee, ledynge þee and techynge þee how þow shalt þenke, how þow shalt praye, what þow shalt werke. So þat in oo fey here þow shalt have moore delit to be by þy self and speke to þi love and þi spowse Jesu Crist þan if þu were lady of a þousand worldes.

Men wene þat we be in pyne and penaunce; but we have moore joye and moore verrey delit in o day þan þei have in þe world al hire lif. Þei seen oure bodies, but þei see no3t oure hertes where oure solace is. If þei sawe þat, manye of hem wolde forsake al þat þei have for to folwen us.

Þerfore be conforted and stalworþe,[31] and dred no noy[32] ne angwissh. But sete al þyn entente in Jesu þat þi lif be God to queme,[33] and þat þer be no þyng þat sholde be myspayinge[34] to hym þat þow ne soone amende it. Þe estat[35] þat þow art inne, þat is moost able of all oþere to revelacion of þe Holy Goost, for whan Seint John was in þe Ile of Pathmos þanne God shewed hym his privetees.

Þe goodnesse of God it is, þat he conforteþ hem wonderfully þat have no confort of þe world. If þei yeve hire herte entierly to hym and coveiteþ and sekeþ no3t but hym, þanne he yeveþ hym self to hem in swetnesse and delit, in brennynge of love, and in joye and in melodie, and dwelleþ ever wiþ hem in hire soule so þat þe confort of hym departeþ never fro hem. And if þei ought bigynne to erre

29. *kynde:* nature   30. *birevynge:* robbing   31. *stalworþe:* strong
32. *noy:* annoyance, harm   33. *queme:* pleasing
34. *myspayinge:* displeasing   35. *estat:* state

þoru3 ignoraunce or freletee,[36] soone he sheweþ hem þe ri3te wey, and al þat þei have nede of, he techeþ hem.

No man comeþ to swich revelacion and grace on þe firste day, but þoru3 long travaille and bisynesse to love Jesu Crist, as þow shalt here afterward. No3t for þan he suffreþ hem to be tempted on sondry maneres, wakynge and slepynge. For evere þe mo temptacions and þe grevouser,[37] and þei stonde ayeins hem and overcome hem, þe moore shal hire joie be in his love, whan þei are passed.

Wakynge, þey are ouþer while tempted wiþ foule þou3tes, vile lustes, wikked delices, wiþ pride, wraþe, and envye, presumpcion, and oþere manye. But hire remedie shal be preiere,[38] wepynge, fastynge, and wakynge.

Þise þynges, if þey be doon with discrecion, þat doþ awey synne and filþe fro þe soule and makeþ it clene, for to receyven þe love of Jesu þat may no3t be loved but in clennesse.

Also som tyme þe fend tempteþ men and wommen þat are solitarie bi hem self in a queynte[39] manere and a subtil. He transfigureþ hym in liknesse of an aungel of light and appereþ to hem, and seiþ þat he is oon of Goddes aungeles come to conforten hem. And so he deceyveþ fooles. But hem þat are wise and wole no3t anoon trowe[40] to all spirites, but askeþ conseil, he may no3t bigilen hem, as I fynde writen of a recluse þat was a good womman, to which þe wikked aungel ofte siþe appered in þe liknesse of a good aungel, and seyde þat he was come to bryngen hire to hevene. Wherfore she was glad and joyeful. But never þe later, she tolde it to hire shrifte fader and he, as a wys man and queynte,[41] yaf hire hise conseil.

"Whan he comeþ," he seyde, "bid hym þat he shewe þee oure ladi, Seinte Marie. Whan he haþ do so, seye, "Ave Maria." She dide so, and þe fend seyde, "Þow hast no nede to seen hire. My presence suffiseþ to þee." And she seide on all maneres she wolde seen hire. He sau3 þat hym bihoved[42] or doon hire wille, or she wolde despisen hym.

Anoon he bro3te forþ þe faireste body of womman þat my3te be as to hire si3te, and shewed it to hire. And she sette hire on hire knees and seyde, "Ave Maria." And also swiþe al vanysshede awey and for shame never siþþe com he at hire.

36. *freletee:* frailty   37. *grevouser:* more grevious   38. *preiere:* prayer
39. *queynte:* crafty, ingenious   40. *trowe:* trust   41. *queynte:* wise
42. *bihoved:* necessary

28

"The Pryk of Conscience"

The fifteen signs of the Last Judgement are here edited from British Museum Ms. Cotton Galba E. IX.

Þe first day of þas[1] fiften days
Þe se sall[2] ryse, als þa bukes says,
Abowen þe heght of ilka[3] mountayne,
Full fourty cubyttes certayne,
And in his stede[4] even upstande   5
Als an heghe hille dus on þe lande.

Þe secunde day þe se sal be swa law[5]
Þat unnethes[6] men sal it knaw

Þe thred[7] day þe se sal seme playne
And stand even in his cours agayne,   10
Als it stode first at þe begynnyng
With outen mare rysyng or fallyng.

1. *þas:* these   2. *se sall:* sea shall   3. *ilka:* that   4. *stede:* place
5. *law:* low   6. *unnethes:* scarcely   7. *thred:* third

Þe fierth day sal swilk[8] a wonder be,
Þe mast wonderful fisshes of þe se
Sal come to gyder and make swilk roryng   15
Þat it sal be hydus til[9] mans heryng.
Bot what þ(a)t roryng sal signify,
Naman may whit bot[10] God almyghty.

Þe fift day þe se sal brynne,[11]
And alle waters als þai sal rynne;[12]   20
And þat sal last fra þe son rysyng
Til þe tyme of þe son doun gangyng.[13]
Þe sext day sal spryng a blody dewe
On grisse and tres, als it sal shewe.

Þe sevent day byggyngs[14] doun sal falle   25
And gret castels and tours with alle.

Þe eght day, hard roches[15] and stanes
Sal strik to gyder[16] alle attanes.
An ilk[17] an of þam sal other doun cast,
And ilk an agayn other hortel[18] fast,   30
Swa þat ilk a[19] stan, on divers wyse,
Sal sonder other in thre partyse.

Þe neghend[20] day gret erthe dyn[21] sal be,
Generaly in ilk a contre
And swa gret erth dyn als[22] sal be þan   35
Was never hard, sythen[23] þ(a)t world bygan.

Þe tend day þar aftir to neven[24]
Þer erthe sal be made playn and even
For hilles and valeis sal turned be
In til playn, and made even to se.   40

Þe ellevend day men sal com out
Of caves, and holes and wend about,

---

8. *swilk:* such   9. *til:* to   10. *whit bot:* know but   11. *brynne:* burn
12. *rynne:* run   13. *gangyng:* going   14. *byggyngs:* buildings
15. *roches:* rocks   16. *to gyder:* at once   17. *ilk:* each   18. *hortel:* hurtle
19. *ilk a:* every   20. *neghend:* ninth   21. *dyn:* din   22. *als:* as
23. *sythen:* since   24. *to neven:* to speak of

Als wode men[25] þat na wut can,[26]
And nane sal speke til other þan.

Þe twelfte day aftir, þe sternes[27] alle   45
And þe signes from þe heven sal falle.

Þe thretend day sal dede men banes[28]
Be sett togyder, and ryse al attanes,
And aboven on þair graves stand.

Þis sal byfalle in ilka[29] land.   50
Þe fourtend day al þat lyves þan
Sal dighe,[30] childe, man and woman,
For þai shalle with þam rys agayn
Þat byfor war dede, outher[31] til joy or payn.

Þe fiftend day, þos sal betyde,[32]   55
Alle þe world sal bryn[33] on ild[34] syde
And þe erthe whar we now dwelle,
Until þe utter[35] ende of alle helle.

25. *men:* mad   26. *na wut can:* have no wit   27. *sternes:* stars
28. *banes:* bones   29. *ilka:* each   30. *dighe:* die   31. *outher:* either
32. *þos sal betyde:* this shall happen   33. *bryn:* burn
34. *ild:* every   35. *utter:* farthest